GOD'S TREES

Trees, forests and wood in the Bible

Julian Evans

GOD'S TREES

Trees, forests and wood in the Bible
An illustrated commentary and compendium

To Fiona & Philip.
Best wishes
Julian Evans

Professor Julian Evans OBE FICFor

Paintings by Veronica Pinchen

© Day One Publications 2014 First printed 2014

ISBN 978-1-84625-410-9

Scripture quotations taken from The Holy Bible, New International Version (Anglicised edition)
Copyright ©1979, 1984, 2011 by Biblica (formerly international Bible Society).
Used by permission of Hodder & Stoughton Publishers, an Hachette UK company.
All rights reserved.
'NIV' is a registered trademark of Biblica (formerly international Bible Society).
UK trademark number 1448790

British Library Cataloguing in Publication Data available

Published by Day One Publications Ryelands Road, Leominster, HR6 8NZ 01568 613 740 FAX 01568 611 473

email—sales@dayone.co.uk web site—www.dayone.co.uk North America—email—usasales@dayone.co.uk

Design by Steve Devane

Printed by PB Print UK

To the memory of my late wife,

Margaret,

who would have rejoiced to see this book

which had its beginnings with us back in the 1980s

CONTENTS

PREFACE **IX**

ACKNOWLEDGEMENTS **X**

1 'AND GOD SAW THAT IT WAS GOOD' **3**
Genesis 1–4

2 FROM ARK TO ARK **15**
Genesis 5–50 and Exodus

3 USE AND ABUSE OF TREES **29**
Leviticus—Deuteronomy

4 DEFINING BOUNDARIES AND SETTING SEALS **41**
Joshua, Judges and Ruth

5 THE BARTER OF KINGS **53**
Samuel—Chronicles

6 METAPHORS OF PEACE, PERMANENCE AND PROSPECT **69**
Ezra—Song of Solomon

7 PROPHETS—PASTORAL AND PAINFUL **87**
Isaiah, Jeremiah and Lamentations

8 TREES IN CONTEXT AND OUT **107**
Ezekiel—Malachi

9 THE NATURAL ILLUSTRATION—
TREES AND WOOD IN JESUS' LIFE AND TIMES **123**
The four gospels, Part 1

10 THE FINAL JOURNEY TO A WOODEN CROSS **135**
The four gospels, Part 2

11 FAITH, FLOTSAM AND A FUTURE IN THE TREE OF LIFE **147**
Acts—Revelation

COMPENDIUM OF TREE SPECIES **161**

SEEING AND GROWING BIBLICAL TREES AND SHRUBS **179**

INDEX OF SCRIPTURAL REFERENCES **181**

TREE SPECIES INDEX **190**

GENERAL INDEX **194**

PREFACE

Writing this book has been something of a personal journey bringing together my career in forestry and my commitment as a Christian. At times I have felt greatly humbled and offer this book with some trepidation. Bible scholars may despair in places at my exegesis while fellow professionals may wonder at the mixing of forestry and faith. Yet, for me, this goes to the heart of what is attempted.

I am no Hebrew or Greek scholar and am conscious that not only do we need to seek the best translation for plants and trees—and there is much uncertainty—but also the harder matter of cultural context. Many references to trees are symbolic, allegorical or used as metaphor. It is difficult for us to take ourselves back 2000 or 3000 years to the world in which the Bible was written and appreciate the frames of reference then current, and how people understood the world and the way it worked. This is none more so than in that greatest of opening chapters, Genesis Chapter 1.

In approaching 'God's Trees: Trees, forests and wood in the Bible' I felt it should have two parts: the main one is a simple commentary book by book through the Old and New Testaments as we come across references or points of interest to our theme. The second and smaller part is a compendium with further details and notes about the trees and shrubs we meet. They are brought together for ease of reference. Throughout, numerous photographs and the artwork immeasurably add to the text.

My own forestry career has focused on both the temperate and the tropical. This undertaking took me to the less familiar world for me of the Mediterranean with its climate of wet winters and dry summers. That said, the germ of this book began in the 1980s and since then visits to Mediterranean or Biblical countries, always with an eye out for trees, have included Cyprus, Egypt, Eritrea, Ethiopia (several), Italy (several), Israel (twice), Malta, northern Iraq, Syria, and Turkey (twice). Recent visits to Turkey and Israel were made with this book very much in mind.

As a forest scientist I have sought accuracy without being guilty of forever hedging around remarks with uncertainties. The latter dulls the reader's interest, but of course exposes the author's fallibility. As noted in the acknowledgements to the many who have helped me, mistakes and shortcomings that remain are mine; as, of course, are my occasional reflective or devotional remarks.

The one overriding aim is to honour the Lord Jesus Christ in these pages.

Julian Evans

June 2013

ACKNOWLEDGEMENTS

A book of this kind relies heavily on the advice, suggestions and contributions from many people.

I am particularly grateful to those who undertook to read the whole of the book in draft:

Revd Clive Anderson, minister

Professor David Cutler, formerly of The Royal Botanic Gardens, Kew

Helen Reid, author

Dr Mike Render, chartered forester, Forestry Commission

and John White, formerly the Forestry Commission's dendrologist at Westonbirt Arboretum, for checking over the details in the compendium of tree species.

Several have kindly contributed illustrations, photographs or sourced pictures via the internet. In most cases the source is acknowledged in the relevant caption.

Clive and Amanda Anderson, Stephen Evans, Martyn Glass, Mr and Mrs R Johnson, Felix Leung, Daniel Luscombe, Tim Pinchen, and the late Bill Stewart.

The bulk of the photographs are unattributed and were taken by my wife, Margaret, or me. (If you have read the dedication you will now realise that I remarried, also to a Margaret, following my first wife's death.) A few photographs were taken in the Forestry Commission's Bedgebury National Pinetum where I was greatly assisted by Chris Reynolds and Daniel Luscombe. Several photographs were taken in the British Museum and this is noted in the captions. Twice Clive Anderson guided me around the Museum to exactly the exhibits I wanted to see!

Assembly and editing of the photographs was kindly undertaken by my son, Stephen.

I must express my gratitude to Veronica Pinchen for her beautiful artwork which has immeasurably added to the book.

In addition, the following provided all sorts of helps—encouragement, factual information, library searches, suggestions of books to refer to, additional contacts, where to find a specimen tree, and more.

Amanda Anderson, Renata Borosova, Dr John Brazier, Jim Carle, Sue Cutler, Paul and Jane Easthope, Kay Fewtrell-Smith, Shahina Ghazanfar, Claire Glaister, Glenn Haines, John Jacobs, Dr Richard Jinks, Dr Gary Kerr, Chris Latham, Peter Latham, Julian Marcroft, Catherine Oldham, Cheryl Pilbeam, Chris Reynolds, Revd. Kelvin and Jane Taylor, Faye Thomsit, Chris Warwick, and Howard Wright.

Two unnamed people—an American lady working in the Jerusalem Botanic Garden who directed us to the new Bible Path she had helped establish and to the groundsman at Kibbutz Ma'agan, Galilee.

The late Nigel Hepper, author of the finest book on Bible plants '*Illustrated Encyclopedia of Bible Plants*' IVP (1992), encouraged me early on in this undertaking saying 'the field was open'. I am grateful, too, to his son, David Hepper.

I would also like to record the interest and support of DayOne's Managing director, Mark Roberts, and book designer, Steve Devane for helping bring this work to completion.

My immediate family, Jon and Christina Evans, Stephen, and Ben and Anna Evans, have been hugely encouraging. I must, too, single out my wife, Margaret, who has been both encouraging and patient when at times things didn't go as smoothly as hoped! But even more, for she read an early draft and she was a great help when we made visits to Israel and Turkey, because she knew Israel well as her father, the late Bill Stewart, had helped train young Jewish men and women in basic farming who were joining the Kibbutz movement in the 1960s and 1970s. A couple of Bill's photographs appear in the book.

Despite all the above helps, any mistakes or errors that remain are mine.

I have prayed much about this book, and have referred above to the many who have given me help, it would be wrong of me and grossly dishonouring not to acknowledge the One who upholds and sustains all life, including our daily toil, and for whom the Christian is to do all things—Colossians 3:23

SPECIFIC ACKNOWLEDGEMENTS

Page 26. The illustration from Queen Hatshepsut's mortuary temple is re-drawn from an original drawing by F. Nigel Hepper (used by permission).

Page 57. Herbarium specimen of *Cedrus libani*. © The Board of Trustees of the Royal Botanic Gardens, Kew. Reproduced with the consent of the Royal Botanic Gardens, Kew.

Page 60. The relief from Seti's temple showing ropes guiding the fall of trees is reproduced from Meiggs (1982) with permission from Oxford University Press.

Internet sourced pictures are credited in the relevant caption in the form: Jastrow (2006)/ Wikimedia Commons

Genesis 1–4

'And God saw that it was good'

God smiled when he made trees. They were perfect; he looked and could find no fault. Yet they appear so ungainly if it was not that we are so used to them—rooted to the ground, but seeming to stretch with abandon in all directions. They are top heavy like a child's toy tree, but endure storms and floods. Some trees live longer than Methuselah. Indeed, some still living today were alive from before Abraham: others are so tall that they would over-top every Egyptian pyramid bar two.

Trees are peculiar in other ways. Some bear flowers of only one sex like the great spreading terebinth (*Pistacia atlantica*), under which the Israelites would come to commit so much idolatry, so both male and female terebinth trees are needed to set fertile seed. Other trees, such as that most prized of all in the eastern Mediterranean, the cedar of Lebanon (*Cedrus libani*), bear flowers of both sexes at once as, indeed, most conifers do. Yet others bear male flowers some years and female ones in others such as our English ash. The wood of trees is similarly variable. It can be more durable than iron or so strong for its weight to be able to make aircraft. We could go on, but this is not a sentimental book. Our journey is tracing trees, forests, timber and wood in scripture to illustrate and magnify God's wisdom and love. But God has not always smiled. For central to the Bible's story is His Son dying on a tree[1] (1 Pet. 2:24). He was the object of God's own wrath to undo for us all the disobedience that plucking that first fruit from a tree led to (Gen. 3:6).

The chapters loosely follow the Bible's chronology and the order of its books with remarks and observations added rather like a commentary. As we come across an identifiable reference to a specific kind of tree, we include its Latin name usually at its first mention, as above for terebinth and cedar of Lebanon, and then stay with the English thereafter. When appropriate we try to place the tree in its setting geographically and, as far as we can, culturally and socially. Some additional notes for each tree species are provided in the compendium. We try to address, too, the following questions. Is there a forest or woodland practice being described or alluded to? How might this help our understanding of the Bible verse? Is there symbolism or deeper meaning? We hope this book is both factual and, to a small degree, devotional, to add interest and to display the beauty and wonder of trees in scripture.

FACING PAGE: *Beautiful Tuscany countryside of cypress and oak, pine and poplar, i.e. conifer and broadleaved intermingled. Though to the north of Rome, perhaps a little like the landscape the Apostles Paul and Peter saw. Photo: S. Evans*

Seed bearing plants

Genesis 1

Trees are first mentioned, along with other seed bearing plants, in the middle of the Bible's opening chapter (Gen. 1:11–13). The Hebrew word for tree (*ets*) is used throughout the Old Testament and is a broad term including stick, wood and timber as well as tree. In one place we have the Aramaic for tree (*ilan*) in Nebuchadnezzar's dream which Daniel interprets (Dan. 4). Compared with the many names of thorns, thistles and spiny plants and shrubs, the Hebrews simply called a tree a tree unless they identified it by name with the difficulties for us of sometimes not being sure of the exact translation species by species.

The trees of the third day of creation have added the special provision that they reproduce after their kind. This reflects the wonder of the ancients that plants grew, dropped seed, and more of the same appeared and could be turned to advantage as the amazing basis of food production.[2] Botanists identify two great classes of seed bearing plants, called angiosperms and gymnosperms, which, for trees, equate with broadleaves and conifers or hardwoods and softwoods. Incidentally these last terms tell us nothing about how hard or dense the wood actually is: strictly speaking balsa is a 'hardwood' and yew is a 'softwood'! The important point, as the Bible asserts, is that pine seed will not give rise to a poplar tree nor a palm nut to a eucalypt.[3] This is an important principle. Continuance of life is not random, the young are as they are because of what their parents were like. We all know this of course, but it reveals order in the universe. This fact impressed many biblical writers. For example, James, in his letter near the end of the New Testament, questions how is it possible that man made in God's likeness can both praise him and curse him with the same lips?(Jas. 3:12). He pressed home his point by observing, 'My brothers, can a fig-tree bear olives, or a grape-vine bear figs?'

In this faithfulness of successive generations, we find in these verses (Gen. 1:11–13) the germ of another biblical principle—the coexistence of young and mature, of the newborn and the elderly, indeed, of family. While there are many forests comprising trees of the same age, both arising naturally as well as, obviously, planted forests, the bulk of woodland and forest is like a family. Of course large mature trees do not in an anthropomorphic sense 'care' for their offspring, the young seedlings, but in many situations the environment of the woodland glade, sheltered from extremes of high winds and desiccating sun, is ideal for seed germination and initial growth. This is well seen in tropical rain forest where recolonisation of a gap left when some giant of the forest crashes down follows a well-defined succession of different species—early colonisers thriving in the new influx of light, secondary species, and then slower growing, long-lived ones. At each stage the trees both thrive in and modify the environment leading, if undisturbed, to the type of forest that there was before. Break this cycle or destroy the orderly succession such as by forest clearance, still so worryingly extensive in the tropics, and irretrievable damage can be done. So too, perhaps, the family unit, but the analogy must not be pressed.

The beautiful picture from the Tel Dan Nature Reserve, through which the Dan River flows as bubbling brooks and gushing torrents from the waters of Mount Hermon, illustrates this diversity. Many kinds of trees and shrubs of many ages are growing together. It is a little bit of paradise, almost 'A Garden of Eden', through which Israel's main tributary to the River Jordan flows.

Verses 11 and 12 of the Bible's first chapter (Gen. 1:11–12) are careful to use the plural emphasising variety and numbers of trees and plants. Trees, which we generally define as plants with a woody stem capable of growing unsupported to 6m (20 ft), form only a small proportion, less than 10 per cent, of the 400,000 or so kinds of flowering plants in the world. In the Mediterranean region as a whole the tree flora is not particularly rich with around 290 indigenous tree species,[4] and in this book we will only be considering 30 or so in any detail. What is interesting, though, is the diversity of plant life not only in the actual Mediterranean region but where its climate, well known by its alliterative 'warm wet winters with westerly winds', occurs elsewhere around the world. Mediterranean type climates are only found in parts of California, central Chile, South Africa's Western Cape Province, and south

ABOVE: *Dan tributary in spate*

and south-western Australia, just two per cent of the world's land surface. But this two per cent has nearly twenty per cent of the world's plant diversity.

Trees and plants are the first things made to inhabit the land God had formed and, as with all creation, God saw it was good. What a masterly and blessed understatement.

But we can say something else unique amongst creation—well almost—about trees and woodland. There are two sides to their benefit. Not only do they provide an astonishing range of products and benefits—posts, poles, paper, timber, firewood, fruits, fodder etc., but the presence of trees and forests protects the soil, modifies the local climate, provides shelter, stores carbon and provides numerous niches for wildlife. Unique among the world's resources, there is a duality: trees offer countless products to enjoy and countless benefits to confer for our and our planet's well-being.

Stewardship
Genesis 1:30

As the creation account of Genesis 1 draws to a close, trees with fruit are given for food (Gen. 1:30) and, along with all else that fills the Earth, the charge that we are to 'subdue' what God has made. Probably approaching half of all trees provide food or some other use for humans or their domestic animals. Consider how goats and camels browse semi-arid scrub as well as our enjoyment of the familiar apples, pears, citrus or olives. But it is the word translated 'subdue' or 'rule over', or 'have dominion' as it is in the Authorised Version, which has raised so many questions. Some see this as licence to exploit and hence explain man's ravaging of the Earth's precious resources. Certainly such exploitation has happened. For me as a forest scientist one of the clearest examples is destruction of Ethiopia's forest cover from forty per cent in the 1850s to less than four per cent of the land today. My visits there with Tearfund showed the consequences: widespread soil erosion, land degraded, and poor crops. No wonder when drought struck, the famine was 'biblical' to quote BBC commentator Michael Buerk as he reported the shocking scenes from the Korem camp in October 1984. As Bob Geldof lamented of the starving children, 'Do they know it's Christmas?'

The Mediterranean region has not escaped. The great savanna forests of North Africa known to the Romans and Carthaginians have long gone. Harbours once used by the Apostle Paul, for

ABOVE: *Looking west from Ephesus. The old harbour is now far inland owing to siltation because of deforestation*

example Miletus and Ephesus in western Turkey, have long silted up and are now miles inland telling of years of muddy rivers and centuries of erosion from deforestation of distant hills inland. When Richard I led the crusade in 1191 at Wadi Felik near Tel Arsuf (Apollonia just north of modern day Tel Aviv) the Saracens lay in wait hiding in forests. A thousand years before, the Jewish historian, Josephus, described another battle in these woodlands. Today they are gone. And today clearance continues. Thirty years ago in northern Iraq one of Saddam Hussain's military tactics against the Kurds was to deforest the hills and so remove cover.

These accounts could be replicated again and again. Russell Meiggs[5] devotes a chapter to Mediterranean deforestation while J V Thirgood's entire book[6] about *Man and the Mediterranean Forest* has the subtitle, '*A history*

of resource depletion'. Probably three-quarters of the pre-civilisation forest cover has gone.[7] We abrogated our God-given position and neglected environmental imperatives because of disregard and greed. But the words translated 'subdue' and 'rule' contain more the idea of civilised government of land under control rather than pillage or rape of resources. Joshua (Josh 17:18 & 18:1) has it exactly—wild, including forested, country being brought under control where it was needed. One aspect of development, including those fostered by Christian organisations, is care for and restoration of land qualities. Thus good land husbandry is an integral part of farming, forestry and rural development.

The first garden
Genesis 2 & 3

Gardens are significant places in the Bible. A mention of Gethsemane or where Christ was buried (John 19:41) and straightaway the Christian is transported to the heart of the gospel. The Bible presents the Garden of Eden (Gen. 2:8–25) not as an imaginary or mythical paradise lost in times long past, but a real place in 'Eden', with real trees, and plenty of 'real' work to do. A garden God planted for man to enjoy and to tend. Moses gives precise, although not now adequately identifiable, details of its location: somewhere in the well watered low lying region of Mesopotamia is the best guess.[8] Much about the Garden foreshadows the rest of the Bible story, but the picture of the Lord God lovingly creating it, planting it, surely delights. The image Genesis conveys is of, 'an enclosed designed landscape planted with trees, a kind of arboretum that was both pleasant to look at and useful as a food supply.[9]

Gardens were important elsewhere and from the earliest times we meet them and how they are the root of the word 'paradise' in Chapter 5.

The account of the Garden of Eden has a particular resonance for foresters. God planting it and Adam working it pictures what foresters mostly do: they take over for a time the care and management of woodland and forest that another created and then pass it on to their successors. Rarely does the same person regenerate or plant a forest and then live to see all its benefits. We see ourselves as stewards of what we have inherited and, as my old professor would say, 'must pass it on in better shape than when we received it'. Of course it's not only foresters who have this sense of being custodians: those caring for orchards or a pedigree herd of cattle built up over the generations, or the great plant collections, botanic gardens, and arboreta such as Kew in England or the Arnold in America know the same sentiment.

Pleasing to the eye
Genesis 2:9a

The great variety of trees and their value as good for food is reiterated in the second creation account of Genesis Chapter 2. But what excites me is the remark God reserves for trees—and trees alone—in all his creation (Gen. 2:9): *trees that were pleasing to the eye.* God saw they were good (Gen. 1:12), but here aesthetic appreciation, beauty and loveliness is declared good and desirable in its own right. Usefulness is important to God, but God shares our appreciation of the aesthetic or, rather, our capacity to admire the sunset or be thrilled by magnificent scenery or take pleasure in an evening stroll is a mark of His image within us. Humans, set apart from animals, are truly closer to God because we both like trees to be around! Thus it is almost to be expected that, later on, part of what tempted Adam and Eve to take the forbidden fruit was that they found its appearance appealing (Gen. 3:6).

This visual appreciation is actually therapeutic, it does us good. It is now well established that recovery from illness or surgery is aided when a patient can look out on greenery as opposed to a brick wall or just the interior of a ward. The converse has also been found. An American study of 18 years data across fifteen states found significantly increased mortality and ill-health in the population where the insect emerald ash borer had killed ash trees and turned once tree-lined streets treeless.[10]

So important today is the visual and aesthetic that in many countries laws protect trees of high amenity value. In Britain there are tree preservation orders with this intention uppermost. A tree evokes strange and powerful emotions, even passions—just consider how we respond to a threat to a much-loved tree, yet it is hardly surprising if God, in fact, made them for us to enjoy with all of our senses. So there is much more than even duality. Trees have uses, they confer benefits and they are lovely to behold: as our creator said, they are both good and pleasing.

Two very special trees
Genesis 2:9b

In the same verse (Gen. 2:9) we are introduced to the first of two kinds of trees singled out by title, the tree of life and the tree of knowledge of good and evil. Regarding the first there is no tree today which can claim to be such an elixir though many healthy foods come from trees, and, as we've noted, forests themselves protect soil and help restore or

ABOVE: *A young African baobab* (Adansonia digitata) *in the foreground with older, larger ones on the horizon: almost a 'tree of life', it's so useful*

heal degraded land. Nevertheless, some trees do symbolise life in the abundance they provide. The olive (*Olea europaea*) is a well-known example, but so too is the great baobab of the dry African bush. It is only in leaf for a few months, but this occurs in the dry season when most other trees have dropped theirs. The leaves themselves are edible, tasting a bit like spinach; the seeds are refreshing to suck and when soaked will make a palatable drink somewhat like coffee; the bark is soft and fibrous and can be used for making cloth, ropes and matting; and, in the crown of the tree, water can be found in tender shoots. During droughts elephants prise up the bark to get at water within. Legends abound about the wonderful baobab, not least that God planted it upside down! In contrast to the baobab's grotesquely fat and stubby appearance is the slender *Leucaena*, once the wonder tree of tropical development. It grows very fast, it enriches the soil, its foliage and pods make excellent fodder, and its woody stem is good for firewood or furniture. Sadly over-reliance on a few clones—trees propagated using the same genetic material—exposed this tree to a devastating pest and its use today is much curtailed.[11]

These remarks are very Western and factual about trees. What intrigued and what puzzled those in ancient times was how can a tree sustain life for hundreds even thousands of years?[12] Human awe at the seemingly immortal 'tree of life' was seen all around in field and forest leading to their worship and reverence. As we find later, even the Israelites succumbed both in what they began to worship, wooden idols, and where, 'beneath every spreading tree'.

Many living trees might rightly claim the title 'tree of life' though none has the abundance and variety or the 'healing' powers of the tree of life we meet at the Bible's end (Rev. 22:3). Almost unique among natural resources is that a tree's usefulness does not stop at death. Indeed, life after death is not putting it too strongly when we consider the years and years of benefit and pleasure an oak table gives or the strength beams and rafters afford in supporting a ceiling or roof. Today we would add that such use of wood keeps the carbon stored. And, for a Christian, the singular importance of the paper of the pages of our Bibles in which are recorded the very words of life and, symbolically, Christ's cross itself as 'the tree of life'.

We return to the tree of life in Chapter 6, as well as in the final chapter. However, it is not only in Genesis and the Bible that we find the idea. Many ancient Near East civilisations from early times portray a tree being honoured or paid homage, though it is not always clear quite what or how. The 9th Century BC reliefs in the British Museum of the Assyrian King, Ashurnasirpal II, show such a tree with an eagle headed spirit—the model for C S Lewis's Tash in the Narnia stories—appearing to offer it a pine cone. This is odd since the tree, albeit stylised, suggests a broadleaf not conifer. With no explanatory text we are left guessing, but it is just one example of the tree motif so common

BELOW: *A mythical, sacred tree paid homage by an eagle-headed spirit, and*

BELOW, LOWER: *by King Ashurnasirpal in ritual robes. (British Museum)*

in Assyrian and Egyptian imagery and religious life.

The tree of knowledge of good and evil we meet only in Genesis. Such super ethical food did not really exist, but by taking fruit that was forbidden the guilt generated by this first act of disobedience would reveal the existence of good and evil to Adam and Eve and hence the fact of alternatives. The revealing of an alternative to what Adam and Eve had known brought new knowledge about the very goodness of the sinless paradise from which they were about to be ejected.

That this knowledge comes symbolically from a tree, seems fitting. Compared with an animal or flower, there is something permanent, solid, immutable about a tree, just as there is about the fact of good and evil: a fact that Adam and Eve could not hide from, just as the trees of the Garden of Eden could not hide them, and their guilt, from God. Fitting too is something negative about trees that planners and the police both know. They can provide cover harbouring criminals. So consideration of where best to site groups of trees and shrubs amongst housing, as well as the provision of lighting, all has to be part of the mix in developing the built environment. Though today society is abandoning absolutes for tolerance, reasonableness, compromise and flexibility in much of life, recognising right from wrong and good from bad remains every functioning community's foundation. Otherwise, we lose our way. The towering stature and spreading umbrella of a tree over us pictures this superior principle that God's absolutes are, for us, larger than life.

Figs
Genesis 3:7

The first identifiable tree (just) is in Genesis 3:7.[13] Adam and Eve sewed fig leaves to cover themselves because they were naked. In the Bible two kinds of fig tree are mentioned, the widely cultivated fruit (probably implied here because even today the large hand-shaped leaves of the common fig (*Ficus carica*) are still sometimes sewn together) and the sycomore-fig (*Ficus sycomorus*) which we remember from Sunday School as the tree the diminutive Zacchaeus climbed to see Jesus (Luke 19:4) on his way through Jericho. The sycomore-fig[14] also produces edible fruits which are not as nutritious or sweet and were known as the poor man's figs. It is a common tree and we meet it again.

The common fig is described as the third classical fruit, after the olive and grape-vine, associated with the beginnings of horticulture in the eastern Mediterranean and south-west Asia.[15] It has a very ancient lineage and history of cultivation and, as with most fruit crops, the key for the grower is to domesticate productive or specially sweet cultivars (genotypes) that arise. Usually this is done by taking cuttings i.e. by means of vegetative propagation. Unusual about the fig is that a single mutation leads to cultivars that produce delicious fruits without requiring pollination and fertilisation, a characteristic called parthenocarpy. Propagation of such desirable forms would have been achieved of old, and still is today, by rooting cuttings of dormant twigs taken in winter.

Adam and Eve used fig leaves to cover themselves. As well as large size, the heavily veined and ribbed leaves sew quite well, not tearing too easily. Ancient Midrash literature[16] suggests a pun or play on words here in that the Hebrew for fig (*t'einah*) sounds very similar to grief or trouble (*to-anah*). Having to sew fig leaves was the beginning, was the first of all the troubles Adam and Eve had begun!

Cursed and expelled from the Garden
Genesis 3:17–18

We end this first chapter with the scene of Adam and Eve doing wrong by a tree, picking what had been forbidden, and being expelled from the Garden of Eden. It continues: doing wrong by trees and forests which are cut down unnecessarily, whether pristine tropical forests for palm oil or English hedges and

hedgerow trees for rape oil. There is plenty of already degraded land suitable for the former, and happily less destruction of the latter than hitherto. But the point remains that, like the first sin, we reap a harvest of toil as soil erodes, floods come, wildlife dies and living becomes more arduous. The cursed ground of Genesis 3:17–18 is an apt description of much degraded land today where forest had been destroyed, soil fertility lost, and often bush and unproductive scrub all that is left.

The beginnings of farming
Genesis 4

The account of Cain and Abel's offerings of their produce in Genesis Chapter 4 not only betrays their contrasting faith in God, but also presents the two sides of farming: arable and livestock. Archaeology has shown that the Middle East was the cradle of agriculture. In Neolithic times the first evidence of domestication of plants is found in the Fertile Crescent and the Levant (Israel, Lebanon and Syria).[17] The place of trees and their early management, beyond forest clearance or gathering fruits, is unclear, but without doubt the olive was cultivated from a very early time with figs and date palms not far behind.

The long years of toil had begun. The principle of hard work to earn reward was well in place. Trees were both a hindrance, if land had to be cleared, and a hope, offering some of the most useful crops of all to cultivate and resources to have available.

Perhaps we should add, too, that Cain and Abel's offerings remind us of something else. Throughout biblical times society was predominantly agrarian, not industrialised. Most of us today are distant, literally and figuratively, from the countryside and what goes on on the farm or in the forest. Looking at these, which are also distant back in time, adds a further challenge just as do the many biblical metaphors, analogies and allegories that draw on the rural and the pastoral with which we are unfamiliar.

FACING PAGE: *Severe erosion in Ethiopia owing to deforestation. The land has lost its farming value and is costly to rehabilitate*

Notes

1 This is the familiar translation. The Greek in 1 Pet. 2:24, and also Acts 5:30 and Gal. 3:13, is *xulon*, not *dendron* the usual word for tree, and it has the wider meaning of wood, pole, timber as well as tree. Most modern English translations have 'pole'.

2 **Walton, J H** (2009) *The Lost World of Genesis One—Ancient cosmology and origins debate*. IVP Academic, Downers Grove, Illinois.

3 The inheritance or passing on of characteristics from generation to generation is more or less fixed in every living cell by a complex pattern of chemicals in the nucleus, the DNA molecules. They make up the genes. DNA has the remarkable capacity to replicate and communicate its structure so that the right kind of growth occurs. The way chemicals (bases) are ordered in the DNA determines that acorns become oaks and that a leaf becomes a leaf and not, say, a root in the wrong place. We have the ability today to intervene in this process (genetic modification or GM) by adding or changing the DNA at certain points to create new characteristics. Also study of DNA in humans shows that we are all descended from one 'super mother' an 'Eve' though the timeline accorded by evolutionary biologists may differ from the biblical.

4 **Fady, B** and **Medail, F** (2004) Mediterranean Forest Ecosystems. In **Burley, J, Evans, J** and **Younquist, J A** (eds) *Encyclopedia of Forest Science* (Oxford: Elseveir Ltd), 1403–1414.

5 **Meiggs, R** (1982) *Trees and Timber in the Ancient Mediterranean World*. Clarendon Press, Oxford

6 **Thirgood, J V** (1982) *Man and the Mediterranean Forest—A history of resource depletion*. Academic Press, London

7 **Fady, B** and **Medail F** (ibid)

8 **Eveson, P H** (2001) *The book of origins—Genesis simply explained*. Evangelical Press, Darlington

9 **Usher, G B** (2012) *Places of Enchantment—meeting God in Landscapes*. SPCK, London.

10 **Donovan, G H, Butry, D T, Michael, Y L, Prestemon, J P, Liebhold, A M, Gatziolis, D** and **Mao, M Y**. (2013) 'The Relationship Between Trees and Human Health', *American Journal of Preventive Medicine*, 2013; 44 (2): 139

11 **Evans, J** and **Turnbull, J W** (2004) *Plantation Forestry in the Tropics*. 3rd Edn. Oxford University Press

12 **Hareuveni, N** (2006) *Tree and Shrub in Our Biblical Heritage*. Neot Kedumim Ltd, Lod, Israel. (Transl. by **Helen Frenkley**).

13 **Zohary, M** (1982) *Plants of the Bible—a complete handbook*. Cambridge University Press, Cambridge

14 Not to be confused with sycamore (a species of maple (*Acer*)), or sycamine, another name for black mulberry.

15 **Zohary, D, Hopf. M**, and **Weiss, E** (2012) *Domestication of Plants in the Old World*. 4th Edition. Oxford University Press.

16 **Hareuveni** (ibid)

17 **Zohary, et al.** (2012). (ibid).

ABOVE: *The first mention of olive in the Bible is the freshly plucked leaf the dove brought back to Noah as a sign that the floodwaters were receding. As a fruit tree it may well have been the first to have been brought into cultivation providing, principally, food and oil—the latter for cooking, lighting, anointing and cleansing—symbolic of a tree of life. The symbolism of olive for peace and prosperity continued through history.*

2

Genesis 5–50 and Exodus

From ark to ark

Of all human undertakings Noah's Ark stands out pre-eminent. Not because of grandeur, nor because it worked, nor even that so vast a structure was built so early in history, but because it was constructed in the face of all reason. Noah's neighbours could not and would not see the purpose of it. Yet the ark was completed, and on time, and without sea trials and commissioning, to do the job required because of Noah's faith—that what God said was true and was going to happen.

Noah's Ark
Genesis 6

We are told the ark was made of wood (Gen. 6:14). It is the first article so described in the Bible, though presumably the harps and flutes (Gen. 4:21), farm implements and many of the buildings in Cain's city (Gen. 4:17) were also. Exactly what kind of wood Noah used we cannot be at all sure: the Hebrew word translated 'gopher wood' in the King James version could be cypress (*Cupressus sempervirens*), and this is what the 2011 NIV has but it footnotes the uncertainty. Some have suggested that the word 'gopher' refers to the way the ark was constructed, with squared or planed beams, or that it is the use of pitch as a sealant for caulking that it signifies. We really don't know. It is possible, too, that the timber is not even available today having been lost in the destruction a flood lasting for months would have wrought. We do

know that in later classical times pitch was a valued and traded commodity not only by the shipwright, but for lining jars, amphora, for storing wine and even, when in liquid form, for flavouring it![1] The best source of pitch is from tapping pine trees and other resinous conifers though the small turpentine tree (*Pistacia terebinthus*) was a prized source of a resin like substance. However, we really know very little about the ark and can only speculate.

The word 'ark' literally means 'box' or 'chest'. Although the same English word is used for the 'ark' of the covenant (Exod. 25–38), the Hebrew for Noah's Ark only occurs again for the basket bearing little baby Moses among the rushes of the Nile (Exod. 2:2–3). The ship-like designs we find adorning so many children's bibles owe much to the artists' colourful imagination, while the famous flood story in the epic of Gilgamesh indicates simply a box structure. The carefully recorded dimensions of the ark (Gen. 6:15–16) clearly suggest a vessel which would be stable and plainly seaworthy. Beyond this we really can't say. It is only in the choice of the same English word that allows the preacher to exhort: that one 'ark', Noah's Ark, saved a few from the destruction brought by sin while the other 'ark', the ark of the covenant, contained the law which exposes what sin is.

Making things out of wood was not as easy as today's ready access to the timber yard and DIY shops might suggest. Trees have to be selected, felled, debranched, and then taken to where they are to be used or processed. Without modern machines, Noah would have dragged logs to a saw or laboriously cut them up on site. It is unlikely they would have been used in the round (as foresters say) like an American log cabin, simply because it is nigh impossible to make their joints watertight. Trees are heavy and felling them is dangerous. A 30 m (100 ft) cypress, perhaps of 50 cm diameter (60 in girth) would weigh 4–5 tons. Felling by axe (made of stone?) would take at least a day and unless direction of fall was guided by ropes, there must have been accidents. Millennia later 'The Teacher' highlights the dangers of splitting logs (Eccles. 10:9). Even today, with numerous safety devices available, forestry work has one of the highest industrial accident rates. We do not know whether Noah began building the ark where the trees were in the middle of a forest or whether he selected a good site, perhaps specially flat and even near a river such as the Tigris or Euphrates, and dragged or floated logs to it. Whichever, it was long, arduous and hard work.

The Bible tells us the ark's dimensions and it was the largest vessel built in the history of the world until the mid 19th Century. It probably had a displacement of around 40–50,000 tons. Several thousand tons of logs would have been used, not to mention all those needed for houses and other infrastructure facilities. If Noah was in the business of clearfelling forests, hundreds of hectares would have been cut while the ark was under construction. If only selected trees were taken then a much larger area of forest would have been stamped with the efforts of the man's labour with all the tracks and trails along which to drag the logs or the pits dug to saw logs to shape. Then there were the shipwright skills, carpentry, administration and even catering to consider. It is staggering to ponder the scale of industry required as Noah obeyed God's instructions .

We are told that when rain began to fall it beat upon the ark's roof incessantly for 40 days. Would Noah's life's work float according to plan? Would they all be safe? Did they have enough food including for all the animals and livestock? Was the caulking of pitch inside and out sufficient or would the ark spring leaks? We can only surmise the thoughts of this man of faith, but he had on his side a unique characteristic of wood. Even if his pitch application wasn't perfect, after a week or so afloat any leaks the ark had would be fewer or perhaps have disappeared altogether because wood is hygroscopic. Wood absorbs or releases moisture depending on its surroundings—hence paper towels and toilet rolls made from wood fibres work. As water is absorbed, wood expands slightly, as sticking doors in damp weather remind us! This 'movement' is the bane of the joiner and furniture maker, but a blessing to the shipwright who sees joints tighten and fit more snugly—the water itself makes the boat more watertight. Though perhaps the long years building the ark and the drying out of the great timbers would have made a leaky vessel, the rain God used to judge mankind was also His own finishing touch to make sure that the few inside the ark were safe and dry.

The verses 7 and 18 of Genesis 6 seem to suggest that trees were not singled out for judgment though obviously prolonged submersion and strong currents would leave few if any alive. Small seedlings, fruits and seeds might have floated on mats of vegetation. Was that where the dove found an olive leaf (Gen. 8:11) though it is described as freshly plucked? Some tree species such as mangroves can grow in water, others, for example, alders, are tolerant of very wet conditions, and some, such as willows (*Salix* spp.), have structures able to transport oxygen molecules to the submerged parts to survive the period of anaerobism. Total submerging for six months as the Bible indicates is quite another thing.

There is another narrative too. Many have thought it, but few articulated it as well as the 'grandfather' of forestry in England, John Evelyn. In his famous *Silva*,[2] presented to the fledgling Royal Society in 1662, and first published in 1664, he writes:

In a word, and to speak a bold and noble truth, trees and woods have twice saved the whole world; first by the ark, then by the cross; making full amends for the evil fruit of the tree in paradise, by that which was born on the tree in Golgotha.

ABOVE: *Hadrian's Wall. Many of the stones have found their way into other buildings. Wouldn't Noah's Ark have been similarly raided for its timbers?*

Might we find remains of the ark?

Various groups have claimed to have found remains of the ark usually on the Mt Ararat complex in the eastern Turkey, Armenia, and southern Russia region. One such investigator, Fernand Navarra,[3] during an expedition in 1955, obtained wood samples from what he thought might be the ark embedded in a glacier. The pieces appeared to be from timbers that had been fashioned by primitive tools, were of oak (*Quercus* spp.) and probably around 5000 years old though carbon dating gave a younger age. Even 5000 years is not as old as many would expect, and suggesting the wood might have come from the ark is speculation. Many other expeditions have been mounted and many claims made as a quick google of Noah's Ark reveals. Evidence for the ark and the flood is attested by reference to them in many mythologies. Josephus, the Jewish historian writing in the 1st Century, asserts that, 'all writers of barbarian histories

make mention of this flood and this ark' and that local people collect pieces of bitumen from it.[4] Most importantly, Jesus speaks of them as plain fact (Matt. 24:37–39; Luke 17:26–27).

But are remains of the ark really likely to be discovered? Wouldn't Noah and his family have raided the great wooden structure for building materials, for fuel and for countless other purposes? One generation is always pilfering the efforts of a preceding one—the gleaming white facing stones gone from the great Egyptian pyramids, the beautifully fashioned blocks comprising Hadrian's Wall now supporting Northumbrian farmhouses, and many a ship's timbers throughout history. We know that in ancient Egypt timber was carefully husbanded. When contemporary buildings were abandoned, the woodwork, flooring, rafters, door and window frames were usually removed and used again.[5]

'Pilfering' is perhaps ungenerous, recycling is

ABOVE: *The great terebinth at the hill top lookout in Tel Dan Nature Reserve. Probably the great tree of Moreh was one.*

a better sentiment. Surely the ark would not have been left untouched where it came to rest?

The story of Noah does not end with the ark landing on Mt Ararat. Indeed, Noah is held up throughout the Bible as an example of faith and the flood as a reminder of God's judgment of sin. The account itself in Genesis concludes with Noah planting a vineyard. Then as now planting is an act of confidence in the future.

From Ur to angels with Abraham
Genesis 10–12

Chapters 10 and 11 of Genesis cover long periods of history. The use of wood and timber must have massively increased as villages, towns and cities grew as domestication and settled farming became increasingly established.[6] Archaeologically wooden artefacts don't often survive because they decay or are perhaps used for fuel when broken or no longer wanted. But with the next great man of faith, Abraham, we find uses and benefits of trees

in the environment which are appreciated by every generation.

What is recorded of Abraham are trees as landmarks, as property, as objects commemorating events, and as providing much needed shade in a hot, dusty land. Indeed, after leaving his home town of Ur, Abraham's first resting place in the promised land of Canaan was at the site of the great tree of Moreh at Shechem (Gen. 12:6). It was probably a magnificent spreading terebinth, or a group of trees, which may have been a striking feature by fact of their size or great age. They are present over several centuries of biblical history: it's where Jacob probably hid the gods and jewellery of his wives (Gen. 35:4), where Joshua set up the witness stone to record the covenant the people made to be true to their God (Josh. 24:26), and where Abimelek had himself crowned (Judges 9:6) though by this time, 600–700 years after Abraham, the wording (pillar) could suggest that only a great hulk is left as is typical of very, very old oaks.

ABOVE: *A solitary tamarisk helping shade visitors to Masada*

Trees for commemoration

Genesis 14, 21 & 23

Both a tree's size and the ability of some kinds to live for hundreds, and in a few cases, thousands of years, and so long outlast our three score and ten, has attracted veneration. In England we find trees, and especially oaks, becoming memorials like the Knightwood Oak in the New Forest or the Wilberforce Oak in Kent under which William Wilberforce, the great Christian social reformer, pondered the evils of the slave trade. And, like Abraham of old who planted a tamarisk tree, (probably the 'leafless tamarisk' (*Tamarix aphylla*)), to commemorate the treaty of Beersheba and the place where he called on the name of the Lord, the Eternal God (Gen. 21:33), we still plant trees to mark an occasion, celebrate a coronation, or honour someone special.

Several tamarisk species occur around Beersheba, all are slow-growing, hardy, and long-lived. Only the 'leafless' tamarisk achieves tree size and grows

as odd individuals in the plains and wadis.[7] An old saying had it that you never planted a tamarisk for yourself but for later generations. It was possibly a tamarisk under which the ejected and disconsolate Hagar placed Ishmael (Gen. 21:15) though a white broom (*Retama raetam*) bush is more likely. Abraham's action of planting may not only have marked a treaty, but perhaps was implying that one day we, my people, will return.

The choice of tree Abraham planted, tamarisk (*eshel* in Hebrew), is explicit in the Bible. It was a good one. The greyish-green clumpy foliage is visible from afar and to sit in its shade, especially in the morning, is pleasant and unusually cool. Tamarisk foliage exudes tiny, very salty droplets (by a process similar to gutation) which, as the droplets evaporate, cool the air. Abraham 'chose the tree whose shade is cooler than that of any other trees'.[8]

Although we no longer use trees to identify legal title—stones, fences, walls and ditches have traditionally been used to delineate boundaries—laying claim to land identified by its trees still occurs. Something very like this Abraham probably did when buying the field near Mamre, specifically with its trees (Gen. 23:17), doubtless because of its past associations for him. It was where he first settled (Gen. 13:18), where he was blessed by Melchizedek, King of Salem (Gen. 14:13); it was where the Lord appeared to him and, perhaps very especially, it was where he first heard the prophecy that at last his ageing wife would conceive the child God had long promised. There is a warmth, too, that Abraham was able to purchase, to repossess as it were, the very field and cave near Mamre with all its trees where such portentous events had occurred, and where to bury his beloved Sarah (Gen. 23:17–20). Such kinds of affections and associations can be found today.

One example of trees used in this way is found in Papua New Guinea, where I worked in the 1970s, and is also the case elsewhere in the South Pacific. Claim to land and identity of ownership among tribal groups often relates to the trees an ancestor planted. The act of tree planting itself is seen as staking a claim. This customary ownership practice and the deeply held commitment to the land it represents, raises all sorts of issues when, say, governments want to carry out afforestation which, of course, usually means planting large numbers of trees! If all the trees our Queen has planted in her long reign were staking a claim, far more than our allegiance would she get! Another example is in my own wood, part of which is a pightle (a medieval word meaning enclosure and pronounced 'pie—tell'). The pightle is square, about five acres, and is bordered by great English oaks (*Quercus robur*), one of which is nearly 300 years old. It is the finest tree in all of our small wood and we've named it 'Mum's Oak' to commemorate my late wife.

Rest and comfort
Genesis 18

Earlier in the account of Abraham and Sarah one other benefit of trees is recorded: resting in their shade (or sheltering from the rain). Three visitors, the three angels, turned up unannounced and Abraham was quick to welcome them and show hospitality by first ushering them under the trees

ABOVE: *Even in England livestock needs the shade when it's hot!*

(Gen. 18:4) for rest and comfort after their journey. Perhaps they were the only trees in the vicinity, perhaps they were becoming scarce in the semi-arid land, though we do find Abraham standing under another tree at a polite distance, and surely consumed with curiosity as he watched them eat (Gen. 18:8).

Shade and shelter is stressed because throughout the Mediterranean region trees serve this purpose. And not only around the Mediterranean; providing this comfort, this amenity, where it has been lost is one of the drivers of social or community forestry—tree planting and woodland management specifically to benefit a village and villagers—in many tropical and sub-tropical countries alongside providing firewood, fodder and building materials. Not only does shade make work more congenial for humans, but even in the heat of the day cattle can graze contentedly whereas in the open grazing is confined to early morning and late afternoon. The barren landscapes of the Middle East, of the Sudan or the Sahel zone of West Africa—a barrenness often of man's making—are all the worse for not only the absence of firewood or protection for the soil, but also for how little shelter and shade there is for the hapless villager who calls the place home.

Three surprises and a request

Before concluding this chapter with the other wooden ark, the ark of the covenant, there are four intriguing episodes between the time of Abraham and the Israelites' exodus from Egypt which involve wood. Of course, many other references to wood and trees occur such as Aaron's staff, the stripping of trees by hail in the plagues, and the wooden door posts and lintels daubed with blood so the angel of death would pass over the firstborn of the Hebrews. These are touched on in another chapter, but here we cannot pass by what Jacob got up to to increase his flock, or his request concerning where he wanted to be buried, and we certainly cannot pass by the burning bush as Moses couldn't, or ignore how Moses made sweet the bitter waters of Marah.

Jacob's sheep and where he wanted to be buried

Genesis 30 & 31

The first surprise occurs when Jacob is in charge of his father-in-law Laban's flocks. Jacob had been tricked into working twice as long for Laban, for 14 years not the agreed seven, to marry his love, Rachel. Now the tables were turned: Jacob rapidly builds his flocks in a surprising way. Laban allowed him to have all the coloured, speckled and spotty sheep and goats and Jacob managed to increase the proportion of these that were born by encouraging mating in front of peeled branches of poplar (*Populus euphratica*), almond (*Prunus dulcis*) and plane (*Platanus orientalis*) trees[9] (Gen. 30:37–43)! The sticks, with the exposed white wood, were placed near or in the drinking trough where the animals would mate. It formed a central part of Jacob's ruse to increase his flock at the expense of Laban's. How we explain it remains a mystery since we know that external factors do not influence what is inherited.

Perhaps we don't need to explain it. Even though Laban had allowed Jacob first to remove (and keep as his wages) all the existing spotty and speckled animals so Jacob only had pure white sheep to work with, the genes for colour would still be in the flock

and something like a quarter of all the offspring would be coloured. Also because Jacob deliberately selected the strongest and healthiest sheep to breed from (and be given this patent treatment), the spotted and speckled ones he was allowed to keep would be robust. So, just laws of inheritance working as if to confirm what was clearly a custom of the time. Jacob had been treated harshly and the clear implication of Genesis 31:12 is that God was allowing the increasing proportion of spotted and speckled animals as a way of recompense.

Many experiments have sought to find out whether outside influences directly affect the nature of offspring—known as the inheritance of acquired characteristics. Apart from a few special cases it is clear that offspring are directly the result of what is passed on (inherited) from their parents which recalls, of course, Genesis Chapter 1 and the refrain of, 'after or according to their kind'. [A pseudo-example of factors influencing progeny occurs in human reproduction where the pH (acidity) of the fluid through which male sperm swims to reach the female egg to fertilise it affects the proportion of male gene-carrying to female gene-carrying sperm. Similarly, gender in some turtle species is influenced by the temperature the egg is incubated.]

The request of Jacob comes at the end of his life. It happens several years after Joseph has been reconciled with his brothers and his ageing father, Jacob, again embraces his beloved son and brings his extended family, the Israelites, to settle in Egypt. He asks before he dies, 'Do not bury me in Egypt, but when I rest with my fathers, carry me out of Egypt and bury me where they are buried' (Gen. 46:29–30). He wants to be buried in the same cave as his fathers in the field Abraham bought (Gen. 49:29–32). As father of the second highest person in the land—his son Joseph was in effect Pharoah's prime minister—his body would have been embalmed and presumably kept in a coffin.

We know from archaeological excavation in Egypt that coffins were made out of both local and imported timbers. Local timbers were cut mostly from the sycomore fig, tamarisk, and sometimes acacia trees. The trunk would be sawn lengthways—so tedious and tiresome with the tools of the day—and then smoothed with an adze

ABOVE: *Outer casing of an Egyptian coffin made from expensive imported cedar wood c. 1850 BC (British Museum)*

and finished off with a rubbing (sanding) stone. The resulting planks were often rough and ready because of all the knots and the crooked shape of the indigenous trees themselves. Thus high ranking officials wanting the best would have expensive coffins made from imported softwood notably cedar of Lebanon, but occasionally of cypress or juniper (*Juniperus excelsa*). These fine, tall conifers produce long straight planks and are readily crafted to a high finish to create an altogether superior product. Did Jacob have a cedar coffin: a coffin fit for a patriarch as well as a Pharoah?

The burning bush and bitter water
Exodus 3 & 15

The phenomenon of the burning bush (Exod. 3:1–3) which appeared not to be consumed, caught Moses'

attention. He knew the wilderness and desert well, from all his years in Midian tending Jethro's flocks, and he had never seen a bush like it. It was how God caught his attention to commission him to return to Egypt to free the enslaved Hebrews. But what was it Moses saw?

There has been much speculation among botanists, one of the more plausible being that a desert acacia tree was covered in the semi-parasitic, scarlet-flowered mistletoe, *Loranthus acacia,* with its arresting fire-red blossoms. Other suggestions are the shrub known as the gas-plant (*Dictamnus albus*) which exude oils that vaporise and can ignite, or the Sinai hawthorn (*Crataegus sinaica*). But as has been pointed out,[10] if we can identify a botanical explanation surely the desert hardened Moses would know it. The account emphasises Moses's

ABOVE: *Desert hawthorn aflame with berries. A possible, but unlikely explanation for the 'burning bush'.*

surprise and his being kept at a distance. This has led to the interesting explanation that Moses saw a mirage of a fire centred on the bush in the way that images are refracted through the atmosphere from tens of miles away. This would be remarkable, is feasible, and would surely catch one's attention like a striking rainbow does, and it would account for the midrash[11] observation that only the upper part of the bush was seen to be aflame. It would also allow the Hebrew for the bush 'sneh' to be the blackberry bush (*Rubus sanctus*) that ancient tradition, Jewish and Christian, has long identified as the burning bush.[12]

Years later something else caught Moses's attention: after crossing the Red Sea the Israelites found the waters of Marah to be bitter (Exod. 15:22–25). It was their very first resting place away from Egypt and it was no good. Everyone started complaining and Moses cried out to the Lord and he was shown a piece of wood (or a tree) to throw into the water. The water became sweet. There is a similar occurrence in 2 Kgs. 2:19–22 where some salt not a piece of wood is added to turn the brackish to drinkable. In this case might the salt have been the conventional coagulant alum which is still used in purification today? We don't know, but what that passage emphasises is God's specific intervention, 'I have healed this water, says the Lord' (2 Kgs. 2:21). But in the case of the wells at Marah it is God who instructs Moses how to purify the water by showing him a piece of wood (or tree) to throw in to turn bitter waters sweet? Is this conceivable: if not, why have the comment about wood or tree?

The surprising answer is 'yes'. One tree of

ABOVE: *Moringa tree at Ein Gedi Nature Reserve. Its long pods are just discernible at top left. Were they what Moses used to turn the bitter waters of Marah sweet?*

the desert has this property, the moringa, where turbid water can be cleared and made drinkable by adding powdered seeds. Moringa seeds contain proteins that act as chemical coagulants which cause impurities, suspended solids and 98 per cent of bacteria to settle out (flocculate) rather as alum does.[13] The best known is *Moringa olifeira* and one tree can provide sufficient seeds to treat 30,000 litres (7000 gals) of water: it is currently recommended for use by rural communities without access to clean running water.[14] What is remarkable is that it only takes a couple of hours at most to give tap-quality water. However, the 14 or so kinds of moringa tree mostly occur in India and the Horn of Africa, but there is one species, *Moringa peregrina*, that is found in the Middle East in Egypt, the Sinai Peninsula, Saudi Arabia, Oman, Israel, Jordan and Syria. It is now scarce and endangered, achieves tree size of up to 10 m, and its seeds possess this water purifying ability. In Israel it is the ben-oil or

bean tree, in Jordan the mazur. Was this the tree God directed Moses to use to clear Marah's turbid waters? We can't be sure. Nevertheless, it is fact that the undrinkable can become drinkable with the help of a tree, and we know there was one such tree species occurring naturally in the Desert of Shur where Moses and the people of Israel made their first halt three days after crossing the Red Sea.

The Israelites next stop (Exod. 16:27) is well provisioned with plenty of springs and seventy palm trees. It must have been good because even the name of the place, Elim, means 'large trees'!

The Ark of the covenant
Exodus 25–27 & 35–39

The ark of the covenant was the wooden chest or box to house the law that God had imparted to Moses on Mt Sinai.

The construction of the tabernacle or tent, including the precious ark, occupies all of the remaining chapters of the book of Exodus from Chapter 25. All the articles and trappings made from wood, the ark itself, the poles and posts, the table and the two altars, and the upright frames and crossbars of the tabernacle are fashioned out of acacia, 'shittim' in Hebrew. Shittim is also a place-name where, presumably, acacia trees abounded (Josh. 2:1). There are several acacia species that occur in the semi-arid conditions of the desert wadis of the Sinai including the extremely hardy desert acacia (*Acacia raddiana*). None is a large tree but are widely available and provide wood that is durable, hard, strong and would take a good finish; just the features required for the skilled craft work and joinery. Sometimes, too, they grow tall enough with substantial enough trunks to provide the longer lengths required by the measurements spelt out e.g. Exod. 26:15–16.[15]

Acacia wood has another valuable property. It shows relatively little 'movement', that is the tiny changes in shape that cause warping and twisting that occur when wood absorbs and loses moisture— the property that helped Noah's Ark to become more watertight the longer it was in the water. This lack of movement was significant because virtually the whole of every article was overlaid with beaten gold except the altar for burnt offerings

ABOVE: *Desert acacias in the Negev (with Arabian oryx). Photo: F. Leung*

where bronze was used. While in their wilderness wanderings acacia wood was probably the only feasible choice, it was still well chosen.

The details of construction were given by God to Moses (Exod. 25:9 and 27:8). They were not a general vision of the kind of thing to make, but a complete set of plans, a blueprint, though how Moses remembered every instruction, along with the laws and commands, greatly impresses. Perhaps it shouldn't. As Jesus promised his disciples that the Spirit would bring all that He had said back to mind after He had gone (John 14:26), Moses was specially blessed of God who not only commands and instructs, but provides enabling gifts as well.

We see this very especially when it comes to whom actually fashioned the ark, the table and the altars. God revealed to Moses that He was going to bless Bezalel with the gift of craftsmanship; his Spirit would come upon him specifically for this work. Bezalel not only worked with wood, but was gifted to undertake all the fine artistry, the cabinet making. He was not alone, he was supported by a right hand man, Oholiab, to oversee the work and who God blessed with the ability to teach others

the necessary skills (Exod. 35:34). Thus everyone would do exactly what was required (Exod. 36:1–2). Although all these gifts were God-given they were not to be exercised on the sabbath. No work was to be done that day, not even such evidently God ordained tasks, and that is a challenge as I write this book in my spare time!

These chapters of Exodus teach something else about working for God, even with things as humble as pieces of wood: the value placed on free giving and willingness. The tabernacle and ark were to be made from materials voluntarily provided by the people as offerings or as their contribution to the work, and this included everyday acacia wood (Exod. 25:5; 35:4; 36:3). In the right spirit nothing is too menial. As we read the actual record of the work (Exod. 35–39) willingness is no less essential for those doing the nitty-gritty (Exod. 36:2) than for those in office. These verses also suggest that the gifts came from what the Israelites may have already had with them in their tents, they were that precious, rather than needing to scour the wilderness for suitable trees and branches.

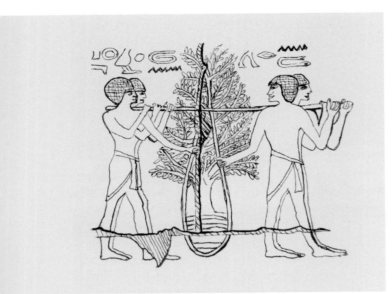

TOP: *Drawing of a slightly damaged relief of a tree (frankincense or myrrh) being transported with a large rootball to help ensure it survived the uprooting, journey to Egypt and transplanting. (redrawn from a drawing by F. Nigel Hepper—used by permission)*

ABOVE: *Iron cage claiming to protect the stump of a tree brought back by Queen Hatshepsut's expedition*

Oil, incense, almonds and pomegranates

Exodus 25, 30, 31 & 37

In the next chapter (Exod. 37) we go to the heart of the sacrificial system, but the latter part of Exodus makes frequent reference to two tree products that are to be used again and again—oil for the lampstand and for anointing, and the burning of incense (Exod. 30:22–38 and 37:25–29). Reference is made too to the symbolic importance of form and decoration in the articles used in worship, namely the explicit requirement that the cups of the lampstand be shaped like almond flowers (Exod. 25:31–36 and 37:17–22) and the hem of the priest's robe of the ephod decorated with pomegranates (*Punica granatum*) (Exod. 28:31–34 and 39:22–25).

Olive oil literally and figuratively oiled the functioning of religious and social life. It was useful for almost everything—lighting, cooking, eating, cleaning, healing and as a cosmetic. Details of how olives were pressed and how different qualities of oil produced are readily available[16] and beyond the scope of this book. What is so understandable is what great store was placed upon olive groves, why they were (and are) so widely cultivated, and what a great crime cutting down or clearing living olive trees was (and still is, in the West Bank for example). The olive, the symbol of faith, hope, mercy and peace, appears by name in almost half the books of the Bible.

Incense was a traded commodity and came mainly from the frankincense tree (*Boswellia*[17] *sacra*). It is not native to Israel or indeed Egypt where it was much used, but to the Horn of Africa. As every forester ought to know, Queen Hatshepsut's famous expedition to Punt (probably modern day Somalia or Eritrea) is the first recorded example of a deliberate tree introduction from one country to another[18] though the Assyrians were doing so not long after.[19] It took place in about 1465 BC with the intention of bringing this, myrrh (*Commiphora myrrha*) and other trees to cultivate in Egypt. Reliefs on one of the walls of the Queen's huge and beautiful mortuary temple, just over the hill from the Valley of the Kings, depict the journey, the boats, the wrapped and cradled tree roots, and the requirement of four men to carry each carefully supported tree slung between two poles. At the foot of the grand entrance to the temple are two twisted metal fences, one on each side, purporting to protect one of the original trees(!)—all you see is a dried up stick. When Moses was growing up in Pharaoh's palace was this famous expedition still fresh in everyone's minds? Were tales of fabled lands far to the south the gossip of the day? Did he even see the incense trees established and growing? There are certainly other records in ancient Egypt recalling this most famous of expeditions.

Other plants of the *Commiphora* genus may also have been used for incense. We return to both the above in Chapter 9 being two of the three gifts the Magi brought to the infant Jesus.

The symbolism of almond flowers and pomegranates recalls the lost fruitfulness of the Garden of Eden, but also the promise held out of prosperity in the promised land. The Israelites would find the almond to be the first tree to flower in spring when for a week or two in February the fertile landscape was be-spangled with white blossom, just like blackthorn in March in the English countryside. Pomegranates with their long season of fruitfulness, their perfect shape, striking orange-red colour, and their sweet seeds so refreshing to eat in summer are all that a fruit should be.

Both arks raise lots of questions, but for me the remarks in this chapter about them and other episodes relevant to our theme, perhaps more than in other chapters, introduce plausible explanations for phenomena. It removes them from being consigned to myth, legend and fairy tales, to facts and history, albeit often hazy in detail and tantalising in what our Western scientific minds long to ask about.

Notes

1 **Meiggs, R** (1982) *Trees and Timber in the Ancient Mediterranean World*. Clarendon Press, Oxford.

2 **Evelyn, J** (1664) *Silva or a Discourse of Forest-trees*. The Royal Society, London.

3 **Navarra, F** (1974) *The Noah's Ark Expedition*. Coverdale Press, London.

4 **Jospehus, Flavius**, *The antiquities of the Jews*. Book 1, ch. 3. pt 6. (Wiston's translation)

5 **Thirgood, J V** (1981) *Man and the Mediterranean Forest—a history of resource depletion*. Academic Press, London

6 **Zohary, D, Hopf, M,** and **Weiss, E.** (2012) *Domestication of Plants in the Old World*. Oxford University Press.

7 **Hepper, F N** (1992) *Illustrated Encyclopedia of Bible Plants*. Inter Varsity Press, Leicester.

8 **Hareuveni, N.** (2006) *Tree and Shrub in our Biblical Heritage*. Neot Kedumim, Lot, Israel. (Transl. **Helen Frenkley**)

9 **Hepper** (ibid)

10 **Hareuveni** (ibid)

11 Midrash is a collection of early rabbinic writings commenting on the Old Testament.

12 **Hareuveni** (ibid)

13 **Jahn, S A A, Musnad, H A** and **Burgstaller, H** (1986) The tree that purifies water: cultivating multipurpose Moringaceae in the Sudan. *Unasylva* **152**: 23–28.

14 **Scharwz, D** (2000) Water clarification using *Moringa oleifera*. Technical Information W1e Gate Information Service, GTZ, Germany.

15 **Musselman, L J** (2012) *A Dictionary of Bible Plants*. Cambridge University Press, New York. [He cites research that makes the point that the tabernacle may not have used solid acacia which would have been very heavy for the oxen and carts (Num. 7:1–9) that transported it, but thin boards.]

16 **Hepper** (ibid)

17 The genus *Boswellia* is named after John Boswell, uncle of James, the famous 18th Century biographer of Dr Samuel Johnson—the conservationist and critic but notably lexicographer creating effectively the first English dictionary.

18 **Evans, J** (2009) *Planted Forests—Uses, Impacts and Sustainability*. CABInternational, Wallingford/UN Food and Agriculture Organisation, Rome.

19 **Dalley, S** (2013) *The mystery of the Hanging Garden of Babylon*. Oxford University Press, Oxford.

3

Leviticus to Deuteronomy

Use and abuse of trees

In the final three books of the Hebrew Torah the question is addressed, 'How may an unholy people approach a holy God?' The Old Testament is clear: it was by means of a carefully ordered system of sacrifices with each one dealing with a different kind of wrong committed or aspect of worship to express.

Fuel for thought

Leviticus 1–6

The first six chapters of Leviticus spell out the sacrificial system: the animals, the other offerings and what the priests are to do in each case. At the heart of all five types of sacrifice is burning, the sign of cleansing, removing, refining and consuming. As several verses record (Lev. 1:7 & 17; 3:5; and 4:12)— and as we would expect—it is done by burning firewood. Indeed, in Lev. 6:12–13 the priests are told that the altar fire must never go out and more wood brought each morning to keep it alight. There is a place set aside for wood ash too. But that is not all.

A moment's reflection raises the question, what about all the other firewood needed by the children of Israel as they journeyed through the wilderness? Leviticus may describe its essential use in the religious life of the nation, but every family would

need to cook, bake, and at times keep warm. We know the miraculously provided manna was boiled in a pot or baked into cakes (Num. 11:18), and presumably the quail were cooked too. What impact would tens of thousands of people have on the surrounding vegetation, sparse as it is likely to be? Gathering firewood might have been a real struggle as perhaps suggested by the man condemned for doing it on the sabbath (Num. 15:32). Families and groups would probably sojourn in the desert wadis where woodland would be a little denser, but even so it wouldn't take very long to exhaust supplies. Indeed, was diminution of firewood availability one reason for moving on, both to find better wooded areas and to allow the tree and bush in the locality where they'd been a chance to recover? The Bible records that the exact timing of breaking camp and moving on was signalled by God as the Israelites were led by the pillar of fire and the cloud.

It is difficult for us in industrialised societies to appreciate firewood. It is startling to discover that even today half of all trees cut down in the world each year, half of all wood consumed, is not for making paper or planks or composite boards and other familiar products, but are burnt for fuel for cooking, curing and keeping warm. Eighty per cent

FACING PAGE: *The burden of firewood—young women in Ethiopia. How much would the Istraelites have used day after day in their years in the wilderness?*

of people living in developing countries have no other source of energy. About two billion tons are burnt as fuel every year. Many more statistics can be cited, but an interesting one is that in reasonably well wooded regions about one ton of wood is consumed per person per year. This is for all purposes including firewood. Firewood, along with its derivative charcoal, remains the most universal of fuels.

Can we estimate what the children of Israel might have consumed? Surveys in communities reliant on firewood and other woody materials like poles and sticks for buildings, and branches and foliage for fencing and fodder, typically show a consumption of 0.5–1 kg per person per day, or about one-third of a ton per person per year. How much forest can sustain this and supply it in perpetuity?

Foresters can readily estimate the amount of new wood a hectare of forest will put on each year, what is termed, the increment. It is the sum of all the wood a tree grows each year and lays down as a new annual ring under the bark and as new woody shoots. When forest is dense and growing conditions good—fertile soil, plenty of rain, and a long growing season—20, 30 or more tons of new wood are added each year in each hectare. But when growing conditions are poor, as would be the scattered acacia trees and scrub of the Sinai and Negev where rain is very meagre, only 1 or 2 tons of new wood each year is the best that could be expected. These figures indicate what can be safely cut sustainably; by just taking the increment the forest is left intact. Problems start when more than this is harvested, but they are not insurmountable. Indeed, very few forests are managed in a way that just takes each year's increment of new wood. Much more is cut and then the forest is left for several years to recover. Trees may be thinned or all be felled then replanted or regenerated. Or trees are severely lopped—pollarded, or even cut back to ground level—coppiced, to give lots of produce, and then left for a long time before returning for more. As the children of Israel moved on, the woodland left behind could recover.

So if there were two million children of Israel each consuming 0.3 t per year, huge areas of 'woodland'

ABOVE: *Firewood on the way to market by camel—Chad*

ABOVE: *Sparse wilderness in the Negev, not promising for gathering fuel Photo: F. Leung*

would be needed. Today the Sinai Peninsula is largely desert[12] but there is striking evidence that it was better wooded at the time of the Exodus. The renowned Egyptologist Flinders Petrie investigated Bronze Age copper mining and smelting operations in Wadi Nash in western Sinai and found a half metre deep bed of wood ash 15 x 30 metres in extent. It seems the adjacent area, now desert, must have borne combustibles—wood or charcoal—during the period when the mines operated.[3] Similarly in the Negev, smelting went on in places that today are completely desert. We can be reasonably certain that there was more woodland around in ancient times, but nevertheless the need for fuel would be one factor prompting the Children of Israel to move on.

The firewood crisis deserves further comment, not because the burnt offerings and sacrifices of Leviticus encourage profligate use—far from it in those times, and, anyway, what more honourable purpose for wood could there be(?)—but because

so many people are affected. It's why programmes with Tearfund, Christian Aid, and other agencies include tree planting and introduction of efficient wood burning stoves as part of rural development. The bare hills of Ethiopia or the deserts of Mali advertise the need of any one of a hundred plus developing countries whose population is largely reliant on firewood and charcoal. To which must be added the peri-urban areas of the mega-cities. What do people in shanty towns and slums use for fuel? Some might illegally tap into overhead electricity wires, but most will burn wood of some kind scavenged from somewhere.

Unintended consequences

Regular supplies of firewood were needed to burn the sacrifices, but what about the livestock kept for the sacrifices and their impact because they would need pasturing somewhere? This is not an issue in Christendom, the Levitical sacrificial system[4] closed when Jesus, the perfect sacrifice, came and died.

ABOVE: *Heavy livestock grazing in the Sahel region of West Africa*

The book of Hebrews spells this out. Jesus' sacrifice ended all sacrifices, He died once and for all (Heb. 10:10). But in Islamic countries today[5] on the 10th and 12th of the month of Dh'ul-Hijja every head of family who can afford to, sacrifices a ram or other animal. On the same day virtually every pilgrim to Mecca sacrifices a ram in the nearby village of Mina in memory of the saving of Abraham's son, Isaac, by the miracle of the ram caught in the thicket (Gen. 22:13). (Back to the theme of firewood, it was the young Isaac who asked his dad, 'The fire and wood are here, but where is the lamb for the burnt offering?' (Gen. 22:7)). Hundreds of thousands of animals are slaughtered each year for this festival in the Islamic world from Senegal to Sinkiang which are largely semi-arid lands wholly unfit for sustaining the huge flocks and herds needed. The maximum number of animals must be kept alive until the 10th Dhu'l-Hijja but, because the Muslim calendar is lunar, the season of this peak is earlier each year. From time to time the festival coincides with the dry season when forage is scarce. Thus overgrazing pressures are not only exacerbated

but at their most destructive. This was partly why Africa's Sahel suffered so much in the 1960s and then again the massive famines of the 1980s and will continue to do so.

Another religious practice, the requirement for cremation in Hinduism causes overcutting and forest clearance in India. The funeral pyre consumes about half a ton of wood each time. It is estimated that 50–60 million trees are felled and burnt each year for this purpose alone.

A medicinal tree?
Leviticus 14
The next reference in Leviticus to wood (Chapter 14) also goes to the heart of everyday life and what might befall people and their property: the scourge of skin diseases and one's house and clothing becoming infested with mould and mildew. They were clearly significant enough threats to merit a whole chapter of instructions as part of a priest's duties. Along with two clean birds, scarlet yarn and hyssop the ritual for cleansing included use of cedar wood. Much fun has been made of these 'primitive'

practices. Surely the God of the Universe should have known better than this concoction from some old wives' tale? Well, I think He did.

I can only comment on the reference to wood, though the hyssop referred to is probably not the wild hyssop of Greece and Turkey after which it is named (*Hyssopus officianalis*) which doesn't occur in Israel, but *Origanum syriaca*. Similarly what is translated cedar wood may not mean cedar of Lebanon, which does not occur in the Sinai or, indeed, Israel, but refers to another conifer, the small widely scattered juniper (*Juniperus phoenicea*).[6,7] This interesting tree occurs throughout the

ABOVE: *The small Phoenician juniper—in this instance far from home in the Bedgebury National Pinetum, Kent*

Mediterranean and has been much researched for biologically and medicinally active extractives from its foliage including anti-cancer and anti-fungal agents.[8] It is famed for being very aromatic and strongly scented, and there are several scientific and medical papers reporting the presence of numerous significant efficacious compounds. If the Levitical instructions point to the wood or foliage of the juniper being burnt inside the home (as suggested by a house having to be closed or sealed for 7 days before re-examining (Lev. 14:38)), both it and infected clothing so fumigated may have helped get rid of the mildew. In Britain such fumigation using our native juniper (*Juniperus communis*) was recommended in old textbooks—early editions of Encyclopedia Britannica describe the process—and may have even been practised as recently as the middle of the last century. The Roman Catholic church still have a ritual for cleansing called Aspergilles, taken from the Levitical account, where the handle of the ladle used to sprinkle the blood is made of cedar wood, but this is symbolic and different from the role the 'wood' actually played.

Is it possible, too, that a paste made from juniper wood ash or a distillation of oils from the foliage might help with skin diseases? I have found no evidence, beyond folklore and the long history of juniper berries being prescribed for ailments 'from leprosy to fumigating the head'.[9] It is, though, the ashes of 'cedar wood', along with hyssop and the red heifer, that are mentioned in Numbers 19:6 in the preparation of water of cleansing. Also we know 'cedar oil' extracted from juniper berries and the heartwood was used to anoint the bodies of the dead in ancient Egypt.[10] Without doubt this small tree is full of biologically active compounds, and this was the one—not any old tree—that the priests were instructed to use. Are the symbolic and the medicinal intertwined?

Fruit trees
Leviticus 19, 23, 26 & 27

The remaining references to trees in this third book of the Bible (Lev. 19:23; 23:40; 26:20; & 27:30) mainly concern fruit trees: almond, fig, olive, date palm, etc. The wisdom of not forcing the harvest and expecting too much too soon (Lev. 19:23–25)

ABOVE: *Great riches in this tropical home garden in Rwanda. Every tree, shrub and plant is of use.*

is reiterated in every gardening and horticultural manual today. While a tree is becoming established its first fruiting will be meagre and unrepresentative of how it will later produce and the picking of the fruit could weaken it. But how welcome to read a law, given years in advance of the Israelites entering the promised land, already talking about the tree planting that's going take place—clearly part and parcel of development. It's not surprising that choice fruit and other produce from trees are the emblem of rejoicing before the Lord in the Feast of Tabernacles (Lev. 23:40). Branches are to be collected of the 'four species' on the first day of the feast. Two are named, palm and willow and two associated by long tradition, myrtle and citrus. The last, *Citrus medica*, and sometimes confusingly called 'citron' in English, is believed to be what is meant by 'luxuriant trees' (2011 NIV) or 'goodly trees'.[11]

All the world over trees provide an astonishing abundance of fruit. In Papua New Guinea, and typical of many equatorial tropical countries, more than 1000 different edible fruits come from the immensely rich rainforest. This huge potential is largely ignored since 95 per cent of food eaten today comes from fewer than twenty kinds of crops, and of these rice, maize, wheat and potatoes dominate. While it is to be expected that fruit from trees was included in the tithes (Lev. 27:30), is not the abundance of provision more than just symbolically related to how we treat God's laws (Lev. 26:4 & 20)? The very things which depress yields and cause crops to fail, or be failures, reflect what is wrong: neglect or lack of care for the crop itself, overuse of land leading to exposure and erosion of soil, wars from tribal fighting and neighbourly animosities to wholesale warfare, and even economic strictures and structures which create and cannot cope with gluts or famines yet aid agri-business, and the flow of dollars that all too easily tempts to corruption. Forgive the rant. No wonder the Lord is scathing (Deut. 28:20–24).

ABOVE: *Almond blossom*

A special fruiting—the puzzle of Aaron's rod

Numbers 17 & 20

The remarkable overnight budding of Aaron's rod is recorded in Numbers Chapter 17. Indeed, more than budding occurred: it bore buds, shoots, flowers and then almonds in less than 24 hours, all natural occurrences but accelerated unnaturally. The circumstances were quite exceptional, and they are the ingredients of a miracle. The lifeless, long dead rod was rejuvenated—life back from the dead, and symbolic of Jesus' resurrection and Christian conversion. The reason it happened was that Moses, and Aaron's, authority was being directly challenged by the tribal elders, there was constant grumbling.

To resolve the matter each of the 12 elders was required to place an identified staff in front of the ark and the one whose rod sprouted was the one God had chosen: it was Aaron's of the tribe of Levi. How the rod budded has no natural explanation.

We've already met the almond, long cultivated in the Middle East and one of the best gifts of the land that Jacob instructed his sons to take to Egypt to placate Joseph (Gen. 43:11). Earlier Jacob had used it along with peeled poplar when breeding the flocks as he laboured for the hard-hearted Laban. We meet the white flowers of almond later on, but they are well known for flowering as early as late January as a herald of spring.

ABOVE: *Well tended olive groves, a distant vineyard, trees and woodland in a prosperous and fertile countryside in late spring. Perhaps a hint of what the 'spies' saw and so refreshing after Egypt and the desert. (Their trophies of grapes, figs and pomegranates suggest the actual exploration was in early autumn.)*

What subsequently happened to Aaron's rod is debated with some evidence suggesting it was the third article inside the ark itself. Was it, also, the same rod Moses had used, which became a snake and devoured the magician's snakes before pharaoh? If so it was certainly old, dry and very dead(!) when it budded, flowered and fruited miraculously. Did it continue to remain in the ark? Was it the rod or staff Moses used to smite the rock (Num. 20:9–11)? All are unanswered questions like the miracle itself.

Longing for the promised land
Numbers 13

In the desert wanderings described in Numbers, trees and wood or wooden articles are only mentioned a few times. This does not diminish the interest and contexts in which we find them as the Children of Israel journey hesitantly and impatiently through 40 years of success and failure. It must have been with some impatience because in the middle of the book (Num. 13), and only months after crossing the Red Sea, there were instructions for the advance party or spies to survey Canaan and report back on what it was like. I like these instructions. The surveyors were tasked with what we call land evaluation. What kind of land is it? Is it good or bad? How is the soil, is it fertile or poor? Are there trees on it or not? And do your best to bring back some of the fruit: you can almost hear Moses shouting after them as they set off! And we know they returned with grapes. We know, too, that except for Joshua and Caleb, the others of the advance party—all leaders of the

Barley	arable crop able to grow in many soils yielding an early harvest in spring.
Wheat	arable crop for the better soils yielding a harvest in early summer.
Vines	perennial yielding fruit every autumn from the coast to the hill country.
Figs	sweet nutritious fruit able to grow in almost any corner apart from desert.
Pomegranates	two crops a year in orchards on fertile soils, and from individual trees.
Olives	live for generations, grow in most soils and climates except wilderness and desert.
Dates	(honey) the fruit tree of the rift valley, oases and wadis in the desert.

people—brought a bad report about how terrifying the inhabitants were. The people rebelled, and God's judgment was to deny that generation the joy of entering the Promised Land by delaying it for 40 years.

Canaan was just as God promised, a land 'flowing with milk and honey' (Num. 13:27); in Joshua and Caleb's words (Num. 14:7), 'exceedingly good'. Words that echo God's declaration concerning creation itself (Gen. 1:12). While perhaps obvious, we can learn a lot about what land is like by what is already growing on it. You don't need a testing kit or to carry out soil analysis, the trees and plants themselves reveal a great deal. How vigorous a tree is growing is readily seen by looking at the length of trunk between whorls of branches on a pine or, pretty well for any tree, how well the current year's shoots have extended. Break off a twig and it's usually not hard to work this out. Is recent growth very slow, almost like a bonzai, or is there a good healthy new shoot? Colour of foliage also gives clues with yellowing perhaps the commonest malady pointing to lack of nitrogen, or lack of iron from chlorosis, or because of diseased roots. Simply observing what trees and plants look like says a lot about conditions more generally.

This observation was taken to an extreme 100 years ago when A J Cajander, a forest scientist in Finland, developed a system of defining forest site types based on the flowers and other plants growing on the forest floor. It worked quite well, and for foresters Cajander has a special place being our only professional to become a prime minister, but then Finland does have two-thirds of its land under trees. In Britain we classify woodlands by the kinds of trees and associated plants present in the National Vegetation Classification (NVC). However, not every case of profuse growth speaks of fertile soil. The fabulously rich and diverse tropical rain forests are mostly on very poor soils—centuries ago the best ones were taken for farming—but they achieve such exuberance owing to astonishing root networks that pretty well capture and recycle again and again every nutrient there is.

Fruit trees as heralds of promise
Deuteronomy 6:11 & 8:8

Four of the famous 'seven' species of the promised land (Deut. 8:8) are fruit trees. They reveal a lot of what the promised land will be like. Verses 7 & 8 of Deuteronomy chapter 8 paint an enticing picture: 'For the Lord your God is bringing you into a good land—a land with brooks, streams and deep springs gushing out into the valleys and hills; a land with wheat, barley, vines and fig trees, pomegranates, olive oil and honey; a land where bread will not be scarce ...'.

Almost everywhere in the promised land something useful would grow.

Canaan was every bit as good as God promised. The advance party were given the right instructions to find out and the evidence was before their eyes. Only Caleb and Joshua were courageous enough to trust the unseen God and urge the people to go forward and not be fearful.

Gods of wood
Deuteronomy 13 & 16

Fear of a different sort was one of Israel's besetting sins. Continually we read of them turning to other

ABOVE: *Date palms, sycomore-figs, and bananas growing beside the Nile* Photo: S. Evans

gods or gods of neighbouring tribes. Such idolatry was specifically forbidden (Deut. 13) and this included wooden carvings and groves of trees (Deut. 16:21). It was perhaps harder for the Children of Israel to resist than we realise.

For 400 years the people of Israel were slaves in Egypt. Throughout that time the 2000 or so gods of Egypt impacted their life at every turn. And this included tree worship—the greatest of Egyptian gods, Osiris, was originally a tree-god. The region of Memphis was known as the land of sycomores (the Bible's sycomore-fig) and the tree was considered sacred.[12] Its durable wood was used for the coffins, the decorated sarcophagi found in the tombs of the Pharaohs. Indeed, in the *Book of the Dead* it is called 'the tree of life'. Many hieroglyphs depict their bounty and a sarcophagus has been found fashioned from a whole trunk where the branches spread to represent the actual body of a deity.[13] What greater veneration could there be? Then and now the world over trees are (inflicted with) sacred or god-inhabiting attributes—classical naiads and dryads, the carved wooden gods of the Hindus, the totem poles of North America, and the miraculously planted tropical fig (*Ficus religiosa*) the Bodhi tree in Sri Lanka.

The theme of Asherah poles and the disastrous distraction of Baal worship turns up again and again. But the point is that the Israelites had been saturated on every side with worship of everything except the one true God, including veneration of trees. No wonder the second commandment was explicit in forbidding worship of or fashioning anything in heaven above or earth beneath (Ex. 20:4–6).

'Are the trees people, that you should besiege them?'
Deuteronomy 19, 20 & 22

Abuses of trees are not confined to worship. The Hebrew law is careful to say, 'Do not destroy trees when laying siege' (Deut. 20:19), after all you are not besieging the trees, nor to pillage bird's nests in a tree to the point of taking the mother as well (Deut. 22:6–7). Indeed, this latter verse makes a clear link between how we treat nature and our well-being.

Provision, too, is made for accidents (Deut. 19:5) such as an axe head flying off while felling a tree—obviously a common enough occurrence to merit inclusion, and another reminder that forestry is one of the most accident prone industries. Someone somewhere in this ancient time discovered that if the socket of the axe head and the shape of the haft into which it fits were not round but distinctly oval (as they are today), losing an axe head was much less likely. Did they also discover that soaking an axe head with its haft overnight tightened the grip immeasurably as the wood swelled—the point noted concerning Noah's Ark? The ancients knew well the importance of a tight fit. In the Bible there is the incident with Elisha (2 Kgs 6:5) and the great consternation when an axe head was lost. His contemporary, the Greek poet Homer, relates that the great bronze axe which Calypso gave to Odysseus had a fine haft of olive wood, well-fitted to the axe.[14]

The emphasis in Deuteronomy when making war is not to cut down fruit trees, since the Israelites would be denying themselves fruit in the future. Permission is given to cut down other trees to build siege works. Even this regulation is hedged about: trees are cut for a specific purpose not wantonly and only for a limited time i.e. just while the siege lasted (Deut. 20:20). The force of this command is brought home by what records we have of actual sieges, in particular of the hapless city of Lachish by Sennacherib which we return to in Chapter 5.

And, of course

We have overlooked the most important of all verses as we conclude the Pentateuch. Deuteronomy 21:22–23 includes, 'anyone who is hung upon a tree (or pole) is under God's curse.' It foreshadows the greatest work of God's Son bearing the curse for us on the cross of wood. We return to it because both Peter and Paul do in the New Testament.

BELOW: *An olive grove never to be wilfully cut*

Notes

1 Interestingly Hepper remarks than when exploring the vicinity of St Catherine's Monastery at the foot of Mt Sinai (Horeb) with a Bedouin guide, 'I was amazed to see running streams supporting poplars, cypress, and groups of olive trees; and some Bedouin, tending small patches of good soil, were actually raising crops of several fruits and vegetables in this barren region.'

2 **Hepper, F N** (1992) *Illustrated Encyclopedia of Bible Plants*, Inter Varsity Press, Leicester.

3 **Thirgood, J V** (1982) *Man and the Mediterranean Forest—A history of Resource Depletion*. Academic Press, London.

4 A hint at the size of flocks kept in Old Testament times is in God's promise, 'I will make their people as numerous as sheep, as numerous as the flocks for offerings at Jerusalem during her appointed festivals.' (Ezek. 36:37–38)

5 **Stewart, P J** (1979) Islamic law as a factor in grazing management: the pilgrimage sacrifice. *Commonwealth Forestry Review* **58**: 27–31.

6 Rabbinical authorities were also much exercised by the reference to 'cedar', some suggesting it was on account of it being the finest of timbers though incredibly difficult to obtain by the wandering Israelites and a number of different woods could actually be used. Hareuveni, in *Tree and Shrub in our Biblical Heritage*, cites Rabbi Tarfon indicating juniper was permissible and makes the case for the likelihood of this species.

7 **Hareuveni, N** (2006) *Tree and Shrub in Our Biblical Heritage*. Neot Kedumim Ltd, Lot, Israel (Translated by **Helen Frenkley**)

8 **Ennajar, M, Bouajila, j, Lebrihi, A, Mathieu, F, Abderraba, M, Raies, A** and **Romdhane, M** (2009) Chemical composition and antimicrobial and antioxidant activities of essential oils and various extracts of *Juniperus phoenicia* L. (Cupressaceae). *Journal of Food Science* **74**(7): M364–371 (Sept. 2009)

9 **Addison, J** (1999) *Treasury of Tree Lore*. Andre Deutsch Ltd, London.

10 **Hepper** (ibid)

11 **Darom, D** (undated) *Beautiful Plants of the Bible*. Palphot Ltd., Herzlia, Israel.

12 **Altman, N** (1994) *Sacred Trees*. Sierra Club Books, San Francisco.

13 **Philpot, J H** (1897) *The sacred tree, or the tree in religion and myth*. Macmillan, London.

14 **Meiggs, R** (1982) *Trees and Timber in the Ancient Mediterranean World*. Clarendon Press, Oxford.

4

Defining boundaries and setting seals

The promised land
Joshua 1–24

Joshua had a lot to do. Taking the mantle of Moses was responsibility enough, but to lead the oft-rebellious Israelites to take the promised land would occupy all his remaining years. Years of battles, conquests and settling disputes, even from within (Josh. 22:12) though wisdom prevailed. It must have seemed a far cry from the agricultural idyll of, 'a land flowing with milk and honey'.

The honey mentioned was probably not referring to that made from the sugary nectar bees collect, as common as this would have been and immortalised in Samson's riddle for the Philistines (Judg. 14), but to a sweet syrup or date honey from the date palm (*Phoenix dactylifera*). This tree, the date palm, ranks among the earliest fruit trees to be brought into cultivation[1] and produces 100–200 kg of fruit every year. The sweet dates are 60–70 per cent sugar and provided the tree has moisture in the soil—'its feet in water'—it can cope with the hottest and most arid of conditions. Thus it is found around oases, beside rivers, and near the Dead Sea in Israel as well

as throughout the Middle East and North Africa. Not only did it provide a staple food, but its trunks serve as beams for buildings, its leaves for roofing, matting and basketry, and its fibrous bark for rope. Truly a blessed provision.

What for me so thrills is that after Joshua is commissioned and the Israelites have crossed the River Jordan, built the memorial and carried out circumcision in accordance with God's instructions, their first challenge is the ancient city of Jericho. It thrills me because this is the 'city of palms' (Deut. 34:3, Judg. 3:13) and so in taking it, in the miraculous way every Sunday School child knows, God has already honoured half of the epithet. They capture a city flowing with honey. And although they destroy it by burning (Josh. 6:24) they will have spared all the trees as instructed by Moses (Deut. 19:20). Here then, at the start of their arduous conquest, was a harbinger of good times to come.

More surveying
Joshua 13–19

As well as conquest the Israelites were concerned about who got what: to what region of the promised land was each tribe apportioned? We saw in the last

FACING PAGE, TOP: *Date palms growing near Jericho* BOTTOM: *View of Jericho city: still well furnished with palms*

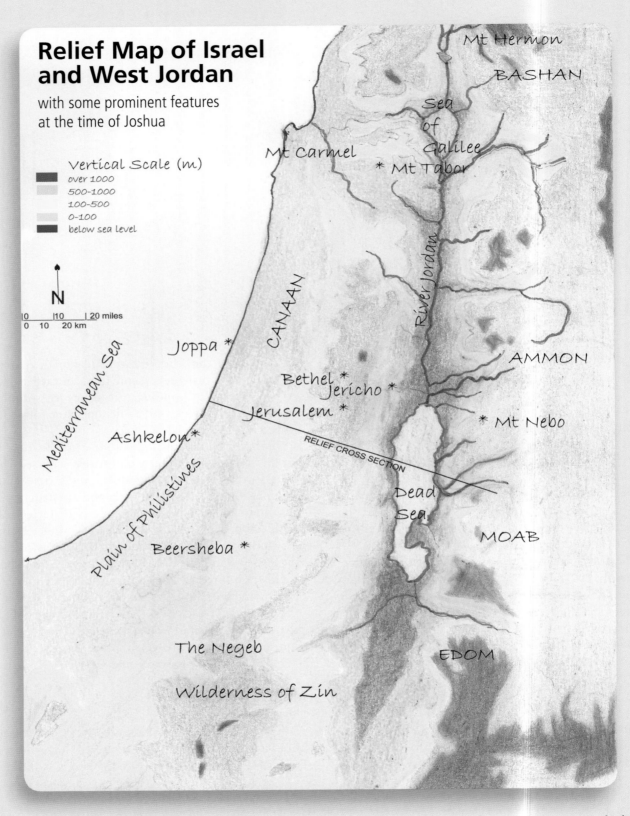

Relief Map of Israel and West Jordan

with some prominent features
at the time of Joshua

Vertical Scale (m)

- over 1000
- 500-1000
- 100-500
- 0-100
- below sea level

N

| 0 | 10 | 20 miles
| 0 | 10 | 20 km

Mt Hermon

BASHAN

Sea
of
Galilee

Mt Carmel

* Mt Tabor

River Jordan

CANAAN

Mediterranean Sea

Joppa *

AMMON

Bethel *
Jericho *

Jerusalem *

* Mt Nebo

Ashkelon *

RELIEF CROSS SECTION

Plain of Philistines

Dead
Sea

MOAB

Beersheba *

The Negeb

EDOM

Wilderness of Zin

ABOVE: *Hand-drawn relief map of Israel and environs with cross-section of elevations. See cross-section overleaf.*

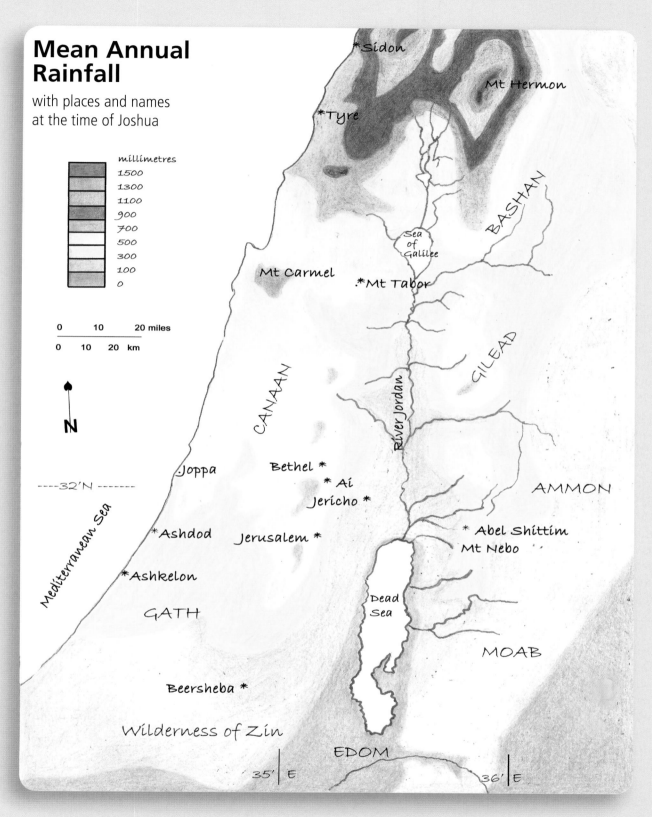

Mean Annual Rainfall

with places and names
at the time of Joshua

millimetres
1500
1300
1100
900
700
500
300
100
0

0   10   20 miles
0   10   20 km

N

*Sidon

Mt Hermon

*Tyre

BASHAN

Sea of Galilee

Mt Carmel

*Mt Tabor

GILEAD

CANAAN

River Jordan

----32'N--------

Joppa

Bethel *

* Ai

Jericho *

AMMON

*Ashdod

Jerusalem *

* Abel Shittim

Mt Nebo

Mediterranean Sea

*Ashkelon

Dead Sea

GATH

MOAB

Beersheba *

Wilderness of Zin

EDOM

35' E

36' E

ABOVE: *Hand-drawn rainfall map of Israel and environs. Boundaries and zones are indicative only; map scales differ*

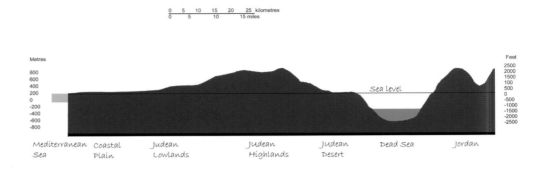

Metres
800
600
400
200
0
-200
-400
-600
-800

Feet
2500
2000
1500
100
500
0
-500
-1000
-1500
-2000
-2500

Sea level

Mediterranean Sea · Coastal Plain · Judean Lowlands · Judean Highlands · Judean Desert · Dead Sea · Jordan

0 5 10 15 20 25 kilometres
0 5 10 15 miles

ABOVE: *Cross-section showing changing elevation from west to east—see relief map*

chapter the instructions to the advance party or spies (Num. 13) to evaluate the land, but land allocation couldn't rely on this one foray. It is clear from Joshua 18:1–10 that explicit surveys were carried out in advance of dividing up the land. This should not surprise us—other than that such a 'modern' approach to land use planning was pursued over 3000 years ago—because Israel's topography is remarkably varied.

Israel is no larger than Scotland,[2] but from west to east there is coastal plain, hill country, semi-desert, rift valley and high plateau (now in Jordan), and from north to south the land ranges from the well-watered to the aridity of parched desert. There are, too, at least nine main kinds of soils from the fertile to the saline, from rich alluvium to nothing but stones and pebbles.[3] The result, the enormous richness of plant life in so small a country, and hard work for Joshua's survey teams to get to grips with, is the land God had promised. It is a rich and diverse country as Moses reminded the people (Deut. 8:6–9), 'Observe the commands of the Lord your God, walking in his ways, and revering him. For the Lord your God is bringing you into a good land—a land with streams and pools of water, with springs flowing in the valleys and hills; a land with wheat and barley, vines, fig-trees, pomegranates, olive oil and honey; a land where bread will not be scarce and you will lack nothing; a land where the rocks are iron and you can dig copper out of the hills.' Joshua was not only a gifted military leader,

but God equipped him to explore well the land of promise.

Twice it is repeated that 'not one of all the Lord's good promises failed' (Josh. 21:45 & 23:14). But like so much in life, the promised land did not come on a plate. As well as battles to fight, in places forest clearance was necessary (Josh. 17:15 & 18) to provide sufficient land for cultivation—in this case for the tribes of Ephraim and Manasseh. Today, as we mentioned in an earlier chapter, this practice goes on in the tropics though rarely now for much lasting benefit since long ago all the best land that could be cultivated sustainably was cleared and settled. The same in Britain: our few ancient and semi-natural woodlands were never cleared for farming because the soils were very heavy clays or poor gravels and sands or simply were on hillsides too steep to cultivate. But what the Joshua reference does reveal is that Israel was far more wooded in Old Testament times than now. Today the hill country of Ephraim is barren.

Tree place names
Joshua 13–21

One of the most revealing ways to learn what a place was once like, is from its name. In Britain all our principal tree species find their way into village and town names. Indeed, within Hampshire where I live there are, for example, the villages of Ashurst (the suffix 'hurst' is medieval for wood), Beech, Lyndhurst (after the lime or linden tree) and

Oakhanger (a steep wooded hillside of oak). We can find the same in the perambulations in Joshua Chapters 14–19 which describe the boundaries of the allotments for each of the twelve tribes. Naphtali's was special because as well as using many kinds of permanent features used to delineate other tribes' land, such as large stones, valleys, rivers, hills, towns and other features, it includes a tree: 'Their boundary went from Heleph and the large tree in Zaanan-nim …' (Josh. 19:33). It must have been an impressive and noteworthy specimen. It recalls the practice in England of 'beating the bounds' (boundaries) of a parish which if an oak tree was incorporated then the gospel was read at the tree, hence the place-name 'Gospel Oak'.[4]

Below we list of some of the towns mentioned in Joshua which were named after or associated with a tree species that can be identified with some confidence, along with some other tree related place names[5]

A place in history
Joshua 24

Near the end of the book of Joshua, with much but not all of the promised land occupied, the covenant is renewed at Shechem. Joshua's own ringing affirmation of faith has been made, 'But as for me and my household we will serve the Lord' (Josh. 24:15), and the people respond equally positively. To seal this renewing of the covenant, Joshua takes, 'a large stone and sets it up under the oak near the holy place of the Lord' (Josh. 24:26). More correctly this should read 'under the terebinth' since the

Hebrew word is 'allah' not 'allon or elon' (oak). As remarked before, both oaks and terebinths are impressive, often growing on their own in the open as great spreading trees, and their bark is not dissimilar. Both are good for shade and a place under which to meet.

In the shade
Judges 1–10

In the book of Judges an awful lot of business takes place under a tree: courts, commissionings, a coronation and clairvoyance. The Bible seems to go out of its way to tell us that these things occurred in the shade of or beneath a tree. Deborah held court under a palm tree (Judg. 4:5), the Palm of Deborah, which served poetically as a symbol of upright stature, justice and righteousness. Gideon met an angel of the Lord who was sitting under an oak that Gideon's father Joash owned (Judg. 6:11). After some thoroughgoing discussion, Gideon was commissioned and sent to save Israel. Abimelek was crowned king beside the great tree at the pillar of Shechem (Judg. 9:6) though, as suggested previously, all that may have been left of the tree was a vast but still impressive hulk. We return to Abimelek as the subject of Jotham's fable.

Three years after his coronation, Abimelek faced revolt from the people of Shechem and so he attacked the city at dawn. In the uncertain light the encroaching army couldn't be made out until Gaal, the leader in Shechem, exclaimed, 'Look, people are coming down from the central hill, and a company is coming from the diviner's (or soothsayer's) tree'

JOSHUA	OTHER		
Shittim—acacia (Josh. 2:1)	**Abel-Shittim**—field of Acacias (Num. 33:49)	**Bethany**—house of figs (Mark 11.1)	**Gethsemane**—olive press (Mark 14:32–42)
Betonim—pistachio (Josh. 13:26)		**Bethphage**—house or place of unripe figs (Matt. 21:1)	
Tappuah—apple[6] (Josh. 15:33; 17:8)	**Allon and elon**—oak, the words are associated with the Hebrew word for god 'el' and quite a number of localities in the Bible bear its name[8] e.g. Beth el)		**Valley of Elah**—terebinths (1 Sam. 17:2)
Luz—almond (Josh. 16:2 & Gen. 28:19)		**Beth-Shittah**—house of Acacia (Judg. 7:22)	**Valley of walnuts** in eastern Jerusalem and also around Genesaret[9]
Rimmon—pomegranate (Josh. 19:7)		**Hazezon Tamar** (Gen. 14:7)—date palms (Tamar, date, a tree much admired for its elegance as well as sweet fruit.	
Nahalal—Tabor oak[7] (Josh. 19:15, 21:35)	**Aroer**—Phoenician juniper (Deut. 2:36)		**Localities where forest (yaar) is included:** forest of Ephraim (2 Sam. 18:6), forest of Hereth (1 Sam. 22:5), and forest of Negev (Ezek. 20:47).
	City of Palms (Jericho, the world's oldest city?) (Deut. 34:3)	**Mount of Olives** (Luke 21:37 & 22:39)	

ABOVE: *The only place to rest, in the shade*

(Judg. 9:37). Was this the same tree beside which Abimelek was crowned and which centuries before was the great tree of Moreh at Shechem (Gen. 12:6) and where the covenant was renewed in Joshua's day as we remarked in the previous paragraph? In the eyes of many, great age and venerable history would invest magical properties in whatever was left of the tree.

Later we read in Samuel that more than once King Saul appeared to hold court under a tree (1 Sam. 14:2; 22:6). Outside the Bible, Alexander the Great is even depicted on a coin sleeping/dreaming under a plane tree. There are many other examples. It's what trees are for. And it is still true of Africa today, especially in drier subtropics: trees are where people meet and where livestock rests in the heat of the day.

Thirty years ago I worshipped at an African Inland Church in Lotubai in north-west Kenya. The Sunday service was simply a gathering beneath a tree—and to my chagrin as a forester I can't now recall what kind of tree it was! But what I do recall, what did make an impression—literally as well as figuratively—was the pew. It was just a pair of long, slender eucalypt poles raised about six inches off the ground. As the service in Turkana went on and on, or so it seemed with my not understanding a word, the poles impressed themselves ever more deeply into the cheeks on my backside. But then I was young.

Gideon's bravery cutting his family's Asherah poles

Judges 6

Gideon was very brave. We know this from the way he whittled down an army of 32,000 to just 300 with which to go to war as he obeyed God's instructions to the letter. But his first act of bravery had happened before this and it raised a hue and cry. He cut down his own family's altar of Baal and Asherah poles and used the wood of the poles to burn an offering of a bull and that from the family herd! (Judg. 6:26). He did all this at night because brave as he was he was still fearful of his family's reaction—though one wonders if the flames of the burnt offering wouldn't have been seen for miles, not to mention the aroma—but all we are told about is the uproar in the morning. And there is a surprising twist. Gideon's father, Joash, appears the least upset and points out with disarming candour, 'If Baal really is a god, he can defend himself when someone breaks down his altar' (Judg. 6:31).

This is an early example of what we meet again and again: the Israelites chasing after or prostituting themselves with foreign gods. As well as Asherah poles many mentions are made of carved images made out of wood and sometimes overlaid. Even itinerant Levites, the priestly caste, had them (Judg. 18). Such was the abandonment of the one true God that inevitably lawlessness followed and the society which Joshua had laboured to bring about on the foundation of Moses' teaching, was revealed in the appalling incident of the concubine gang-raped all night and whose dead body was cut up and dispatched to all corners of 'the land flowing with milk and honey' (Judg. 19). This shocking affair had the desired affect, at least for a time.

What were Asherah poles? We can't be totally sure but it seems clear from archaeology and the reference to banning them in Deuteronomy 16:21 (and many more references in Kings and Chronicles) that this Canannite way of honouring the fertility goddess Asherah, was either to plant a sacred tree or grove of trees, or to erect a sacred wooden pole or carved figurine. Sacred trees and groves are not the preserve of ancient times. They were common in medieval England, such as the 'Green man' and common today in 'New Age' Earth worship. From

ABOVE: *Christ-thorn tree growing near Korazin in Galilee.*

time to time I help advise new owners of small woodlands and on one such visit the owner, who was upset, pointed out the signs of dark or satanic use of her wood where twigs were broken, totems placed, and other signs left.

Jotham's parable of the trees
Judges 9

Jotham had just witnessed his half-brother, Abimelek, kill seventy of their siblings. He fled the scene, climbed the nearby hill, Mt Gerizim, and from a vantage point regaled the people of Shechem with a story. It was a truly eastern fable to make a powerful point. Like all good stories it began, 'Once upon a time the trees went out to anoint a king for themselves.' (Judg. 9:8). First the trees asked the olive to reign over them, then the fig, then a vine to be king, but each declined saying their benefit, their fruit, would be forfeited if they did. Finally, says Jotham our storyteller, the trees ask the thorn-bush, and the thorn-bush's answer was different. If you

really want me to be king then come and find refuge in my shade.

The point of the story is that the ruthless and bloodthirsty Abimelek, who the people of Shechem have persuaded themselves they want as their king, is not what he appears. His baby brother suggests that like the thorn-bush he will be abrasive, he will yield no fruit, he will be a threat and scourge. But the story doesn't somehow seem quite right: how can a fig or olive, which grow up to 20 or 25ft high, find shade under a thorn-bush? It's worse where translators of the Hebrew '*atad*' give 'bramble' as the meaning in English. Most commentators suggest that Jotham is being deliberately sarcastic by suggesting such lowly plants. However, Jewish writers such as Nogah Hareuveni[10] and Michael Zohary[11] using the Hebrew bible argue persuasively that 'atad' is the Christ-thorn (*Ziziphus spina-Christi*).

Christ-thorn, a common tree in Israel, grows quite big enough to shade olives and figs—indeed

47

it casts good shade even when leafless—and has all the negative connotations needed to make Jotham's point. It is very thorny, it produces barely edible fruit, and importantly it is 'unfriendly' to other fruit trees because of its voracious far spreading root system. Like a walnut tree it takes no captives, not even other Christ-thorn trees in the immediate vicinity, a phenomenon called allelopathy. When new olive orchards or vineyards are prepared, every effort is made to clear the land of Christ-thorn. Added to this, so unpalatable is its foliage that even goats reject it and thus bunches of twigs often hang low touching the ground. And these twigs have one other characteristic: they burn very easily, very hot and almost smokeless. The locals of Shechem would have known this and so understand the strange reference (Judg. 9:15) to 'fire coming out of the thorn-bush' to consume the local top-brass—the cedars of Lebanon metaphor in this verse.

Christ-thorn seems much the best fit for the 'thorn-bush' metaphor for the unsavoury King Abimelek. And, like its zig-zaggy twigs, there is a cruel twist later in the Bible.

Abimelek gets worse. The rest of Judges chapter 9 relates more of the attack on Shechem and finally his own downfall as a woman drops an upper millstone on his head. As he is dying he pathetically gets his armour bearer to finish him off so that people can't say, 'A woman killed him'. Yet it's recorded in the Bible and for more than 3000 years everyone has known that is what happened. Just before his end, Abimilek had resorted to a common military tactic, of which the Assyrians later became masters, of an accelerated siege.

In Judges 9:46–49 Abimelek tells his men to take their axes, go into the forest where they were on Mt Zalmon, cut off branches and carry them to the stronghold at Shechem. The besieged people, about a thousand in number, were cowering in the tower for safety. Abimelek piles the branchwood against the tower and sets light to it. It does its work perhaps burning the door and other wood used in the tower's construction and causing the stones to shatter[12] and doubtless the tower to fall. The slaughter was complete. When he tried it again in Thebez, the tower was stronger and there was a woman on the roof with a millstone.

A pause for Samson
Judges 16

This inappropriate heading for such an active and angry judge of Israel is to mention the massive city gates he tore from their footings (Judg. 16:3). An example of such gates has survived from the 9th Century BC—the gates of Balawat—which once guarded a palace of the Assyrian king Shalmaneser III.[13] They are made of cedar held together by great bands of copper engraved with grizzly depictions and what look like stylised cedar trees—you can see cones on top of the branches as is characteristic of the cedar family. Looking at a replica of them in the British Museum we can only be awed at Samson's strength; the gates are 7 m (20ft) high and half as broad.

Ruth
Ruth 1–4

The book of Ruth provides several insights into Middle Eastern farming practices and society around 1100 BC. The fact that famine drove Naomi, her husband Elimelech and their two sons to leave Bethlehem and trek eastwards to the land of Moab reveals the subsistence nature of day to day survival. Their journey would have taken them through the Judean desert descending to the Dead Sea, perhaps passing Jericho on the way, across the River Jordan and up the mountains into the land we now know as Jordan. They may have followed the Annon River gorge up to the high table land to a narrow fertile belt that was fairly well watered. Though east of the Jordan the land was a little higher than Bethlehem in the Judaean hills and, being west-facing like the slopes of Israel itself to the west of Jerusalem, it probably attracted sufficient extra rain to stave off severe drought. The area was densely populated and prosperous in biblical times.[14]

Just how prosperous is seen from the tribute Moab was paying the Israelites in the 8th Century BC. During the reign of King Ahab 100,000 lambs and the wool of 100,000 rams were being exported to Israel (2 Kg. 3:4). Naomi and her family chose a sensible place to settle, but, as the book of Ruth tells us, the famine in Bethlehem didn't last (Ruth 1:6) and, after the trauma of the deaths of her husband

ABOVE: *In the background, a reproduction of the massive gates of Balawat (British Museum).*
© *M Chohan (2007)/Wikimedia Commons*

and both her sons, Naomi decides to return home with her daughter-in-law, Ruth.

The two travellers arrived back in Bethlehem at the time of the barley harvest, which begins in late March or early April, and Naomi sends Ruth to glean in the fields—to pick up leftover grain dropped by the harvesters. She began to glean in the fields their owner Boaz was harvesting. We find her working hard with just an occasional rest, perhaps in the heat of midday, in a shelter (Ruth 2:7).

The word 'shelter' is the common word for 'house', but different versions of the bible translate it in this verse as 'booth' or even 'in the shade', as well as house or shelter, indicating some uncertainty

of meaning. Shelter was often provided by a tree, but sometimes temporary booths were (and are) made just for the period of harvest or for the duration of the summer heat.[15] I saw these in northern Iraq for use by shepherds. They were of oak foliage and branches cut from multi-stemmed pollards or by cropping side branches, a practice known as 'shredding'[16] which was once widespread in England. The branches were loosely spread between the trunks to create a roof. The leaves would dry out but not fall because the corky layer that develops in the autumn and causes leaves to separate from the twig (abscission) hadn't happened. Two common oaks of the Middle East, both also native to Israel,

TOP LEFT: *Foliage drying in a pollarded multi-stemmed Tabor oak for temporary roofing, or for fodder or bedding for livestock. Notice the fresh regrowth sprouting.*

BELOW LEFT: *Oaks where side branches have been cropped (shredded) for the same purpose.*

Both photos taken in the mountains to the north of ancient Nineveh in northern Iraq

TOP RIGHT: *Traditional threshing board showing sharp stones in holes, Nazareth Village*

were being used: Aleppo oak (*Quercus infectoria* or *Q. boissieri*) and Tabor oak. If such shelters were where Ruth and Boaz's workers rested then with the barley harvest in the spring only foliage of the evergreen Kermes oak would have been suitable. This tough tree is still plentiful in the Judaean hills today.

The drama of Ruth reaches a climax when she secretly offers herself in marriage to Boaz who was asleep with his newly threshed grain (Ruth 3:7). Threshing grain changed little over the centuries and even today threshing boards with sharp stones to help separate the grains are used as can be seen in the illustration. The board my wife photographed in Nazareth looked as if it is made of cypress.

The story of Ruth has a happy ending indeed. Her grandson is Jesse who is father of the great King David and thus an ancestor of Jesus himself. Thus through Ruth arise two of the great titles given to Jesus with their tree related metaphors, 'A shoot will come up from the stump of Jesse, from his roots a Branch will bear fruit' (Is. 11:1) and, says Jesus, 'I am the root and offspring of David' (Rev. 22:16).

Notes

1 **Zohary, D, Hopf, M,** and **Weiss, E** (2012) *Domestication of Plants in the Old World*. Oxford University Press, Oxford.

2 The frequent changes of border make exact comparison difficult.

3 **Zohary, M** (1982) *Plants of the Bible*. Cambridge University Press, Cambridge.

4 **Carey, F** (2012) *The Tree—meaning and myth*. The British Museum Press, London

5 **Zohary M** (ibid)

6 **Musselman, L J** (2012) *A Dictionary of Bible Plants*. Cambridge University Press, New York. [Mussleman, following Moldenke and Moldenke (1952) *Plants of The Bible*. The Ronald Press Company, New York, argues the case for apricot not apple, but see entry in Compendium.]

7 **Hareuveni, N** (2006) *Tree and Shrub in Our Biblical Heritage*. Neot Kedumim, Lod, Israel. (translation by **Helen Frenkley**).

8 **Zohary M** (ibid)

9 **Zohary M** (ibid)

10 **Hareuveni** (ibid)

11 **Zohary M** (ibid)

12 Heating rock leads to shattering in a not dissimilar way to the meteorite that broke up over Russia on 15 February 2013 causing over a thousand injuries.

13 **Edwards, B** and **Anderson, C** (2011) *Through the British Museum—with the Bible*. DayOne, Leominster.

14 **Bimson, J J** (1985) *New Bible Atlas*. Inter Varsity Press/Lion Publishing, Leicester.

15 Ruth gleaned from the barley harvest to the end of the wheat harvest (Ruth 2:23). The wheat harvest begins 50 days after the barley harvest, so she gleaned from April to mid-June, well into the hottest and driest time of the year..

16 **Rackham, O** (2006) *Woodlands*. The New Naturalist Library, Collins, London.

ABOVE: *A stand of cedar of Lebanon in southern Turkey showing straight stems and log potential quite unlike the open spreading cedars we are used to. Photo: D. Luscombe*

5

Samuel—Chronicles

The barter of kings

More of the Old Testament concerns the period of about 500 years from Israel choosing their first king to the time they went into exile, than any other. There is much history and much prophecy. This chapter covers six of the books of history. It begins with Samuel, the last of the judges, who appoints Saul as king, followed by the golden era of David and Solomon and their building of palaces and the temple, and then there is decline. Israel is divided into two, a few good but mostly bad kings rule who turn their back on God, and finally the nation goes into exile in two stages. Without doubt for our theme the building work by David and especially Solomon, and the necessary trading arrangements to find all the timber, feature strongly. But as throughout we try to touch on all relevant incidents book by book.

Giving directions

1 Samuel 10 & 2 Samuel 5

In 1 Samuel 10 we find the elderly prophet, Samuel, telling Saul what he must do in preparation for ascending the throne of Israel as its first king. He must accomplish several tasks to demonstrate how God has changed him. After Saul leaves Samuel his instructions are that he will first meet two men near Rachel's tomb at Zelzah, who will tell him that the lost donkeys he was looking for have been found, and then Samuel says. '… you will go on from there until you reach the great tree of Tabor …' where he will meet three men carrying goats, bread and wine. This is quite a journey from the district of Zuph, via Bethlehem (Rachel's tomb), on to Mt Tabor—if that is the Tabor referred to—and then back to Gibeah and finally to meet Samuel again at Gilgal. Of course we have highlighted this royal progress because of the great tree of Tabor used as a rendezvous point, as one of the directions for the journey. It must have been very well known. It is likely to have been an oak, a Tabor oak, named after the mountain on which they comprise much of the woodland on its slopes.

I like this incident because my wife is always complaining that I give directions by, 'turn left after the line of poplars' or 'it's on the corner where the Scots pine is'. But then she gives directions by such and such a pub, at least in Hampshire, in her case recalling a career with the county constabulary!

We find more directions being given in 2 Samuel, this time to Saul's more illustrious successor, David, as he too takes the reins of kingship. The Philistines are forever Israel's goad and before David takes Jebus (Jerusalem) to establish his capital, he is confronted by the Philistine army in the valley of Rephaim (2 Sam. 5:23–24 and 1 Chron. 14:8–17). David seeks God (via Abiathar the High Priest) about what to do. And God gives him clear directions both how and where to marshal his

ABOVE: *Tall poplars in the valley at Banias, striking and easily identified*

forces for battle and when to commence hostilities. The poplar trees[1] in the valley are key: it is where the trees are sited that he is to engage the enemy. With great stealth David is to circle around behind the Philistine army and once in front of the poplars to prepare to attack. Famously, he is only to begin the attack, 'as soon as you hear the sound of marching in the tops of the poplar trees.' (2 Sam. 5:24). The unusual rustling of another poplar's leaves, trembling aspen, will be familiar to readers in Britain. The Philistines, perhaps taken by surprise, are vanquished as God has gone before and David's army completes the rout chasing them westward down the slopes all the way to Gezer some 30 miles away.

Trees and forests have played significant roles in many battles in history. Indeed a little farther on we meet Absalom's army lost in a forest and Absalom himself caught by a tree, literally. But a battle in thick forest worth highlighting, for what it tells of a certain Roman general, was the complete loss of three legions under the weak, ineffectual command of one Publius Quintilius Varus in AD 9. He failed to follow directions and his forces were ambushed in the Teutoberger Forest (Germany). It is known

as the 'Varian disaster'. It was the worst setback at the height of Rome's powers from a failure to plan, or to scout out the route through a dark and dank forest, or even to have his troops ready. Varus lost around 15–20,000 soldiers and committed suicide. Popular historians give him a castigating.[2] He was the same Varus who was governor of Syria when Jesus was born around 5 BC. Incidentally critics are quick to point out that Luke says in his gospel that Quirinius was governor (Luke 2:1–3) not Varus, but anybody ill-prepared enough to lose an entire army to ambush in a forest can't have been much of a governor, and we know Quirinius was, to all intents and purposes, the real power and authority in the region at the time. So Luke is right.

This and that
1 Samuel 14, 22 & 31)

As we have remarked before, much takes place in the shade of trees. Perhaps surprisingly King Saul rests or holds court under a fruit tree, a pomegranate, (1 Sam. 14:2). Pomegranates can grow quite large displaying their brilliant orange and red flowers and swelling fruit hanging like Christmas tree baubles against the dark foliage. They cast heavy shade.

Later, and still battling with David who has moved to the Forest of Hereth, Saul knowing where David and his men are hiding, sits, spear in hand, under the tamarisk tree on the hill of Gibeah (1 Sam. 22:6). His officials are standing nearby and a discussion ensues about intrigues, accusations and counter accusations. And later still, the ashes of Saul's decapitated body are, perhaps fittingly, buried under a tamarisk tree at Jabesh (1 Sam. 31:13). This was thanks to the men from Jabesh Gilead who journeyed through the night to recover his body hung on the walls of Beth Shan by the Philistines. Unusually in Old Testament times, Saul's remains were burned. Though God had rejected Saul, these brave men, like David himself, still honoured the one who was once the Lord's anointed. There is some suggestion that as well as the comfort of shade, that tree-worship or undue reverence was practised so using trees for meetings and places for burials are to be expected.

Next we have the strange incident of Jonathan eating honey (1 Sam. 14:24–45). He dips his staff into a honeycomb, and in so doing disobeys his father's, Saul's, explicit instructions that no one can refresh themselves until he, Saul, is avenged and victory complete. Saul places pride and selfishness over common sense. As Napoleon said, an army marches on its stomach. But, for us, it is verses 25 and 26 that demand explanation, 'The entire army entered the woods, and there was honey on the ground. When they went in the woods, they saw honey oozing out …' Despite being faint no-one dared eat it because of the oath to Saul except Jonathan who hadn't heard about it. But clearly the quantity of honey was striking enough to be remarked upon. Ground nesting bees don't produce honey since they feed on caterpillars, but some bumblebee species do have small colonies in ground nests, make wax combs and store nectar, albeit much less efficiently than honey bees. Consultation with entomologists hasn't fully resolved this question of quantity of honey on the ground which clearly was so striking as to attract comment.

The log trade
1 Kings 5–7 & 1 Chronicles 28 & 2 Chronicles 2–3
The Bible makes clear that King David being able

ABOVE: *Pomegranates in flower*

to build a fine palace in Jerusalem, a palace of cedar (1 Chron. 17:1), was one way the Lord showed he was now established as king over Israel (2 Sam. 5:11 and 1 Chron. 14:1). The peace and prosperity such building work suggests indicates rest from his enemies, though perhaps not from his now numerous wives, concubines and offspring! But we meet here for the first time King Hiram of Tyre getting in touch and offering logs of cedar and the skilled craftsmen to do the construction. It is but a brief mention, but tells of trade in logs which we know was commonplace around the shores of the Levant. Egypt especially sought much of their timber from Lebanon, Syria, Cyprus and Cilicia (southern Turkey) as did Assyria for more than a millennium with reference to cedar logs being obtained from Amanus (Syria) as far back as Sargon of Akkad in 2200 BC. There is no doubt that the wars waged by the Assyrians, the Babylonians and the Persians in the countries to their west, in which Israel and Judah got caught up, was in part to do with resources and obtaining the precious coniferous timbers of cedar, fir and juniper, which were so sought after for their

TOP: *Terebinth branches hanging just head high—a few have recently been pruned to avoid accidents!*

ABOVE: *Unmanaged natural oak and terebinth woodland: pleasant enough, but it would be easy to get lost*

Entrapped by forest and tree
2 Samuel 17 &18

It is sad indeed to read of the elderly King David fighting his own son, Absalom (2 Sam. 18). The revolt comes to a head in the Forest of Ephraim to the east of the Jordan. Twenty thousand are slain, but scripture records that more were taken by the forest than by the sword. The battle must have spread out, and perhaps the forest had few tracks and paths and there were doubtless wild animals such as lions and bears. More significantly Absalom's army had probably marched for several days, first downhill into exhausting and enervating heat of the lowest point on earth, the rift valley of the Jordan and the Dead Sea, and then up the slopes to where David's men were holding out in the Forest of Ephraim. Absalom's army was ill-prepared to fight.

The battle would have exacerbated the hunger and thirst, the empty stomachs and parched mouths, of Absalom's soldiers and if we add in fear of getting lost, then the ingredients are all there for a rout. One is reminded of Merry and Pippin getting lost in the forest of Ents in Tolkein's *Lord of the Rings*. But there is also a fear of forests. In Japan it is where people commit suicide, in Britain it is where murderers try to hide their victims, and where even animals, such as a deer hit in road accidents, retreat to die. Did David's men, on the run and battle hardened, cope better in wild country? Did they know hidden tracks and paths or where dangerous terrain was, or where wells and springs could be found? They had been well fed before the battle (2 Sam. 17:29), but had Absalom's army of Israel? Were they already exhausted by the time they reached David's forces who were at home in friendly territory?

Getting lost and disorientated in forest may well explain the account of Absalom himself and his 'happening to meet' David's men (2 Sam. 18:9). It suggests he was alone and lost. As he rode his mule, no doubt hurrying to escape, his hair got caught in the thick branches of a large 'oak'—it should read terebinth—and he was left hanging in mid-air. Caught by tree and by the enemy, he was killed where he hung and buried in the forest. Sad too is Joab's disobedience to David by killing Absalom hanging defenceless by his hair. David had issued strict

fine palaces and temples but largely absent from their countries, the modern day Iraq and Iran.

We return to this below when Solomon starts the greatest of undertakings, building the Temple, as so much detail is provided. But it is good to record the peace that must have prevailed that allowed great capital works to be undertaken after all the battles and wars David faced and sad, therefore, to relate the next incident involving trees and forests.

KEW HERBARIUM
0003615

FROM
OXFORD UNIVERSITY
DEPARTMENT OF FORESTRY
FOREST HERBARIUM
(FHO)

Sheet 4

FLORA OF   Lebanon

Leaf specimens are from a young
(7 m. tall) tree at the well
known stand of Cedars at Beharre,
high on the western slope of the
Lebanon, altitude 1900 m.   The
cones are from older trees in the
grove.   The seedling is from the
same area, likewise the wood sliver.

(See also Beals, E.W. in J. Ecol.
53, 679-694, Nov. 1965).
Arabic name Arz.

5.9.1966.

Cedrus libani A. Rich.
var. libani
Det. A. Farjon (RBG Kew) Nov 2008

COLL.   J.D.Chapman.   No.   4.

ABOVE: *Herbarium specimen of cedar of Lebanon which botanists use for making exact descriptions and precise classifications.*

instructions not to kill his son; perhaps seeing him hanging by his hair was too good an opportunity for the battle-hardened Joab to pass up. And then Joab goads David, grieving inconsolably for his own son, as failing in his duty as leader by neglecting all the faithful soldiers who had fought so valiantly. All lose, no one wins when battles are fought.

This episode is particularly poignant for me. Although I, personally, prefer forests to open country in the sense of feeling safe and knowing

where I am, for most it is the other way round when in unfamiliar territory. And in my own family, my youngest son, Ben, was lost for hours in forest in Chile. It was a year after his mother had died suddenly when she was just 55, that Ben and a friend, also Ben, took a gap year to travel the world. They had left their hostel with only a light bag and gone hiking in a national park and they got lost. The once clear track they had followed seemed to disappear. No one knew where they were least of all me, his dad, 8000 miles away. Thrashing increasingly anxiously through head-high undergrowth Ben and Ben resorted to going downhill. Hot, flustered and desperately thirsty they finally found a track and found their way out. It's easy to get lost and disorientated in forest and wilderness and the shocking facts of 2 Samuel 18 ring so true.

Solomon the scientist
1 Kings 4

What a CV of Solomon's accomplishments are in 1 Kings 4:29–34! And how interesting to single out, 'He described plant life from cedar of Lebanon to hyssop that grows out of walls.' If only we had the record of these descriptions, or labelled etchings on pottery, papyrus or hide, much of the trouble accurately identifying the Hebrew name of a tree or shrub with its modern equivalent would vanish. But we don't and we have to content ourselves with hints in Proverbs and luxuriate in the metaphor laden Song of Solomon where images from horticulture, viticulture and silviculture express the joys of beauty, love and desire.

We do have detailed accounts in Greek of trees and plants in the Mediterranean 600 years after Solomon by the industrious Theophrastus who became Aristotle's pupil. But even his descriptions and distinctions of types of oak, pine, cedar and cypress can't always be reconciled with today's botany. We have in Latin Pliny the Elder's *Natural History*, completed in AD 77, which drew on numerous earlier accounts. Indeed, he lists 123 authors on which he based his information about trees, but as to reliability Meiggs[3] says, 'Unlike Theophrastus he (Pliny) was no botanist and it is doubtful how many species he would have recognised himself in the forest.'

Preparations for Solomon's temple

1 Kings 5–8 & 2 Chronicles 2–7

High in the Taurus Mountains axes swung, birds took flight, and cedars fell. Across the Levant, in Lebanon, and possibly Amanus (Syria) and Cyprus, logs of cedar, and probably fir and juniper were on their way.[56] The great undertaking, anticipated for a generation, began in earnest. Great King David 'rested with his ancestors', and his son Solomon began to build what his father had longed to do and for which he had even left preparations (1 Chron. 22 & 28). Chapters 5 to 8 of 1 Kings and 2 to 7 of 2 Chronicles record how it all went. Eleven years later, after four more of preparation and seven of building, God's House was open for worship. Arguably it is the finest building ever erected and crafted using God's blueprint and overseen by the wisest of men. At last the ark of the covenant had a permanent home. On that momentous day was heard that momentous promise, 'If my people, who are called by my name, will humble themselves and pray and seek my face and turn from their wicked ways, then will I hear from heaven and forgive their sin and will heal their land.' (2 Chron. 7:14).

Two more temples would come and go, and by the time of Jesus the second of these, Herod's, magnificent and newly finished, was less than 40 years from utter destruction. The enormous and impressive stones that underpinned the whole temple complex itself, some weighing hundreds of tons, are still there buried in Temple Mount, but that's all. Just as Jesus said, it would be destroyed; indeed, this was the one trumped up charge that was made to stick at his trial by twisting his words (Matt. 26:61).

Supplying timber destined for such a great undertaking described in Kings and Chronicles calls for dedication far beyond the everyday. Like Noah, millennia before, the undertaking was gargantuan. And in the accounts of Kings and Chronicles we are told a great deal: how Solomon bartered food and land for logs with King Hiram of Tyre; how Israelites were pressed into service and foreigners in the land enslaved so that tens of thousands were put to work; how villages and territories changed hands, how the ark was brought and, above all; how God inhabited this new place. The logging went on not only in Turkey's Taurus Mountains (in old Cilicia), but much, even the bulk of it, in the Lebanon mountain range in present day Lebanon and Syria for cedar and probably fir and juniper with pine logs possibly coming from Cyprus. The whole undertaking called for remarkable organisation.

Were all motivated by the great project of the age, building God's house? We know silence reigned on the building site itself (1 Kgs 6:7), but was the whole nation caught up with this giant of public works? Did the enthusiasm and commitment touch

ABOVE: *Foliage of cedar with characteristic cone erect on the branch*

Hiram's skilled tree felling gangs far away? Was it like the hysteria that gripped all France in the 1880s when the ageing hero of Suez, Ferdinand de Lesseps, nourished by national pride, announced that another canal, one at Panama, was next? Or when President Kennedy committed America to go to the moon? We don't know, we can only guess.

We know they worked silently on the temple site, so important, so holy, was the building, but did the tree felling gangs also honour God in their work? Did they pray at the start of each day? Did they sing the late King David's psalms as they worked? What about health and safety or a biblical risk assessment? Was the incredibly hard and exhausting work assigned to slaves—the 'hewers of wood and drawers of water' of Joshua 9:21 & 23? All sorts of questions arise.

Logging operations
1 King 5 & 2 Chronicles 2

There were many very practical issues. Were all trees in a stand cut down, what is called clearfelling, or were only the best thinned out from the forest? The Bible tells us that King Hiram's Sidonians were skilled in felling (2 Chron. 2:8) and their rations ran into hundreds of tons of wheat and thousands of gallons of olive oil so great was the number of 'woodsmen who cut the timber'. Felling all the trees is easier and safer than thinning and is the main system used today in commercial forestry, particularly for forest plantations. Almost certainly, though, the forests supplying Solomon were natural, though diminishing in extent. So there may have been some clearfelling or forest clearance to gain farmland, as centuries before Joshua (Josh. 17:15 & 18) had encouraged the people of Joseph (Ephraim and Manasseh) to do. Probably, though, most of the logs came from thinning out the best trees. This is a sustainable practice because the smaller ones are left to grow and mature and new seedlings, what foresters call regeneration, fill the larger gaps where there is plenty of light. The foresters and their gangs will have had plenty on their hands.

Were individual cedars selected to meet pre-assigned uses in the temple, like the bent limbs of oak providing the 'knees' for the ships of Nelson's navy 200 years ago or, today, only the most super straight Douglas fir trees for telegraph poles? If, yes, how were they identified to ensure safe delivery from stump to stanchion, from tree to treasury? It's what we call chain of custody and why we see the FSC (Forest Stewardship Council) and other logos on timber we buy from B & Q, Wickes or other builders merchants. Or were just the best logs sent to Israel where the carpenters and craftsmen would then make their selections? This is more likely in view of the route the logs had to take—hauled to the sea, floated in rafts and then hauled inland up to the vicinity of Jerusalem (1 Kgs 5:8) and in view of the huge quantities of which the bible speaks (1 Chron. 22:4).

Back in the cedar forest selected trees were doubtless marked with a slash from an axe—no paint aerosol cans in those days! Was an official seal of King Hiram stamped on the newly exposed slash mark, creamy-white and oozing resin, to avoid fraud and theft? I own an old Forestry Commission hand axe with a crown engraved on the back of the head to do just this, to show the slash mark was authorised. After all, once a tree is felled you can never put it back up.

How long did it take to fell a cedar or juniper relying only on axes? Was direction of fall aided by ropes? Imagine standing before a moderate cedar tree. If you can just about hug the trunk with your finger tips touching, it will be about 40 cm diameter and probably 15 or 20 m tall and will weigh approximately one ton. High in the mountains of Lebanon and Syria cedars would have grown to 30 m or more tall with diameters so great that two or even three men with outstretched arms could just encompass it.[7] So a fine, mature cedar of Lebanon confronts the tree fellers with a weight of many tons.

Felling was probably with double headed bronze axes and professional sharpeners would be on site to renew the cutting edge again and again throughout the day. This was so important that 'The teacher' warns of the folly of using the dulled axe (Eccl. 10:10). Axe men would first clear undergrowth from around the tree and then probably start cutting at about 50–80 cm above ground or above any buttresses that older trees might have developed. Normally one cuts a wedge out of the side of the trunk facing the direction where you judge the tree

will safely fall: the wedge is cut deeply, to about one-third of the way in. Felling then switches to the other side and starts a little higher up. A tree begins to become unstable and starts to fall when the remaining thickness of wood between the two cuts, the hinge, falls below ten per cent or so of the cross-section. But if there are high winds, or the tree is leaning, or its is crown lop-sided, or there's decay in the butt … it's good that Hiram's tree fellers were renowned for their skill (1 Kgs 5:6)! They are likely to have used ropes too: a relief in the temple at Karnak (Egypt) in the time of Seti I, more than 300 years before Solomon, shows just this, ropes guiding the fall of cedar trees being felled in Lebanon.

Once on the ground trunks were de-limbed by axes (Jeremiah 10:3) to produce the logs. We are then told by King Hiram, 'my men will haul them down from Lebanon to the sea' (1 Kgs 5:9). Almost certainly draught animals were used, probably

FACING PAGE: *Fine cedar of Lebanon in Hillier Arboretum, Hampshire showing dimensions fit for a temple!*

BELOW: *Relief of highly stylised trees, probably cedars, from the recorded campaign of Seti 1 in the temple of Amun at Karnak showing ropes attached to a tree being felled. (Berlin State Museums) Reproduced from Meiggs (1982) with permission from Oxford University Press.*

TOP: *Relief showing rafts of cedar logs destined for the palace. (The Louvre) © Jastrow (2006)/Wikimedia Commons*

ABOVE: *Slaves hauling balks or logs of cedar from Lebanon's forests. Is it a road or canal in the forest at top left? (The Louvre) © Jastrow (2006)/Wikimedia Commons*

teams of yoked oxen or mules. When we match weight of log to traction power, a really fine cedar might require 10 or 20 yoke. There is evidence that when Nebuchadnezzar wanted cedar logs for Babylon both specially prepared roads for hauling and a canal for floating them were excavated.[8] Once at the coast Hiram's logs were bound together into rafts and transported to a suitable point on the Palestine coast (1 Kgs 5:9). The account written later in Chronicles indicates to Joppa (2 Chron. 3:16) but this may have been because the second temple, built by the returning exiles, used this port (Ezra 3:7). Rafts had long been used to float logs from Lebanon all the way to Egypt and thence up the Nile.[9] Egypt had long nurtured aspirations of annexing Lebanon to secure its log supplies as had the Assyrians. There is an Assyrian bas-relief, now at the Louvre, that depicts galleys towing cedar logs. A similar scene, probably on the River Tigris at Nineveh, of a large raft of logs lashed together is in Sennacherib's relief in the British Museum.

Storing and floating logs by canal, river or in the sea does them no harm, they do not decay. Indeed, the opposite is the case. When the great storm of 1987 blew down millions of trees in south-east England the Forestry Commission salvaged 70,000 tons of the best pine logs and, in a special store in Thetford, kept them fresh and blemish free by continually soaking them from overhead sprinklers. Five years later the logs were still in good condition and marketable, though the slime over the soggy wood pile was something else!

Building the temple

1 King 6 & 2 Chronicles 3–4

1 Kings 6 tells how the temple was built and what the different materials were used for. We find that the cedar, so expensively assembled, provided the beams and the planks for the roof, the panelling throughout from floor to ceiling in every chamber, and even the altar itself. So complete was the use of cedar that not a stone was seen, 'everything was cedar' (1 Kgs 6:18). Everything, that is, except for the floor which we are told (vs 15) was probably of juniper (pine, as in the old NIV is unlikely). In the inner chamber, even the finest cedar was not sufficient for the perfection aimed at and it was all,

Species	Dry wood density (kg/m³)	Strength	Hardness	Durability	Nailing/ glueing	Working
Cedar (Cedrus libani)	560	low-moderate	soft & brittle	durable	excellent	easy to work, finishes well
Juniper (Juniperus excelsa)	550 – 600?	moderate	hard	very durable	tends to split	fragrant like cedar, finishes well
Fir (Abies cilicica)	450 – 500?	low-moderate	soft	poor, but good submerged	splits easily	easy to work, good joinery
Olive (Olea europaea)	900 – 990	high	very hard	moderate	glues well	season slowly to avoid warping, finishes well

including the altar, overlaid with pure gold (1 Kgs 6:19–22). What a sight!

Olive wood, hard and durable, was used for the intricate carving of the cherubim above the altar and for some of the doors;[10] others were made out of juniper (1 Kgs 6:34). On the walls around the temple and on the olive wood doors motifs were carved of cherubim, palm trees and open flowers. These beautiful adornments would remind worshippers of the Garden of Eden, from which man had been driven, and the welcome here in God's temple in the heart of the land 'flowing with milk and honey'.

This choice of timbers is remarkable. Today we have lists of the technical properties of different woods as a result of exhaustive testing and research. It's why, for example, the wood used for your staircase is different from that for the roof trusses and barge boards. It was just the same in Solomon's time, he knew the right wood for the right job.

In the Table we list a selection of relevant properties of the main timbers used in the temple.

The principal use of cedar was as panelling requiring little strength but needing excellent properties for attaching the gold overlay (i.e. nailing) and for the carving, and this is just what is found. The use of cedar beams for roofing is fine since it is easy enough to overcome inherent weakness by simply increasing dimensions—you need a somewhat thicker beam of cedar to offer the same strength as juniper. It's the same in Britain where our home-grown softwoods like spruce, larch and pine tend to be very slightly weaker than the imported equivalent, but which is readily overcome when specifying them in construction because they are stress graded at the sawmill so the architect or builder know they are fit for purpose.

A SECRET

Who would have known the secret? Certainly those working with the temple, those privileged to be invited to King David's palace, indeed almost anyone in Jerusalem owing to the vast quantities of cedar logs imported (1 Chron. 22:4), and even those far away tree felling gangs; all would have known it. But only on entering the finished temple would the worshipper have suddenly and wondrously become aware of it. The sight would have been awe inspiring like our great cathedrals, but what would surely linger long in the memory, indeed, perhaps God intended what would most prompt recollection of worship in His house, was the fragrance! All cedars and many junipers have highly volatile oils that are natural antiseptics and are a delight to the nostrils. Not only the sight and sounds of the place, but the aroma all around would evoke God's house: so powerful is smell in triggering recollection. The fragrance doesn't last for ever and, of course, in the temple itself the daily sacrifices and the many incenses offered would soon disguise the lovely, delicate essence of cedar.

Join those first worshippers, the first priests, and King Solomon himself going to the newly finished temple. It looked, it felt and it smelt new and fresh and fit for God's wonderful house. (A demeaning analogy is the smell of a new car—for the first weeks and months you are reminded of its newness each time you get in.) But what a wonderful thought about Solomon's temple: how suitable, then, to use cedar wood so very generously.

Tidying up
1 Kings 10 & 2 Chronicles 1, 2 & 9

When the Queen of Sheba comes to visit Solomon, the temple and his palace completed, we meet a new wood, almug in 1 Kings 10:11–12 and algum in 2 Chron. 2:8 & 9:10–11, used to make the steps for the temple. Incidentally we also learn that so popular was cedar—did it become fashionable to build with the lovely fragrant softwood?—that it was as plentiful in Jerusalem as the everyday sycomore-fig trees (2 Chron. 1:15 & 9:27).[11] Almug and algum have sometimes been considered as variants, but Hepper[12] reviews the evidence and the research of others to conclude that two timbers are referred to: almug is probably red sandalwood (*Pterocarpus santalinus*) imported from India (Ophir), but algum, supplied by Hiram from the forests of Lebanon, is possibly the Grecian juniper (*Juniperus excelsa*). However the latter is usually '*berosh*' in Hebrew and uncertainty over identification remains.[13] Whatever is right, it appears that algum wood wears well as a tread just like another conifer, Parana pine (*Araucaria angustifolia*) from southern Brazil, was long used in Britain for stairs and staircases until supplies dwindled as forests were logged out. Assuming algum was specially used, it just adds further to the picture of a sophisticated logging trade and to the skill of carpenters and joiners in selecting timbers fit for each job.

Under every spreading tree
2 Kings 12, 16–18, & 22

The glory of the temple and Solomon's reign would not last. Every bible student knows the history, the break-up of the kingdom, and the eventual exile as God's judgment. But sad to relate trees emerge as a weathervane of religious life from the glories of the cedar panelled temple to the glaring and brazen rejection of the One at its heart. We mentioned asherah groves and poles in the previous chapter; they have not gone away and in Kings and Chronicles the Israelites' apostasy and idolatry are laid bare. Not all was black all of the time, good kings like Asa, Josiah and Hezekiah stand out as exceptions and, incidentally, repair the temple and order yet more logs! (2 Kgs 12:2 & 22:6)

What pain, desolation and abandonment of Israel's God is portrayed by 2 Kings 16:4 & 17:10! On every hill top and under every spreading tree—great spreading oaks and fine terebinths—false gods proliferate. We read the words uncomprehending: imagine, everywhere and in every place, littering the landscape, wherever you pause on a walk, was this offence to God. What took place is too appalling to contemplate (2 Kgs 17:16–17)—child sacrifice, sorcery, divination—and the consequent immorality too shocking to detail (Ezek. 16–23).

Rather more than one hundred years earlier, even the great Elijah had felt alone (1 Kgs 18:22) when he challenged the priests of Baal. Appropriately on a hill top, Mt Carmel, the great contest was enacted, firewood was piled high and the challenge issued as to which god would send fire to consume the bull sacrifice. It was no contest, the mute people turned back to God, but only for a time. Things deteriorated again, indeed, got even worse. Everyone, bar a few, regressed to Baal worship and so, in this promised land flowing with milk and honey, in its every corner detestable practices occurred, and Scripture says they occurred, 'under every spreading tree'. I've found it hard to picture a worse indicator of the totality of the Israelites rejection of God—'under every spreading tree'.

But if trees are embraced by idolaters they will also be part of our rejoicing. David's exultant psalm of thanks and praise (1 Chron. 16:8–36) proclaims, 'then the trees of the forest will sing, they sing for joy before the Lord, for he comes to judge the earth'.

Weapons of war in judgment
1 Kings 18 & 24

The separation of the Kingdoms, their sackings and the killing or exiling of many of the people is laid out vividly in the latter pages of Kings and Chronicles. None more so than what we know of the fate of fortress Lachish in the Judean lowlands.

ABOVE: *Great dome-shaped crown of the terebinth tree on the outlook hill top in Dan Nature Reserve—a great spreading tree*

Many times in its history it was attacked and of the sieges by Sennacherib in 701 and Nebuchadnezzar in 586 we have the conquerors' accounts. Biased they may be, but whenever we read that Sennacherib '… attacked all the fortified cities and captured them.' (2 Kings 18:13) or that Nebuchadnezzar laid siege to Jerusalem (2 Kings 24:10) let's remember what we know befell Lachish.

Sennacherib's scribes set the scene,[14] the king crowing over his accomplishments:

As for Hezekiah the Judean, who had not submitted to my yoke, I besieged forty-six of his fortified walled cities and surrounding smaller towns, which were without number. Using packed-down ramps and by applying battering rams, infantry attacks by mines, breeches, and siege machines I conquered. I took out 200,150 people, young and old, male

ABOVE: *Seige and sacking of Lachish by Sennacherib's army. Even a date palm is cut down, something the Israelites were forbidden to do when they went to war (Deut. 20:19–20) (British Museum)*

and female, horses, mules, donkeys, camels, cattle, and sheep, without number, and counted them as spoil.

The fall of mighty Lachish was singled out. Sennacherib lined a room at the heart of his immense palace in Nineveh—the palace to astonish the nations—with relief panels recording how he laid siege to, captured, and crushed the city.[15] It's all there, the wooden weapons of war: the bows and arrows, the spears and javelins, the chariots, the huge siege engines and battering rams thrusting up specially built ramps, and the storming ladders. There, too, emerging from the city gate, are the citizenry destined for exile or execution.

But Sennacherib had his comeuppance: the very panels which depict what he inflicted on Lachish are blackened and scorched from the fire that later raged through his own palace and the city of Nineveh just as Nahum prophesied (Nahum 2:15). Though God may execute judgment by any means, it doesn't exempt the conduct of those involved.

One hundred and twenty years later, it was Nebuchadnezzar's turn and he added a further dimension requiring wood foraging parties to scour the countryside. Layers of wood ash several metres thick still remain today[16] testifying that wood and timber were stacked high against Lachish's walls, ignited, and kept burning for days by replenishing the fuel again and again until the stones, white hot, shattered and the walls tumbled. (It was a common method and may, as we commented, have been implied in the account of Abimelek's attack on the people of Shechem hundreds of years before (Judg. 9:49)). But think for a moment of families huddled inside Lachish, of terrified children staring at the sky lit up with flame night after night and hearing the great stones explode one after the other. As each frightening hour passed it was an hour nearer to capture. What awful memories, what terror, what sadness, what desolation for the former inhabitants of Lachish, and of Jerusalem, and of all the once well fortified cities as they were forced into exile. 'So Judah went into captivity, away from her land' (2 Kgs 25:21).

Notes

1 Many older translations have balsam trees, but this is not right because they are a subtropical species at home in the rift valley and around Jericho not in the cooler hills to the west of Jerusalem where the battle took place.

2 **Johnson, B** (2006) *The Dream of Rome*. Harper Perennial, London. [In chapter 1 about the Varian disaster shambles, Boris Johnson calls Varus, besides many other disparaging things, a 'cock-up artist'.]

3 **Meiggs, R** (1982) *Trees and Timber in the Ancient Mediterranean World*. The Clarendon Press, Oxford.

4 **Zohary, M** (1982) *Plants of the Bible*. Cambridge University Press, Cambridge.

5 **Farjon, A** (2008) *Natural History of Conifers*. Timber Press, London.

6 These species often occur together in these mountains and, in the case of cedar, even distinguishing Atlas cedar (*C. atlantica*) from cedar of Lebanon is uncertain as cone shape and appearance intergrade—see Farjon (2008).

7 **Meiggs** (ibid)

8 **Moscati, S** (ed.) (2001) *The Phoenicians*. I B Tauris, London.

9 **Hepper, F N** (1992) *Illustrated Encyclopedia of Bible Plants*, Inter Varsity Press, Leicester.

10 **Musselman, L J** (2012) *A Dictionary of Bible Plants*. Cambridge University Press, New York. [Musselman suggests olive is unlikely for doors and that the wood referred to, an 'oil or resin' producing wood, is in fact pine.]

11 It could be that as well as importing cedar logs Solomon planted cedar saplings in and around Jerusalem, as perhaps implied by Psalm 92:13–14. The climate is reasonably suitable and healthy cedars can be seen today e.g. in Jerusalem Botanic Garden.

12 **Hepper** (ibid)

13 **Musselman** (ibid) [Musselman agrees with Hepper's identification of almug as possibly red sandalwood, but suggests algum is boxwood (*Buxus sempervirens*), a mainly temperate species which does occur as far south as the mountains of southern Turkey and northern Syria and so could well have been imported along with cedar (2 Chron. 2:8–11)]

14 **Cogan, M** (1998) Into Exile: from the Assyrian conquest of Israel to the Fall of Babylon, In **Coogan, M D** (ed) *The Oxford History of the Biblical World*. Oxford University Press. pp 242–275.

15 **Collins, P** (2008) *Assyrian Palace Sculptures*, British Museum Press, London.

16 **Thirgood, J V** (1982) *Man and the Mediterranean Forest—a history of resource depletion*. Academic Press, London.

Metaphors of peace, permanence and prospect

In our narrative we have three more books of history, Ezra, Nehemiah and Esther, which shed light on the exiled Israelites and their return, before we luxuriate in metaphor and imagery that so enrich Psalms, Proverbs, Ecclesiastes, and Song of Solomon.

Starting again

Ezra 1–10 and Esther 1–9

We've already noted that in Ezra (3:7) cedar logs are again imported from Lebanon via Joppa for rebuilding the temple when the exiles return. Progress reports are sent to King Darius including how the logs have been used to provide timber for the walls (Ezra 5:8), but this king's subsequent decree has a grizzly penalty. Darius had the archives searched to check that rebuilding the temple had been authorised. It had, in the reign of King Cyrus, so Darius issues a decree himself specifically concerning the temple in Jerusalem (Ezra 6:3). An outline of its dimensions are given, the provisions needed—stone and timber, that no one is to interfere, and the expenses are covered by the royal treasury. But then comes the penalty for disobedience: 'I decree that if anyone changes this edict, a beam is to be pulled from his house and he is to be lifted up and impaled on it. And for this crime his house is to be made a pile of rubble.'

This severe and brutal penalty tells us a bit about house construction and a lot about the cruel method of execution in Persia. The later book of Esther graphically details the death the scheming and conceited Haman planned for Mordecai; to hang him on gallows 75 feet high. Probably death was by impalement followed by hanging the corpse high for all to see. As Esther records, tables were turned and Haman was the one so executed.

Impalement was widely practised by the Persians and was a deliberately cruel execution. And it was probably under the Persians that impalement evolved into crucifixion which came to be used with such relish and such cruelty by the Romans. It foreshadowed the execution of Christ on the cross. The victim of impalement was forced down onto a pointed wooden stake which was slightly angled to avoid overly damaging the internal organs. Even worse was that the stake itself was of a size to 'plug' the entry point to limit bleeding. Death was designed to be slow and excruciatingly painful. Later the victim would be hoisted high and left hanging or gradually sliding down the pole.

FACING PAGE: *A beautiful cedar of Lebanon in old Cilicia (S. Turkey). It was the metaphor of choice for greatnes, power and authority.* Photo: D. Luscombe

ABOVE: *Impalement, and other gruesome details, depicted in a bronze band near the base of the gates of Balawat (British Museum)*

BELOW: *Great beauty and intimacy in Tresco Gardens, Isles of Scilly*

In the same way as James marvels that both cursing and praising come out of the same mouth (Jas. 2:10), this forester is pained by the thought that trees and wood are used for both great blessing, such as the wonderful panelled temple and the beauty of countryside, and for great cursing—stakes to impale, crosses to crucify, gibbets to hang, and racks and treadmills to torture.

Keeper of the king's forest
Nehemiah 2

It is easy to gloss over this title in Nehemiah 2:8, but the importance of adequate timber supplies loomed large in the mind of King Artaxerxes's cup-bearer—and shortly to be leader of the returning exiles. Indeed, his book finishes with his achievements (Neh. 13:31) which specifically highlights securing wood at designated times; in this instance, the daily

necessity the Levites had of fuelling the altar fires to keep them burning (Neh. 10:34).

The prayerful, godly and savvy Nehemiah, who plainly knew his way around court, asks for a letter from King Artaxerxes with two requests. The first is safe passage and the second to secure supplies of timber for the gates of the citadel by the temple, the great gates in the walls of Jerusalem, and for his own residence. As a top official he knows Persian administration and who the keeper of the king's forests is, one Asaph. His requests are granted, but as patently competent as Nehemiah was, he attributes the king's favourable response to the gracious hand of God.

Before asking what a keeper of forests does, the word translated as 'forest' (Neh. 2:8) in older versions of the Bible, is not the usual one in Hebrew '*yaar*' but the word '*pardes*' or the Septuagint's Greek '*paradeisos*'. The 2011 NIV has translated it as 'royal park' which is better since what is implied is from the Old Persian meaning 'an enclosure'. From it we get the word 'paradise'. The same word is in Ecclesiastes 2:5 as 'park' and in Song of Solomon 4:13 as 'orchard'. In the New Testament it occurs three times with its modern meaning of a place of serenity and blessing for the soul after death. Most famously it is referred to in the comforting promise of the crucified Christ to the dying thief that they will both be in paradise that very day (Luke 23:43).

The idea of a park or enclosure was popular in Assyrian and Persian times where woodland or

specially planted trees were enclosed and sometimes specially populated with wild animals for sport and interest. Kings and rulers would proudly display their magnificent parks, often whole hills or larger in extent. The reliefs of Ashurbanipal's lion hunt in the British Museum shows this in tragic and terrifying beauty, always remembering that it was sculpted to underline the king's own greatness. It is clear, too, that creating beautiful gardens, which included exotic trees and plants gathered from afar during foreign conquests, was a means to display or advertise greatness of which Sargon and his son Sennacherib were foremost exponents.[1] Meiggs[2] cites a quote from the days of Alexander the Great, in which Quintus Curtius wrote: '*There is no better indication of the great wealth of the Bazaioi than the herds of noble beasts confined in large forests and open woodland. They choose for the purpose wide spreading forests relieved by abundant springs or running water; the woods are surrounded by walls and there are towers in them for use of hunters.*' In

medieval Britain enclosed wood pastures and deer parks, with their boundary wood-banks, such as Staverton, Richmond or Moccas, fulfilled the same function as does our pleasure today in the great game parks of Africa. But Nehemiah's request for an introduction to Asaph suggests more extensive forest than royal hunting parks to obtain the quantities of timber he needed. Probably Asaph was responsible for all trees and forests under Artaxerxes' jurisdiction.

The title or position of 'Keeper of the king's forest' is perhaps strange as trees don't need shepherding and they are not kept in zoos! The old style park keeper or modern green keeper in golf are better parallels. But what would a keeper of forests do? We can be pretty sure. Trees might not escape like animals, but their management throughout history has three elements. Although the Bible tells us little of forest management we know that as long ago as 1750 BC the early Assyrian King of Babylon, Hammurabi, bequeathed us his codified laws on a

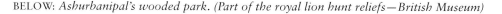

BELOW: *Ashurbanipal's wooded park. (Part of the royal lion hunt reliefs—British Museum)*

IMP HAD AUG
DEFINITO SILVARUM

IMP HAD AUG
ABORUM GENERA IV CETERA PRIVATO

ABOVE: *Hadrian's inscriptions exercising imperial prerogative over certain trees. The abbreviated Latin translates: 'The demarcation of the forests of the Emperor Hadrian; four species of trees; the rest are private' (i.e are not claimed by the emperor.)*

stele.[3] Many refer to agriculture and caring for land and property and one spells out the penalty, a stiff fine of silver, for illegal tree felling.[4] The limestone rocks of northern Lebanon bear witness to a much later example. More than one hundred inscriptions of Hadrian have been found dating to AD 138 demarcating great tracts of forest and warning that four of the tree species are the Emperor's.[5] We are not told which ones, but doubtless the best and most important economically: probably cedar, juniper, fir and oak.

In Nehemiah's time laws will have regulated forest use along the following lines.

First, because forests are often remote and often with ill-defined borders, the first job of a keeper is to stop theft of trees and logs and encroachment by squatters or expropriation. The keeper has to maintain the forest's integrity: it is property like anything else, not free-for-all, and people in history are no different from today when it comes to trying to get away with it. Equally threatening is trespass by livestock which will browse young trees and strip bark from older ones. The worst culprit is the ubiquitous goat, though camels, horses, sheep and cattle are all up there as capable of appalling damage. Attempts to exclude them would only make Asaph's forests all the more appealing to animal and animal owner alike!

Secondly, the keeper will keep an eye on the exercise of rights within a forest. If permission has been given, like Nehemiah requests, are the provisions being complied with? Are only permitted trees being cut or are others being filched and sneaked out? Are sufficient smaller ones left for the future? Where livestock is permitted to graze, are the number of days for grazing properly monitored? A Norman example comes from a forest designated by William the Conqueror, the New Forest in Hampshire, where the right of pannage is to graze pigs in the forest at certain times of the year, and the gathering of firewood 'by hook or by crook' restricts collection to what can be broken off, i.e. dead, or is on the ground.

Only once the keeper is on top of the forest's integrity and exercise of legitimate rights, can decisions about the third element be addressed: where can timber be harvested. Put simply, forests are subdivided in three ways: (a) by predominant species—where are the good oaks and cedars, where are the unthrifty patches, (b) by age—where are the mature trees and where are young ones coming on as the forest of the future, what foresters call 'regeneration', and (c) by access—where can trees be felled safely and logs extracted easily? In Britain areas of forest that are worked as a unit, like a farmer's field, are typically of 5 to 50 ha or more and called 'compartments'. Within a compartment particular groups of trees to be thinned or felled are called 'stands'. There is no doubt that chief forester Asaph will have divided the king's forest in some way as an aid to management. But he may have done one more thing too.

To cut timber sustainably, it is important not to cut more than the whole forest is adding each year. Think of all the trees in the forest each with their annual ring of new wood—the rings we count to find out a tree's age. Add together all the new wood in the current year's ring that each tree grows and

ABOVE: *Forest on the western slopes of Mt Carmel; it might look unmanaged, but isn't*

that tells you how much is available to cut from the forest. Cutting consistently more than this will deplete the forest. There are sophisticated ways of calculating this quantity—estimating the increment as it is called—and it is probable that Asaph had a way of knowing what quantities could safely be cut. I don't think we are exaggerating. Why else would one of the most senior officials, Nehemiah, the king's cupbearer, have asked the king himself for a letter to the keeper of the king's forest? It suggests firm management and control of this greatly valued resource.

Exactly where the forests were that Asaph managed we don't know. The timber Nehemiah sought for beams for the gates of the citadel, and for the great gates in Jerusalem's walls, not to mention his own residence, needn't have been the famed and expensive imported cedar Ezra used 60 or so years earlier to rebuild the temple. Native cypress, oaks, sycomore-fig, poplar, terebinth and possibly pine would have been suitable depending on sizes needed. Were Solomon's wooded parks (Eccles. 2:4) still surviving, managed and protected 600 years on or had the waves of destruction from Assyrian, Babylonian and Persian armies long since laid them waste?

ABOVE: *Suckers at the base of a very old olive (Gethsemane) are normally removed so as not to deprive the tree, but would make acceptable coppice if the tree itself was lost*

Tree branches to make shelters for the feast of tabernacles

Nehemiah 8:15–16

In their rediscovery of the law and the festivals after returning from exile, Nehemiah included re-instigating the feast of tabernacles. He specifically instructs the people to, '"Go out into the hill country and bring back branches from olive and wild olive trees, and from myrtles, palms and other leafy trees, to make temporary shelters"— as it is written'. (Neh. 8:15). The choice of these trees harks back to the instruction about the 'four species' of Leviticus 23:40, the reference in the verse to 'as it is written'. Though actually they are not directly for the festival itself, but to make shelters or booths to be built on the roofs of the people's houses. This may account for the slight discrepancy in species, namely, no mention of citrus by Nehemiah. The slightly odd double mention of 'olives' and 'wild olive trees' (Hebrew '*ets shemen*') is mistaken according to Zohary[6] and the latter should be Aleppo pine, as it is in the King James version. Other translations suggest fig, though most now have 'wild olive trees'. Nevertheless the list

shows what was readily available in the countryside in Israel in the 5th Century BC.

Two analogies of Job's and one question of God's

Job 14, 19 & 40

Job's trials and testing last throughout much of the book of his name. Dispirited, Job in his reply to Zophar is wistful, almost plaintive, in contrasting the lot of a tree with his own (Job 14:7–9), 'At least there is hope for a tree. If it is cut down, it will sprout again and its new shoots will not fail.' Job is referring to the ability of most broadleaved trees to coppice, when new shoots sprout from the old stump; Isaiah, too, knew it well (Isa. 6:29). The stump (or stool as it is called when coppicing), appears dead, but dormant buds spring to life usually the following year or next wet season. And Job is right, the new shoots very rarely fail and will often far outpace a seedling in early growth. In Britain this system was relied on in medieval times when most woodland was regenerated by coppicing, such as hazel, oak, mixed coppices or copses, and more recently sweet chestnut. More recently still modern biomass energy crops of poplar and willow are being coppiced. There is evidence that 5000 years ago coppicing was practised in the Somerset Levels indicated by the corduroy laid timbers on the Sweet Track.

Not all broadleaved trees coppice. A few like some alders, beech in dry climates and shining gum in Australia (*Eucalyptus nitens*) for example won't coppice or do so only poorly. And others, of which English ash (*Fraxinus excelsior*) is an outstanding example, may initially remain dormant for a year after cutting. Stumps of summer felled ash will often not sprout coppice until the year after next. Few conifers coppice, exceptions are the redwoods, the monkey puzzle, a few cypresses and one or two pines.

The contrast Job draws is right, resumption of growth after felling a mighty tree is astonishing. And the hope is that we know it will happen, that's why we rely on the practice. Job also remarks about the ability of some roots of semi-desert trees and shrubs that, when left in the ground, can hang on for months and then spring to life when the rains return (Job 14:8–9). One example is with olive and

ABOVE: *Poplars and willows by the stream in Banias, Israel*

the shoots, or offshoots (*netzer*) which arise from the roots, and which helps explain how the messiah is an offshoot of Jesse (Isa. 11:1 & 10).[7] The nearest comparison in Britain is root suckering by cherry trees as anyone with a lawn next to this tree will know! Shoot growth comes again and again and even seems stimulated when the parent tree itself is cut down. As Job adds next, such recovery is beyond the lot of man, at least until faith arises in Christ and which, perhaps, Job distantly foresaw.

When Job next compares his lot to a tree (Job 19:10) he is in even deeper despair. Of God he wails, 'He tears me down on every side till I am gone; he uproots my hope like a tree'. How heart-rending —gone like the blast of a storm overturning a great tree, wrenching its roots from the ground, with the finality of the tree's end never again to stand tall and upright. But then, only a few verses later (Job 19:25–26), we read that paean of faith (or is it the last gasp despair dug out from the very pits?), 'I know

that my Redeemer lives … and in my flesh I will see God'. What assurance in times of deep trouble: knowing that the impossible can happen, as if an uprooted tree is restored fully to its former glory.

While identification of the behemoth (Job 40:15), God's beast par excellence in Hebrew, is uncertain, suggestions of great herbivores like the hippopotamus or possibly elephant fit well with the habitat of reeds and marsh land and where poplars occur by the stream (Job 40:21–22). However the tail swaying like a cedar fits neither creature unless it refers to the elephant's trunk. Both these animals once occurred in the wetlands which form part of the headwaters of the Jordan north of the Sea of Galilee,[8] but may have been extinct when the Old Testament was written though the hippo is thought to have still been present as late as the 8th Century BC.[9] Surely their renown was known to Job, who lived much earlier, and would not be lost on him as his Creator questioned him about the behemoth.

BELOW: *Desert acacias and umbrella thorns marking out where water must sometimes flow*

Six tree similes in Psalms

Psalms 1, 37, 52, 74, 83 & 92

All the psalmists delight in simile. They delight in likening a spiritual teaching to an earthly illustration, just as Jesus did in his many parables. And the inclusion of trees and forests does not disappoint.

The Psalms open with the picture of the honourable, upright man who shuns bad company and meditates on God's laws. He is compared to a tree that can cope with any threat (Ps. 1:3), 'He is like a tree planted by streams of water which yields its fruit in season and whose leaf does not wither.' This compelling simile is repeated almost word for word in Jeremiah 17:7–8 who adds that heat and drought are not feared either. Clearly it was a powerful image in thirsty Israel. It reflects, of course,

ABOVE: *A solitary tree in the Judean desert thriving because its roots must tap water beneath the dried-up river bed*

the common observation of riverine woodland, that fringe of greenery hugging every twist and bend of a stream or river flowing through desert. While plants have contact with a source of water they can survive whatever heat or drought stresses their foliage. More extreme is the individual tree or shrub seemingly alone in a desert yet flourishing. It too will be garnering moisture in one of three ways: roots which spread out far beyond the reach of the crown, roots which have tapped supplies at exceptional depths, or in a few cases foliage able to utilise morning dew and mist as occurs in Chile's famed Atacama desert.

Many will have admired Africa's game parks, in person or on television, and perhaps seen a sleek leopard lolling on the branch of a spreading acacia. Less obvious is that the trees rarely form forest thicket, unless close to water, but are scattered across the landscape. They appear at random, but this is not so. Their crowns of branches may not touch, but beneath the soil their roots, extending great distances, will be competing with all the neighbouring trees for what little moisture is on offer. They survive, they flourish from possessing huge spreading root systems far more extensive than their above-ground size suggests.

It is deep rooting, however, which we commonly, but quite wrongly, associate with trees. Most trees only root in the top one metre of soil, as examination of an uprooted tree will usually show. Really deep rooting is confined to soil and rock types that permit it. Occasionally very great depths have been recorded. Many years ago as a consultant I was asked if some huge eucalyptus trees could be maintaining an artificially deep water table on a site in South Africa. In the course of the investigation we identified live tree roots, presumably of eucalyptus, at an astonishing depth of 19 m (60 ft). Over a period of 30 or 40 years the roots appeared to have followed the water table ever downwards in a profile that was shattered, fissured and rootable through crevices.

These examples explain how trees, with their massive daily demand for water, can survive and flourish where it is barren and dry. All that's needed is for their roots to access by some means a reliable water supply. Just as the psalmist says, like a tree planted by streams of water.

Psalm 37 is wonderful. It is so full of promises and encouragements, but near the end David passes comment about wicked and ruthless men appearing to do well, 'flourishing like a green tree in its native soil'. Soon, he says, they are gone despite having been so secure, healthy and prosperous. The remark about 'native soil' is the contrast it draws with a tree planted on the wrong site or in non-native soil to which it is ill-suited. There are numerous examples. If Scots pine trees are planted on chalky soils they usually start well, but will be dead from lime-induced chlorosis by age 25 just as would azaleas or rhododendrons or similar lime-hating or lime-fleeing plants called 'calcifuges'. A different example is Britain's bread and butter timber producer, Sitka spruce. Although introduced from western North America it is at home on the peaty soils of the hills and mountains of the moist, temperate Atlantic side of the country. Plant it in the drier east and it struggles. There is a science of getting this right, of matching tree species with site.

Rich in meaning and beautiful as a thought is David comparing himself to an olive tree in God's house (Ps. 52:8). As we have remarked already olive trees are incredibly long lived, almost impossible to kill, fruitful and useful for so many different purposes. Secure and safe in God's house the olive would yield every one of its blessings. Despite setbacks, on a spiritual high David cries, 'I am like an olive tree flourishing in the house of God'.

Psalm 74 is so different. Like Psalm 73 reflecting on why the wicked seem to prosper, Psalm 74 wonders aloud how God's foes get away with it. Their appalling behaviour is likened to men wielding axes to fell thickets of trees and smash carved panelling (Ps. 74:5–6). Was this the destruction wrought by the Babylonians when sacking Jerusalem and taking the Israelites into exile? The image of felled trees is powerful: what was green, vibrant and healthy becomes 'overnight' brown, dried up and destroyed. Foresters are forever receiving complaints both from planting up land and the change that introduces and also, and very especially, from the sudden, shattering change wrought by tree felling. None of us likes change.

Psalm 83 is set alight by verse 14, 'as fire consumes the forest or a flame sets the mountains ablaze' to express the way the psalmist implores God to judge. It is an imprecatory psalm, one that calls on God to condemn and to visit judgment. Like the complete destruction uprooting conjures, so the image of out of control forest fires leaves little to the imagination. All burnt, blackened and beyond recovery—there for all to see, for all to ponder the after-fire silence, for all to whiff the singular smell of burnt land. Early in my career I once worked in what was then Britain's most fire-prone forest region, the dying industrial valleys of South Wales: you never forget your first experience of a forest fire and its aftermath.

My favourite simile is Psalm 92:12. 'The righteous will flourish like a palm tree, they will grow like a cedar of Lebanon.' The psalmist's straightforward meaning is that the righteous will be both fruitful year after year and strong and firm. But this lovely pairing of two different trees has something more: a desert species, the palm, thriving in the dry, hot and arid contrasted with a mountain species, the cedar, growing tall in the cool, exposed hill country. They also represent angiosperm and gymnosperm, the full spread of what botanists call 'higher plants'. One yields abundant sweet fruit, the other the finest timber then known. The picture is of God's breadth and blessing—all walks of life and people from all corners of the world; none is left out or excluded. The point is clear, that wherever we are and

whoever we are who seek God and his righteousness we are are included.

There is a further point. The psalmist may also be implying that both these trees were growing together in Jerusalem though neither would do so naturally.[10] Had Solomon facilitated this to impress his many influential visitors (2 Chron. 9:23) with richly diverse gardens and parks—the arboreta and botanic gardens of the day?

Is there, too, even more symbolism in the pair of trees. We have commented several times that cedar of Lebanon symbolises the best and finest, the stately and impressive. But the date palm with its numerous uses and abundant provision was widely admired, indeed it was used as a decorative motif in the main hall of the temple (2 Chron. 3:5). In other cultures it was revered and worshipped: the great Sennacherib took to himself the remarkable title, 'Date palm of Assyria', probably for religious reasons.[11] We cannot know the Psalmist's thoughts, but without doubt the pairing of palm and cedar has all sorts of resonances evoking a wonderful picture of 'the righteous'.

Six evocations of power and praise
Psalm 29, 50, 96, 104, 105 and 148
David knows his trees. In Psalm 29:9 he writes, 'The voice of the Lord twists the oaks and strips the forest bare'. Stripping the forest pictures the havoc wreaked by a great storm, but why oaks twisted; why not pine, or cedar, or sycomore-fig? Because oaks are brittle.[12] When storms come, gusts that would uproot some kinds of trees more often than not tear branches from an oak as if twisting them off. It might be sturdy and strong, but a bit brittle. David knows his trees, and the power of his God. And I think God knows something else. The oak, of all the trees, was most likely to be worshipped in ancient times[13] as Isaiah (Isa. 1:29) bemoans: but it too is subject to God.

The words of God in Psalm 50:10, '... for every animal of the forest is mine, and the cattle on a thousand hills' resonate with authority. It is said not out of boasting, but plain fact.

Several times in scripture, trees are symbolically presented as rejoicing. In Psalm 96:12 they 'sing', 'Then all the trees of the forest will sing for joy'. It pictures creation entering in to the restoration God will bring about (Rom. 8:21–22).

Our next evocation is in Psalm 104:16, 'The trees of the Lord are well watered, the cedars of Lebanon that he planted.' The psalmist goes on to rejoice in God's provision in creation that birds nest in the junipers (vs 17) and wild animals prowl in the forest at night (vs 20). Under the title, 'Trees of God' the great Baptist preacher Spurgeon, in his inimitable way, draws out much from vs 16 for a morning devotion. 'Like cedars', writes Spurgeon, 'Christians are full of sap. There is a life force flowing through us, the life of Christ. Finally the majesty of the cedars is for the glory of God alone. In the believer there is nothing that can magnify man. The Lord has done it all. To Him be all the glory.'

Ancient Jewish tradition drew out even more. Quoting Psalm 104:16, Rabbi Johanan taught that the glorious cedar tree was actually created for the sake of the Temple.[14] Indeed, the Jews took a positive view about Lebanon and its wonderful cedars, perhaps spelled out most fully in Hosea 14:5–8.

In the very next psalm God's power and authority in rescuing the Israelites from Egypt is recounted. In two of the verses (Ps 105:32–33) the appalling hailstorm is recalled. Exodus 9:24 tells us it was the worst storm in Egypt since it had become a nation. So severe was the hail that it stripped the forest bare, but tellingly in Psalm 105:33 we are told their vines and fig trees were struck down and trees of the country shattered. It is difficult for us to envisage.

When we look at where hail storms are most destructive it is often in sub-tropical regions and where local topography channels winds. In Swaziland, where I once worked and continue to visit regularly, hail is such a problem that special rockets were, for a time, used to fire into hail bearing clouds to shatter the hail stones into mush or sleet. Such clouds are dark, lowering and tinged greenish or purplish and hang like draped curtains. In this way fields of pineapples and maize and orchards of citrus were protected. As well as the physical destruction hail wreaks, in forests the scarring of bark can permit fungal infection. One 20 minute hail storm in northern Swaziland destroyed over 3000 acres of pine killed by a fungal blight that took hold called Diplodia.[15] With Egypt suffering a plague of hail which was the worst ever experienced physical and biological destruction would have been total. There were no half measures when it came to the ten plagues.

The concluding psalms are filled with praise which, symbolically, embraces all that God has made. Psalm 148:9 exclaims, 'Praise the Lord from the earth … you mountains and all hills, fruit trees and cedars …' Again cedar is singled out as representing the best, as praise goes up from the created to the creator.

A tree of life
Proverbs 3, 11, 13 & 14
We met the tree of life in Chapter 1 (Gen. 3:22) with its implication of living for ever. We meet it again in all its abundance and fruitfulness at the very end of the Bible (Rev. 22:2). Here in Proverbs four blessings are likened to it: wisdom itself; the fruit of righteousness; a longing fulfilled; and kindly words that bring healing (Prov. 3:18; 11:30; 13:12; and 15:4). Not only does the tree of life last, but as these lasting analogies show it endows, blesses, gladdens, and comforts. Who would doubt this of great trees? It is not surprising that many kinds of tree are given the scientific name 'green and flourishing' i.e. the Latin sempervirens. Included are the widespread Italian or evergreen cypress, the cypress of the Bible, Cupressus sempervirens, the Cretan maple of the eastern Mediterranean, Acer sempervirens, the famed coast redwood of western North America,

Sequoia sempervirens, and the box tree, Buxus sempervirens,[16] native from the chalk downs of southern England all the way to the Mediterranean and North Africa.

Even closer to a tree of life is the wood traded as 'lignum vitae' meaning 'wood of life'. It got the name from its many medicinal properties and is a slow growing tree of tropical America and the Caribbean. The wood is incredibly hard and dense, so dense in fact that it doesn't float in water but sinks. Its hardness makes it usable as a bearing. Harrison's[17] famous tower clock at Brocklesby Park, which has run continuously since 1722, is made almost entirely of wood! It never needs oiling because he used lignum vitae bushes as self-lubricating bearings:[18] perhaps a life-giving wood!

The world's oldest living trees manage at most 5000 years, the bristlecone pine (Pinus aristata), the redwoods (Sequoia sempervirens and Sequoiadendron giganteum), and a recently discovered Norway spruce (Picea abies) growing in Sweden. Some olive trees have reportedly achieved 2000 years, yews (Taxus baccata) may just exceed 1000 years, and oaks (Quercus spp.) many hundreds. Most trees commonly seen typically live only for many decades or one to three hundred years, depending on species, site, and environment. Longer life is associated with testing conditions like drought and cold: shorter life with fast growth on fertile soils with plentiful moisture.

Horticultural cameos of the teacher
Ecclesiastes 2, 3, 11 & 12
Ecclesiastes always brings us down to earth. The work Solomon describes of cultivating vineyards and orchards or wooded parks, irrigating them, and seeing them flourish (Eccles. 2:4–7) shows the sophistication of horticulture a millennium before Christ. No wonder, too, that Solomon the scientist and farmer understands the cycles of work and of crop and includes, 'a time to plant and a time to uproot' (Eccles. 3:2). And he is right. Even the best orchards need replacing as fruitfulness finally declines with age and, in forestry, growth of trees peaks and then slows down. Foresters use the word rotation as the length of time or age at which trees are felled and harvested.

ABOVE: *Cretan maple in Hillier Arboretum, Hampshire. The apostle Paul would have seen these maples in his travels and perhaps been encouraged that they were 'always green and flourishing' in line with today's scientific name*

But Solomon talks about uprooting—a time to plant and a time to uproot. Is this because some fruit and tree crops, to be over-dramatic, 'poison' the ground for their successor? Citrus, apple, cherry and peach suffer from this 'specific replant disease' such that the next crop, if of the same kind, grows poorly although not exhibiting symptoms of ill-health.[19] Did Solomon know this and hence advocate uprooting and the implication of complete change? If not, why didn't he say, 'a time to plant and a time to harvest'?

Forestry examples of 'replant diseases' include the common garden scourge of honey fungus killing trees and shrubs planted on infected ground from

ABOVE: *Gap regeneration from a fallen giant. The moss covered trunk is now barely discernible but new trees have all sprung up from where it fell. (Olympic National Park, Washington, USA)*

a previously diseased woody plant and Fomes damage to successor pine trees on chalky soils. In both cases rigorous removal of the preceding crop's stumps and roots—uprooting—largely eliminates the threat. This subject is of special interest to me since my research has examined whether successive crops of trees can be grown on the same site again and again. The answer is almost always 'yes' because trees take little from the soil compared with farm crops and often return much over their life.

Solomon's next cameo (Eccles. 11:3) is plain: where a tree falls, whatever the direction, there it lies. This recalls what happens naturally in forest whether temperate, Mediterranean or tropical and underlies what we call 'gap dynamics' as mentioned in Chapter 1 of this book. An ageing forest giant, weakened by decay in root or trunk, finally succumbs to a tropical squall or temperate storm and crashes to the ground. There it lies, immovable, and there begins regeneration: the influx of light may reinvigorate branches or stimulate germination and growth of seedlings on the forest floor, or even promote coppice around the upturned base. In natural forest the pattern of trees is the pattern of where their predecessors fell. This is well shown in many New England states where natural woodland is revealed by the fact of uneven ground of humps and hollows or 'tip mounds' left by uprooted and overturned trees from hurricanes of the past.[20]

The last tree metaphor is precious; it speaks of old age (Eccles. 12:5). 'When the almond tree blossoms ...' pictures turning grey and for some a white head of hair and beard. No flower is more exquisitely white in the near East than almond, not only because they are the first to appear at the end of winter but because, like ash trees in Britain and the glorious blue of jacaranda (so common now in the towns and cities of the Mediterranean), flowering occurs before the leaves flush. Thus an almond bush is bedecked unsullied in blossom, like a snow-white cloud in the landscape exclaims Zohary,[21] a sign of hastening events and herald of spring. A foretaste, perhaps, for the ageing believer of heaven that awaits when, '... his spirit returns to God who gave it.' (Eccles. 12:7).

The greatest of songs

Song of Solomon 1–3, & 5

The lovers admiration of the other is illustrated by just about every fruit, every spice, every incense, and the best of trees. The verses drip perfume and the sensuous; they employ nature's bounty and beauty to portray the deepest feelings and yearnings. It cannot be bettered: 'My lover is to me a sachet of myrrh resting between my breasts. My lover is to me a cluster of henna blossoms from the vineyards of En Gedi.' (Song 1:13–14). Myrrh, the reddish aromatic resin from the diminutive desert shrub, *Commiphora myrrha*, was famed throughout the East as a perfume to wear e.g. Esther 2:12 and even to scent royal nuptial robes (Ps. 45:8). So precious and so royal was it that the Magi brought to Jesus this gift fit for a King. And henna (*Lawsonia inermis*), with its numerous white petalled and powerfully fragrant flowers, is, too, a desert shrub found in the hottest and driest parts such as at En Gedi, the oasis west of the Dead Sea where, famously, David was

ABOVE: *Almond blossom*

hiding in the very cave where his pursuer, King Saul, went to relieve himself.

We can pause and smile at the sharp change of tone three verses later (Song 1:17) as our more practical lover, the man, the breadwinner, announces that his 'house' is built only of the best, the queen of timbers—cedar (and fir for the rafters)—fit for a queen. As we know from Kings and Chronicles, Solomon's palace was a wonder of cedar. Three hundred years later it was still known as 'the Palace of the Forest' (Isa. 22:8), such was its renown.[22]

The metaphors and analogies continue. Picture the apple[23] tree (Song 2:3), perhaps in blossom or laden with delicious fruit, alone and surrounded by forest trees that only offer timber, contrasting the desirable with the utilitarian, the exceptional with the ordinary, the singular with the commonplace. And then as verse follows verse and love and desire excite, the senses become aroused: the caressing taste of raisins and sweet apples, the abandon of wild gazelles, the yearning for the other watching

ABOVE: *Walnut leaves, fruit and nut*

and hoping for their arrival. And then winter is past (Song 2:11), spring has come, love is in the air: flowers appear, the fig tree its early fruit, the vines flush with new growth. Only those in love could write such poetry.

While a few have questioned the authorship, the many references to Solomon are suggestive and consistent. As we've seen, he sought timber from Lebanon and here he is using the same to build a sumptuous carriage (Song 3:9).

In Chapter 4 the lover's eulogy takes the breath away. Its delicacy and tenderness and the aroma of love and intimacy of verse 6, a mountain of myrrh and hill of incense, leads to the ultimate exultation: there is no flaw in you. But our lover, surely King Solomon who described plant life, reveals in verse 8 (by the reference to the haunts of wild animals) where great forests remained, namely Mt Hermon on Israel's northern border, through Lebanon to Amanus (Syria). How sad today that so little is left, barely a stand of cedar, and none on Mt Hermon. But none can pass over Solomon's luxuriating in perfumes, scents and incense and all the finest spices in verses 13 and 14.

The excitement of the beloved anticipating her lover's arrival (Song 5:4)—hands dripping with lotion of myrrh, fingers flowing myrrh (vs 5)—wonderfully leaves everything to the imagination. So too her description of him (Song 5:10–16): head, hair, cheeks, lips, arms and legs and how we can understand his appearance, that sense of presence—like the finest of cedars of Lebanon: the most impressive, tall, strong, and stately of trees and perhaps as an evergreen too in constancy and faithfulness?

We cannot leave this extraordinary song and poem of love and desire, with sexual intimacy fulfilled in the final three chapters, to the neglect of the practical and the allegorical. Throughout references to orchards, the grove of nut trees, probably walnuts (*Juglans regia*) (Song 6:11), vines and pomegranates, the gardens, while plainly metaphorical, also convey a sense of place. The lovers know this somewhere special and share their recollections and joy of where they courted. May it have been the gardens or wooded park of the kind we discussed earlier (Neh. 2:8) and which Ecclesiastes 2:4–7 tells us Solomon created?

Josephus (*Antiquities* 8.7.3) records that Solomon delighted in the gardens at Etham six miles south of Jerusalem.

But allegory remains. For all the delight in each other, for all the exchanges of intimacy, for the sheer joy this Song of Songs conveys, there remains that greater love and greater devotion of Christ to his church, of God for his creatures. In the past this was emphasised to the detriment of the obvious meaning of this beautiful poem, but it ever remains that the Christian can say with the beloved (Song 2:4), 'His banner over me is love.'

Notes

1 **Dalley, S** (2013) *The mystery of the Hanging Garden of Babylon*. Oxford University Press, Oxford.

2 **Meiggs, R** (1982) *Trees and Timber of the Ancient Mediterranean World*. Clarendon Press, Oxford.

3 An upright pillar with writing, inscriptions, or sculpture engraved.

4 **Richardson, M E J** (2000) *Hammurabi's Laws*. Sheffield Academic Press, Sheffield.

5 **Meiggs** (ibid)

6 **Zohary, M** (1982) *Plants of the Bible*. Cambridge University Press, Cambridge.

7 **Hareuveni, N** (2006) *Tree and Shrub in our Biblical Heritage*. Neot Kedumim, Lod, Israel. (transl. **Helen Frenkley**)

8 **Alon, A** (1969) *The Natural History of the Land of the Bible*. Jerusalem Publishing House & Hamlyn, London.

9 **Curtis, A** (2008) *Oxford Bible Atlas* (4th Edn) Oxford University Press.

10 **Hareuveni** (ibid)

11 **Dalley** (2013) (ibid)

12 Half an hour after writing this I was sitting in the garden. It was a summer's day. Beyond the hedge I heard a car in the lane followed by a crash, but not that of an accident. A branch had fallen on the carriageway; from an oak!

13 **Carey, F** (2012) *The Tree—Meaning and Myth*. British Museum Press, London. [Carey cites the example that at the heart of Zeus's sanctuary at Dodona in NW Greece was an ancient oak invested with much power. Zeus was the greatest of Greek gods, and Dodona the most ancient of Hellenic oracles. Wreaths of gold oak leaves are listed in inventories of Greek temples.] We also know that garlands of oak leaves would adorn sacrificial bulls, such as featured on a frieze at the entrance to the Baths of Constantius, Ephesus, and the oak leaf and acorn motif often decorates the base of temple columns. When the inhabitants of Lystra tried to worship Paul and Barnabas, thinking they were the gods Hermes and Zeus (Acts 14:13), the wreaths brought from the temple are likely to have been of oak leaves, perhaps even of gold.

14 **Hareuveni** (ibid)

15 **Evans, J** and **Turbull, J W** (2004) *Plantation Forestry in the Tropics*. Oxford University Press.

16 **Musselman, L J** (2012) *A Dictionary of Bible Plants*. Cambridge University Press, New York. [Musselman in noting the very wide distribution of this essentially temperate species, believes boxwood may be the mysterious algum wood of 2 Chron. 2:8–11)]

17 The 18th Century clockmaker who won the prize to enable ships to measure their longitude accurately. His early attempts can be seen working in the Royal Observatory at Greenwich.

18 **Taylor, J C** and **Wolfendale, A W** (2007) John Harrison: clockmaker and Copley Medallist. A public memorial at last. *Notes and Records of the Royal Society* 22 January 2007 **61**(1): 53–62

19 **Savory, B M** (1966) *Specific Replant Diseases*. Research Review No. 1, Bureau of Horticulture, Plantation Crops, East Malling, Kent.

20 **Rackham, O** (2006) *Woodlands*. Collins, London.

21 **Zohary** (ibid)

22 Some suggest (see Hareuveni) that 'The Palace of the Forest' was a cool summer mansion built by Solomon (1 Kg. 7:2–5) with pillars of cedar trunks with branch stumps still attached for effect and as beam supports. The roof was of cedar planks. It was impressive and long remembered. A hint of the effect conveyed might be like that of the trees gracing the aisle of Westminster Abbey for Prince William and Katherine Middleton's wedding.

23 **Musselman** (ibid) [Musselman strongly argues that references to apple in Song of Solomon and elsewhere for the Hebrew word '*tappuah*' refers to apricot. This is unlikely since apricot only arrived in the Mediterranean region in Roman times while archaeological evidence for apple cultivation around 10th C BC i.e. the time of Solomon, comes from an Iron Age site around Kadesh Barnea between the Negev and Sinai (Zohary, et al. (2012) *Domestication of Plants in the Old World*. Oxford.

7

Prophets—pastoral and painful

The remaining books of the Old Testament—the prophets—largely comment on or proclaim what God is teaching the Israelites through their life and times and the events that beset them. They are not in chronological order historically, but that doesn't prevent us from helping to enlarge upon a rich metaphor or analyse an allegory. We begin with the greatest of all; great in portraying more clearly than any other Old Testament book the coming of a Messiah and great in Isaiah's use of the pastoral— he loved his people, he loved his country and he surely loved his countryside.

However, the very number of tree-related metaphors and analogies in Isaiah, and to an extent in all the remaining prophetic books, makes worthwhile commentary more challenging compared with the books of history or poetry. Quite often an image is repeated or a point is obscure for us today. Also there is the sense at times of going on and on about the same issue which to our ears is tiring to the point of boring and becoming a 'turn-off'.

Shame and humbling of oak and cedar
Isaiah 1 & 2

We've already mentioned that oaks were worshipped and their name, *allon* and *elon*, associated with the Hebrew for 'god'. Here in the opening chapter of Isaiah (Isa. 1:29) the shame and offence of such animism is spelt out. Isaiah presses home the oak imagery in the next verse, 'like an oak with fading leaves, like a garden without water'. Is he referring to drought: figuratively of a drought of God's word, of obedience to His commands and of love for Him, and literally too? Oaks are deep rooted and take a long time to die of drought, but as they do, leaves of evergreen ones will fade and fall and those of deciduous species, like Tabor oak, may actually persist longer as reminders of the slow death that has befallen. Premature browning of leaves from drought arrests the natural processes of autumnal leaf ageing (senescence). The corky layer that forms at the leaf base in autumn to separate it from the twig does not develop; botanically, there is no abscission. This was seen in the picture on page 50 of oak foliage being dried. Is 'An oak with fading leaves' (Isa. 1:30) a reminder of spiritual drought, and a reminder of the foolishness of worshipping an oak tree, all dried up and useless?

Oaks, with cedar this time, come in for a second humbling (Isa. 2:13). The greatest tree of the East, the cedar of Lebanon, and the finest tree in Israel,

FACING PAGE: *A distant hillside of oaks and terebinths in Bashan*

ABOVE: *Young Tabor oak in mid October showing no sign of changing leaf colour, nearby terebinth foliage just starting*

the oak, are humbled so that 'the Lord alone will be exalted' (vs 11). Bashan to the east of the Jordan in the region of Caesarea Philippi, was famed for its oaks. These symbols of pride, wealth, majesty and permanence are just that, symbols. 'The arrogance of man will be brought low, the pride of men will be humbled' (vs 17).

Hope and despair in a tree stump
Isaiah 6–11

In Isaiah 6:13, and famously in Isaiah 11:1, we meet the tree stump and its powers of regeneration. The prophet uses this analogy as Job did (Job 14:7–9) though this time to express great hope not Job's despair. But the NIV translation for stump in Isaiah 6:13 and its implied meaning along with the slightly curious, 'the holy seed will be the stump in the land', may be not be the best. Nogah Hareuveni, in his fine book *Tree and Shrub in our Biblical Heritage* using the Hebrew Bible, gives an alternative reading and explains why: '... Like the oak and the terebinth in their fall (season) their (dormant) trunk remains carrying the holy seed within'.[1] Isaiah, suggests

Hareuveni, does not simply pair the trees for poetic effect, but because he understands their biology, particularly leaf fall in the autumn, and uses them as a simile.

The two trees behave differently. At the beginning of the rainy season in November the terebinth stands out from all other forest trees as its leaves turn to reds and yellows and surpass all others in beauty. But the glory is fleeting, in days the leaves are gone. Judah, says Isaiah, is like this, glorious for a time but soon to fall. The Tabor oak does not show autumnal colour before leaf fall, the trunk and branches just become bare, though only for two or three weeks! New buds soon burst forth fresh and green, acorns on the ground germinate with the rains: everywhere growth springs forth. Destruction is not total, says Isaiah, there is hope, the seed, for the future, for the long-term—consider the terebinth and oak—the hope of Messiah.

In Chapter 7 Isaiah begins the prophecies against Judah. Ahaz, of David's dynasty, is not to fear the alliance against him even though he was defeated before by Aram and Israel (2 Chron. 28:5–8) and even though now, '... the hearts of Ahaz and his people were shaken as the trees of the forest are shaken by the wind.' Though Judah tries God's patience (Isa. 7:13) the next verse is that wonderful encouragement and sign of the coming Messiah— the virgin shall be with child—but only as an interlude before God announces that Assyria will be his instrument of judgment (Isa. 7:17). Destruction will lead to desolation, to fruitful land becoming a wilderness of briers and thorns (Isa. 7:23). And then in Chapter 9 the Christmas message of promise is followed by downfall of the proud who show off by exclaiming, '... the fig trees have been felled, but we will replace them with cedars.' (Isa. 9:10) How impressive cedars must have been, a byword for greatness just as the burning and consuming forest fire is a byword for wickedness and the smoke that goes up of God's wrath (Isa. 9:18–19).

It is Chapter 10 where God's judgment of Assyria draws most heavily on our metaphors, and with irony too. Woe to Assyria, who may be God's instrument but who does not escape responsibility: 'Does the axe raise itself above him who swings it, or the saw against him who uses it?' (Isa. 10:15).

ABOVE: *One-year-old shoots of hazel coppice over 7 ft (2.3 m) high*

took it and, in 701 BC, his great army was forced to retreat to Nineveh.

Back to our tree stump. An exquisite contrast is drawn between Isaiah 10:34, the mighty cedars, namely Assyria, falling, and the very next verse (Isa. 11:1) the tender shoot from the stump of Jesse, the shoot of Isaiah 53:2. God delights in choosing and nourishing the weak and vulnerable (1 Cor. 1:27).

Though apparently dead, there is life in the lifeless stump, hidden for now, waiting to spring forth with vigour. Growth of coppice shoots which stumps throw is often astonishing and far exceeds a seedling. This is because of a massive root system supplying nutrients and sap so that the bud can burst forth and grow rapidly just like the resources of God, hidden but immense. In Rev. 5:5 Jesus Himself is described in these terms, 'the root of David' i.e. Jesse's son.

Foresters sometimes harness this vigour, not only with the familiar practice of coppicing, but also when a seedling isn't doing very well. It is called, 'stumping back'. Sometimes an oak or walnut will take time to establish, the young plant struggles to grow or develops poorly. The problem can be that the shoot part is out of proportion with the root, too few roots to meet the demands of all the leaves. (It's the same problem newly transplanted semi-mature trees suffer from). After two or three years of slow growth, difficult as it seems, the best medicine can sometimes be to cut back everything to ground level. The following year the new shoot can grow so rapidly that it may exceed in one year what the original plant had struggled to achieve in three or four. It enriches even more the picture of hope that Isaiah 11:1 conveys.

Different images and outcomes of judgment
Isaiah 14, 17, 22, 29, 32 & 35

In Chapters 13–35 up to the historical insertion about King Hezekiah, Isaiah's prophecies first concern each of Israel's neighbours (13–24)—though Chapter 22 concerns Jerusalem—and then he turns to his own people both with encouragement and cause for great rejoicing and with warnings and distress. Trees are pressed into service to picture the judgments coming and their different outworkings.

The first of these is clear (Isa. 14:8), and it is no

The picture of judgment is spelt out in verses 18 and 19, 'The splendour of his forests and fertile fields it will completely destroy, as when a sick man wastes away, and the remaining trees of his forest will be so few that a child could write them down.' This is deforestation writ large, ugly and stark, but plainly refers to the Assyrian army itself as the later verses in the chapter (Isa. 10:33–34) make clear, 'See the Lord, the Almighty One, will lop off the boughs with great power. The lofty trees will be felled, the tall ones will be brought low. He will cut down the forest thickets with an axe; Lebanon will fall before the Mighty One.' The irony would not be lost. Sennacherib's proud claim was complete mastery of Lebanon's forest resources, but, though he extracted much tribute from Jerusalem he never

ABOVE: *Natural juniper woodland with regeneration (Turkey) Photo: D. Luscombe*

wonder. 'Even the junipers and cedars of Lebanon gloat over you and say, "Now that you have been laid low, no one comes to cut us down"'. It is no wonder because it concerns Babylon and one of Sennacherib's great boasts[2] was the clearance of forests in Lebanon and the vast quantities of cedar trees he, like his predecessors, had hauled to his capital (Isa. 37:24). As if to underscore the humbling of the mighty and the scale of the impact, Isaiah reflects that now the distant forests are quiet, birdsong not battle cry is heard, and the woods are safe from the axe, at least for the time being.

The second picture of judgment is where Isaiah uses a familiar tree and a familiar sight: gathering ripe olives. He uses it twice, concerning both Damascus (Isa. 17:6) and then in the more general judgment and blessing of the final days (Isa. 24:13). The picture is of beating an olive tree to release its fruit and always a few get left, hanging on in the topmost branches. Devastation is so complete that all that's left is likened to just an olive or two remaining: gone are the fruit laden, fertile orchards and groves.

The word translated 'beaten' can also be understood as shaking. Olive branches were shaken or beaten with sticks and the fruits collected in nets on the ground, but care was needed not to bruise the olives themselves. Damaged fruits would quickly ferment and the resulting oil be inferior. Maybe there is another thought conveyed: was the beating also to stimulate the following year's fruiting? This is commonly held to be so for another Mediterranean tree, the walnut; some even saying, 'it is best manured by beating'. I'm not sure today we agree with Taylor, the water-poet, 'A woman, a spaniel and a walnut tree, the more you beat them the better they be', but there is a scientific basis for it, the beating of the walnut tree that is, not the lady or her dog! Partial ring barking or other stresses will often induce or promote flowering in trees, known as distress flowering, and the technique is sometimes used to increase seed production from stands of selected trees. Isaiah's picture was that of so little left—just the gleanings—after judgment had come, but did the practice itself have this second purpose?

The picture we come across in Isaiah 29:17 of Lebanon becoming a field, probably harks back to Assyria's eventual demise, namely, mighty cedars

ABOVE: *Olives being harvested*

no longer. By contrast the rather similar words in Isaiah 32:15, 'the desert becomes a fertile field, and the fertile field a forest' is so full of hope and of future because it is the way Isaiah speaks of God's Spirit poured out. We are familiar with the day of Pentecost recorded in Acts 2 when the apostles spoke many languages praising God, when Peter preached the first and perhaps greatest sermon, and when 3000 converts were added: we see this as the Holy Spirit poured out as Joel prophesied (Joel 2:28–32). Here in Isaiah the same abundance, the same overflowing, the same transforming is presented in pastoral terms, the greening of the desert (Isa. 35:1–2). The link is even more explicit

in Isaiah 44:3–4. One day God will pour out his Spirit and it will be like the desert blooming: the parched becoming productive, the arid arable. We return to this theme a little later in my favourite Old Testament chapter to delight in wilderness becoming prosperous, and where there is perhaps an additional dimension.

We must backpedal a moment to Isaiah chapter 22 concerning Jerusalem. 'Palace of the Forest' (Isa. 22:8) is Solomon's palace built from top to bottom with cedar, which we remarked on in the previous chapter, and then later in the chapter there is a picture of a peg and its usefulness (Isa. 22:23 & 25). Normally pegs in the Bible refer to tent pegs but here

ABOVE: *Enormous shear strength of wood.*
A familiar enough picture of a tree (an oak at Korazin)
but consider how strong wood is to support a great branch

it is more like a coat peg—a wooden dowel driven in on which to hang things or pin things together in joinery. It is vivid. A strong dependable support when driven home into some firm place. It recalls the rock climber driving pitons into the tiniest of cracks and crevices and then belaying himself and hanging his life upon it!

Wood makes excellent pegs because most wood fibres run lengthwise and thus have very high shear strength—logs can't be split crossways. It can be seen in a branch, stretching far out from a tree and very rarely shearing off. It's like a giant peg. Maybe there is more, for verse 22 is suggestively Messianic, recalling Isaiah 9:6, as is the honour accorded in the next verse. What a typology of Christ—a peg! Strong, dependable, always there, somewhere to fasten our lives. As He hung upon the tree (1 Pet. 2:24), the cross, like a peg God hung on Him the sins of the world. In Isaiah's words, he bore the sin of many (Isa. 53:12).

Judgment is equally pictured (Isa. 22:25) as when a peg is sheared off and in that instant becomes utterly useless. We meet the peg again in our next chapter in Ezekiel's prophecy.

Sennacherib's comeuppance and forest is spared

Isaiah 36 & 37

Chapters 36 to 39 are tense with argument and counter argument. Sennacherib's envoy tempts and taunts the inhabitants besieged in Jerusalem. He tells them not to listen to King Hezekiah but to hear the words of his king, the King of Assyria (Isa. 36:16), 'Make peace with me … then everyone of you will eat from his own vine and fig-tree and drink water from his own cistern …' This is no allegory but a proposition. Lay down your arms, surrender, and once again you can enjoy health and well-being and the fruits of your own labour, or so he claims.

We know how further exchanges of news and letters with the assailants terrified King Hezekiah until Isaiah sent a message to him to say his prayer about Sennacherib was answered. This is the word of the Lord to one who insults Israel, to the one who boasts that, 'I have ascended the heights of the mountains, the utmost heights of Lebanon. I have cut down its tallest cedars the choicest of its junipers. I have reached its remotest heights, the finest of its forests.' (Isa. 37:24). He who boasted of destroying forests would himself be destroyed. The irony of Isaiah 14:8 would not be lost. As we saw the great trees would gloat and exult and the forests, for a time, be spared as Sennacherib's star declined, his army routed by death[3] and he became holed up in Nineveh, and later murdered by his sons.

Chapter 40 at last!

Isaiah 40, 41, 44, 53 & 55

Now begins some of the greatest of blessings ever prophesied as well as Isaiah despairing at the stupidity of worshipping wooden idols fashioned by man's hand (Isa. 40:19–20). How can such be compared with the true God? But our focus from Isaiah chapters 40 to 55 is the blessing God pours out as portrayed by wilderness and wasteland becoming fertile and fruitful. Four kinds of tree God lists as he transforms the desert (Isa. 41:19)—cedar, acacia, myrtle, and olive, and three the wasteland—juniper, fir and cypress.

ABOVE: *Magnificent white poplars beside the Hermon stream in Banias*

Desert and wasteland are not synonymous in Hebrew, the latter being a mix of the arid with fertile gulleys. Only acacia and, at the desert edge, myrtle, are really suited to the desert environment, so seeing these others, the cedar and olive, is miraculous or suggestive of far greater change. It is designed to make us reflect, '… that the people may see and know, may consider and understand, that the hand of the Lord has done this …' (Isa. 41:20). And the consequence? As God pours water on the thirsty land and streams flow so His Spirit on Israel's descendants who will, 'spring up like grass in a meadow, like poplar trees by flowing streams.' (Isa. 44:4). (Isaiah knows his poplar ecology as an earlier comment about the ravine of poplars at the border of Moab and Edom (Isa. 15:7) reveals; it is the only place you would find them in such land.) The picture of Banias and the towering white poplars display profusion and luxuriance.

After such riches, it is no wonder Isaiah's sarcasm knows no bounds when he compares all this that God will do with the stupidity of the wooden idol (Isa. 44:12–20). You cut wood, cypress or oak, some

93

TOP: *Prickly Kermes oak foliage*

ABOVE: *Myrtle foliage*

bits you burn for cooking or keeping warm, other bits you make into a god! Half for fuel, half for a god! It's laughable. Shall I bow down to a block of wood? (Isa. 44:19). No-one stops to think, says Isaiah, or, at best, people are simply ignorant (Isa. 45:20).

But Isaiah has a greater message. A day will come when Israel, indeed all of earth and heaven, will burst into song with the trees and forests for the Lord has redeemed his people (Isa. 44:23). A little later we are to go out in joy and peace and all the trees of the field will clap their hands (Isa. 55:12–13). It comes about because between these verses is Isaiah chapter 53, the greatest of Old Testament messianic prophecies so completely fulfilled in Christ. And there in verse two (Isa. 53:2) is the impossible, 'He grew up before him like a tender shoot, and like a root out of dry ground'. Great blessing comes because 'He bore our sin and made intercession for us' (Isa. 53:12); the kernel of Isaiah's greater message.

Isaiah begins chapter 55 with an image so apposite for a parched country. He proclaims, he shouts (Isa. 55:1), 'Come, all you who are thirsty, come to the waters … that your soul may delight in the richest of fare.' This, my favourite of chapters, has it all—invitation, the Almighty being found of the seeker, his thoughts not like ours, his word convicting and converting—all to conclude that we will go out in joy and be led in peace (Isa. 55:12). It finishes (Isa. 55:13) with an everlasting sign that it will be so and that it is God's work.

What is this everlasting sign? It is an explicit change, 'Instead of the thornbush will grow the juniper, and instead of briers the myrtle will grow'. The picture is familiar; waste or abandoned land becomes productive and beautiful again. The thornbush may well be the common, evergreen (or Kermes) oak which produces prickly thickets of almost holly-like leaves when young coppice sprouts from stumps. The briers are probably a myrtle look-alike which is found in dry wadis and has a skin irritant sap. Isaiah's immediate prospect is that unpleasant abandoned countryside will become fertile and fruitful when the exiles return, graced by the lovely juniper and the delightful and fragrant myrtle. Perhaps, too, Isaiah has a longer prospect in view, if only dimly?

TOP AND MIDDLE: *The similarity of flowers of (a) native myrtle and (b) exotic eucalypt*

ABOVE: *Hinnom Valley to the west of Old Jerusalem —certainly pleasant enough now with its scattered cypresses*

On the journey today from Tel Aviv up to Jerusalem the once barren hills are now clothed with pines (and some cypresses) which are either native or at least eastern Mediterranean species. There is another tree present, though not in large plantations. It is now everywhere in Israel, the Australian gum tree, the eucalypt. Mostly they are red river gum (*Eucalyptus camaldulensis*), but some are the blue gum (*E. globulus*) so common throughout the Mediterranean. Why mention gums from Australia? Because they are in the same plant family as the delightful myrtle bush, from which the family name derives, the Myrtaceae. The similarity in their flowers, numerous small delicate stamens, is striking! This thrills, because of all the trees used in development in the tropics the eucalypt has pre-eminence, it is the most widely planted.[4] Almost every village in the developing world has some planted for firewood, building poles or fencing materials. Even the paper of this book, and many of our bibles will be from fibre from plantations of this tree. It is not a panacea species, eucalypts make great demands on soil moisture and can out compete adjacent farm crops. But I believe there is more than a hint that the prophecy (Isa. 55:13) extends far beyond Isaiah's own world, just as his even greater prophecy concerning the work of Christ spreads far beyond his own people, as the next chapter in Isaiah so clearly spells out (Isa. 56:8).

In Britain the eucalypt is quite common, especially cider gum (*E. gunnii*) as a lanky garden tree that almost grows too fast and which is just hardy enough for our winters. It too displays the characteristic delicate cream flowers of the Myrtaceae family.

Accusations and acclaim

Isaiah 57, 60, 61 & 65

The final chapters of Isaiah have their share of tree analogies and metaphors, and thus challenge those who question his authorship of them. The simple wickedness of what was going on and where, is highlighted once again in Isaiah 57:5 with the now familiar idolatry of oak and probably terebinth (the spreading tree). Some suggest that the ravine where children were sacrificed was the Hinnom Valley, '*Ge Hinnom*' in Hebrew, where the awful Molech

ABOVE: *Great oak at the High Place of Dan (incidentally it is a eucalypt to the left)*

was worshipped. It gives us the word Gehenna, and became a byword for hell. The valley is below the old city walls of Jerusalem on the south-west side and, today, with its many cypresses, pines and exotic trees is far more picturesque than its more famous counterpart on the east side, the Kidron Valley.

More comforting is the return to the symbolism of blessing (Isa. 60:13) with the now equally familiar glory of Lebanon (cedars) along with other fine forest trees of juniper, fir and cypress returning to the people of Israel. This verse and Isa. 41:19 are the only references to true fir trees in the NIV, and are probably the elegant Cilician fir (*Abies cilicica*) which grows in Lebanon in mixed stands amongst the cedars, but doesn't occur naturally as far south

as Israel. However the Hebrew '*berosh*', translated here as fir, includes other needle conifers such as juniper and cypress.[5] Fir was well known and according to Hepper[6] Cilician fir logs were imported into Egypt for ships' masts.

More comforting still is Isaiah chapter 61 which begins with the words Jesus quoted (Matt. 11:5; Luke 7:22) when relaying to the imprisoned John the Baptist that he really was the One. Jesus' quote didn't reach as far as our next tree verse where believers are called, 'oaks of righteousness, a planting of the Lord for the display of his splendour' (Isa. 61:3). The oak metaphor is that of enduring, firm, unwavering and sure; a far cry and ironic contrast to the oaks that were worshipped and under which child sacrifice was offered. A planting of the Lord speaks of God's initiative, intentions and purposes and what an interesting description of conversion to become, 'a planting of the Lord'!

Planting is done with care, with preparation and forethought, followed by nurturing the young tree. In forestry, seeds are sown in beds with fine tilth in specialised nurseries with every attention given to encourage germination and growth. On the site where the tree is to grow the soil is dug, the tender seedling's roots are placed gently in the ground, the soil firmed home, competing weeds are kept in check, and browsing and other damage prevented. Much care attends what is planted.

The best comfort of all is the picture of the new heaven and new earth (Isa. 65:17–25) containing the well-known prospect, 'The wolf and lamb will feed together, and the lion will eat straw like the ox'. And this will not be fleeting, but will last, 'For as the days of a tree, so will be the days of my people' (Isa. 65:22). Not only longevity, but echoes too of Psalm 92:12–14 that we remarked on earlier, 'The righteous will flourish like a palm tree, they will grow like a cedar of Lebanon.'

Warnings ignored about what goes on under every spreading tree
Jeremiah 1–5, 7 & 10

Jeremiah, writing a hundred or so years after Isaiah, repeats many of the same warnings over Israel's abandonment of God and chasing after other religions. His reputation for being all doom and judgment is proverbial and is seen clearly enough in the opening Chapters 1–10, but throughout his great prophecy there are precious, indeed unique encouragements.

The first warning within our theme is Jeremiah's own wake-up call in verse 11 of Chapter One. God asks, what does he see? An almond branch. Does this, the earliest flowering of all fruit and nut trees, symbolise that things are beginning, the time has come? The Hebrew for almond, 'shaqed', means waker or watcher and in the next verse God says, I am watching (shoqed) you, which sounds very similar, to see that His word is fulfilled. A play on words with a powerful message: everyone knew about the almond tree, Jeremiah wouldn't miss the point.

ABOVE: *Profuse almond blossom*

Now follows the charge. Where? On every high hill and under every spreading tree (Jer. 2:20)—and therefore far removed from the temple. What? The worship of idols made of stone and wood (Jer. 2:27). Hence the charge of prostitution, real as in pagan and ritual practices and symbolic in chasing after what was not their own and rightful. In Chapter 3 the charge is repeated, (Jer. 3:6 & 9) and this time compared to adultery—deliberate abandoning past promises and undertakings and leaving the one true God, in order to worship a piece of wood.

Jeremiah moves on: he spells out the consequences, or rather God does through him as his mouthpiece. Chapter 4 begins with invitations and entreaties. Even now turn to me, says God, abandon your foolish ways, and you will be blessed. We are given a lovely pastoral image, 'Break up your unploughed ground and do not sow among thorns' (Jer. 4:3). A similar appeal occurs in Hosea 10:12 and the message seems clear: start again, start afresh—repent and turn—become productive and fruitful again, do not let the world's affairs choke you. Jesus explains it best in his famous parable of the sower (Matt. 13:1–23). Jeremiah's hearers ignore the prophet.

Soon, however, Jeremiah returns to warnings telling his hearers what judgment will be like. When the Babylonians (the North) come some will try to hide in the wasteland and bush, others in the

ABOVE: *A mature olive grove still yielding its crop year after year* Photo: W. Stewart

mountains (Jer. 4:29), but wild animals, lions from the forest, wolves from the desert and the ever artful leopard will lie in wait (Jer. 5:6). Quite a picture of top mammals in the food chain still present in Israel in 600 BC. Worse is to come. Their carefully tended and husbanded crops are taken by invaders—as always—flocks and herds, vines and fig trees are devoured (Jer. 5:17). Even their own trees are pressed into war against them as God appears to instruct the Babylonian army what to do (Jer. 6:6), 'Cut down trees and build siege ramps against Jerusalem. The city must be punished, it is filled with oppression.' Sennacherib made it to Lachish, but failed to take Jerusalem when death struck the Assyrian camp (Isa. 37:36). This time, warns

Jeremiah, Nebuchadnezzar will not be thwarted he will succeed as God's instrument of judgment, Jerusalem will fall.

Now follows four awful chapters. One sub-theme is the disaster they paint for nature because of the stupidity of people worshipping nature. Jeremiah 7:18 'The children gather wood, the fathers light a fire, and the women knead the dough and bake cakes of bread for the Queen of Heaven' (the Babylonian God, Ishtar). Every member of the family is involved. God's wrath falls on everything which, of course, includes trees: 'trees of the field'— fruit and nut trees in orchards (Jer. 7:20)—because of the appalling sin spelt out yet again in the account of child sacrifice later in the chapter (Jer. 7:30–33).

Children gather wood for pagan worship and are themselves burned in sacrifice by it. The utter stupidity of it, the terrible evil is summed up at the end of these four chapters in the opening verses of Chapter 10:2–5, 'This is what the Lord says: "Do not learn the ways of the nations or be terrified by signs in the sky, though the nations are terrified by them. For the customs of the peoples are worthless; they cut a tree out of the forest, and a craftsman shapes it with his chisel. They adorn it with silver and gold;[7] they fasten it with hammer and nails so that it will not totter. Like a scarecrow in a melon patch, their idols cannot speak, they must be carried because they cannot walk. Do not fear them; they can do no harm nor can they do any good."' To such gods you sacrifice your children, to senseless, worthless wooden idols.

A sandwich of olive trees with a bitter filling
Jeremiah 11, 12, 15 & 17

Chapters 11 to 17 of Jeremiah are topped and tailed by reminders of what the Israelites once were like and what they may still return to with dire warnings in between: it's like a sandwich. In Jeremiah 11:16 God likens Israel to a thriving olive tree with fruit beautiful in form, but it is about to be destroyed, broken and burnt. The picture of an old and venerable olive tree is rich in meaning. It speaks of enduring over the centuries, of faithful yielding of crops—the very best crops, and of a treasured possession. Even today censure falls on any who cut down olive trees; they are pruned but never cleared away unless, very unusually, they have died. The olive is a symbol of Israel prospering with her true God. At the end of these six chapters, Jeremiah 17, verses 7 and 8 have the sentiments and almost the same words as Psalm 1 repeating that the one who trusts in the Lord is like a tree planted by streams. The whole of Chapter 17 is a yearning by God that His people would return to Him and an affirmation of God's character and faithfulness by Jeremiah.

Sandwiched in between is a litany of complaint and condemnation. Complaints about Jeremiah by the unbelieving people of Anathoth who didn't like what they heard (Jer. 11:18–23); complaints by Jeremiah to God (Jer. 12:2), 'Why to do the faithless live at ease? You have planted them, and

they have taken root; they grow and bear fruit. You are always on their lips, but far from their hearts.' God's complaints, which are many, and a condemnation of which one is all too familiar (Jer. 17:1–2), 'Judah's sin is engraved with an iron tool … Even their children remember their altars and Asherah poles beside every spreading tree and on the high hills.' So bad have things become that, 'Even if Moses and Samuel were to stand before me, my heart would not go out to this people' (Jer. 15:1). The condemnation and disaster that will befall is foreshadowed in what happened to the beautiful olive tree. In the same verse (Jer. 11:16) Jeremiah prophecies, 'But with the roar of a mighty storm he will set it on fire, and its branches will be broken. The Lord Almighty, who planted you, has decreed disaster for you'. Then, after likening wayward Israel to a lion in the forest, wild, untamed and roaring at God (Jer. 12:8) and whose crops will fail who sow wheat but reap thorns (Jer. 12:13), there is a tenderness, a love, a compassion, of a long-suffering God. 'But after I uproot them, I will again have compassion and will bring each of them back to their own inheritance and their own country' (Jer. 12:15).

True greatness is more than a cedar palace
Jeremiah 21 & 22

Jeremiah chapter 22 is a remarkable indictment. It is against a King, Jehoiakim, who thought that kingship and leadership were all about what he was able to show off. It is no different today as Vance Packard's 1950s classic, *The Status Seekers*, showed a couple of generations ago, or in our time those presidents, dictators and heads of industries and organisations who revel in the trappings of power rather than the wise exercise of it.

The irony is that immediately preceding this chapter the last verse of Chapter 21 describes a military tactic of burning forest to frighten the inhabitants and destroy a precious resource. The word 'forest' in Jeremiah 21:14 is singular and it may refer symbolically to Solomon's Palace of the Forest, his cedar-clad royal residence built 350 years before and still of renown. This leads us to Jeremiah's invective and what King Jehoiakim was up to.

Jehoiakim's palace was of fine cedar (Jer. 22:7, 14&15) and plenty of it. Jeremiah weighs in, 'Does it make you a king to have more and more cedar?' His father, the godly Josiah, had enjoyed God's favour by defending the cause of the poor and needy (Jer. 22:16), but all you do, says Jeremiah, is chase dishonest gain, shed innocent blood, and feather-bed yourself. He warns, 'You who in live in "Lebanon" (a reference to Solomon's Palace in Jerusalem), who are nestled in cedar buildings, how will you groan …' (Jer. 22:23). Was this weak king, importing vast amounts of expensive cedar, just to try and keep up with the Sennacheribs and Nebuchadnezzars? The latter, his contemporary, would humiliate him in his first siege of Jerusalem when Daniel and companions, the intelligentsia,

were carried into exile. We meet this accusation again in Haggai (1:4) when, 100 years later, the returning Israelites were again distracted by attention to their own properties to the neglect of the house of the Lord.

Cedar was the Rolls-Royce or Ferrari to display on the forecourts of the day. This lovely, precious and increasingly scarce timber was used for great works like the temple, and greatly used by the greedy as a status symbol.

The righteous branch
Jeremiah 23

'Branch' is a messianic title both here (Jer. 23:5) and in Isaiah (Isa. 4:2) and is linked to the shoot from the stump of Jesse we mentioned earlier. It

BELOW: *The cedar at Old Childrey Rectory, Wantage; one of the original introductions planted in about 1638. Cedars of Lebanon became fashionable in the 18th Century to adorn the gardens and parks of the wealthy   Photo: Mr and Mrs R. Johnson*

ABOVE: *Baskets of good and bad figs*

is a metaphor for great strength and great spread, shade and shelter, bearing of flowers and fruit and, all the while, irrevocably part of the main trunk. A lone spreading cedar of Lebanon, or Tabor oak or terebinth readily come to mind—their glory is their branches! The glory of the prophecy in these verses is the wise reign of the foreshadowed king doing what is just and right in the land for the good and salvation of God's people.

Two baskets of figs and two fates
Jeremiah 24

The good figs and bad figs of Chapter 24 reflect reality and symbolise here the contrast of destiny of those sent into exile—the cream of the citizens—whom God will watch over, and those who tried to escape to Egypt or struggle on under a bad king.

The two kinds of figs are not comparing normal figs with those of the sycomore fig tree—the poor man's figs. The good figs are the early ones, ripening in late May or June, the bad ones are overripe figs old and unfit to eat. Rich promises are given to those likened to good figs, sweet and nutritious figs: 'My eyes will watch over them for their good … I will build them up and not tear them down; I will plant them and not uproot them. I will give them a heart to know me, that I am the Lord. They will be my people, and I will be their God, for they will return to me with all their heart.' Perhaps implied is: would the idol of wood or effigy of stone ever express such care, compassion and love even if it had the capacity to do so?

Jeremiah's prophecy was not well received, he was given a hard time and threatened with death

(Jer. 26:8). They didn't want to hear the truth about their predicament, just as Paul warned some 600 years later (2 Tim. 4:3). But some of the elders did defend him and quote from Micah (3:12) in the days of King Hezekiah, that you shouldn't shoot the messenger. Incidentally this is the only time in the Old Testament that one prophet cites another and quotes their words verbatim. Micah had prophesied that Jerusalem would become rubble and the temple mount, probably the whole hill area, be overgrown with thickets. 'Thickets' is the same word in Hebrew usually translated forest and describes what happens when land is abandoned and cultivation and grazing cease. It can be dramatic.

Just how dramatic I recall from my childhood. I would walk a mile and a quarter to school from

BELOW: *Nothing has been planted: this woodland in southern England has entirely grown up because land was abandoned and browsing by animals ceased*

Petts Wood to Crofton in today's London borough of Bromley. Just off our route was a great place to muck about. I think it was abandoned farmland surrounded by housing, but was itself protected green belt. Over the years it turned from rough pasture to 'scrub' of hawthorn, oak, sallow and birch, and when I last saw it, now decades ago, was well on the way to becoming woodland. A quick google shows the area today as Roundabout Wood and Sparrow Wood. The same happened across much of England because of myxomatosis. Rabbits all but died out in the 1950s from the disease. This gave relief from browsing which led to woodland regenerating on pretty well every patch of wasteland. With seedlings no longer cropped back and few deer about in those days trees readily got away and became established. The transformation Jeremiah was suggesting for beloved Jerusalem—from the civilised and settled to desolation and waste, seemed unbelievable as well as unpalatable.

Bleak as the prospect of 70 years exile seems, the next chapters are full of encouragement and hope. Numerous promises, messianic allusions, and the assurance of eventual return are summed up in the pastoral idyll, 'Again you will plant vineyards on the hills of Samaria; the farmers will plant them and enjoy their fruit.' (Jer. 31:5). As I write I want to quote thrilling verses like Jeremiah 29:11–14 or 31:31–34 or note in passing the prophecy (Jer. 31:15) that was fulfilled when Herod murdered all the under-twos in Bethlehem, but we stray too far from our theme. Suffice to say that simile and metaphor speak of good times returning: they will be like a well-watered garden, God will plant, not uproot, fields and land will be bought and sold—it is one of the living parables Jeremiah is instructed to enact (Jer. 32). It culminates in his reiterating the promise (Jer. 33:15), 'In those days and at that time I will make a righteous Branch sprout from David's line; he will do what is just and right in the land.'

Jeremiah's lot worsens. Still King Zedekiah, his leaders and officials want to shut him up. He is imprisoned then thrown into a cistern. Finally everything Jeremiah has been warning comes true. In 586 BC Jerusalem is taken. The feared Nebuchadnezzar lays seige and in 18 months the city wall is breached. The cowardly Zedekiah flees in secret at the dead of night, is quickly overtaken, sees his sons slaughtered, is blinded and shackled and taken captive to Babylon. And then we read the awful words (Jer. 39:8), 'The Babylonians set fire to the royal palace (so full of inflammable cedar) and the houses of the people and broke down the walls of Jerusalem.' But Jeremiah is taken care of, he is freed and is allowed to remain with the remnant or do whatever he pleased. Jewish tradition suggests he ended his days in Egypt where he was stoned to death.

Jeremiah continues to prophecy and to warn his fellow Jews in Egypt, the Egyptians themselves, and old enemies like the Philistines, Moabites and Ammonites. The warnings to the Egyptians are particularly graphic in terms of our theme (Jer. 46:22–23), 'Egypt will hiss like a fleeing serpent as the enemy advances in force; they come against her with axes like men who cut down trees. They will chop down her forest, declares the Lord, dense though it be.' The first part is simile, likening destruction of the Egyptian army to clear-felling forest, but the latter may refer to a better wooded Egypt than it is today. There is good evidence that despite the aridity of the climate parts of Egypt originally had trees and woodlands, doubtless mainly of acacias and probably sycomore-figs in moister parts, and that considerable blocks still existed as recently as 700 years ago.[8]

The end
Jeremiah 50, 52 and Lamentations
Jeremiah has a message for his people's captors, Babylon (Jer. 50). Though used by God to judge the Israelites, it will not itself escape judgment. As we know it fell to the armies of the Medes and Persians and all that the once feared Nebuchadnezzar had built up was lost. The overthrow of Babylon is pictured with Jeremiah's favourite simile of lions hiding in the forests and thickets (Jer. 50:44) with the power, stealth, cunning and, above all, suddenness we can readily appreciate from many a David Attenborough television documentary. Jeremiah had used the same simile in warning Edom (Jer. 49:19). The end of both evokes horror, with Babylon itself nothing more than a heap of ruins and a haunt of jackals ... where no one lives (Jer. 51:37).

ABOVE: *Well tended olive groves beneath Jerusalem's eastern wall*

Their greatness had come to nought, the labour had been in vain (Jer. 51:58). So ended Jeremiah's words (51:64).

The final chapter is like an appendix. It expands on details of the fall of Jerusalem, what was destroyed, what was captured as booty, and who was taken into exile. There is, however, a wise if self-serving order from the commander of the Babylonian Imperial Guard, the poorest people were left behind to work the vineyards and fields (Jer. 52:16). The command not to destroy fruit trees when at war and laying siege (Deut. 20:19) was understood by the Babylonians. Was it a comfort through the years of captivity knowing that, although much of the city would become waste and overgrown, at least the olive groves and vineyards, and perhaps a favourite fig tree or two, were being looked after—a down payment against the day of their promised return?

In exile, firewood has to be paid for

Lamentations 3 & 5

Lamentations is like Jeremiah's epilogue, a funeral song over Jerusalem. But in the midst of mourning and wailing of what has befallen, is depicted the changing economic circumstances. Water and wood must be paid for (Lam. 5:6) and firewood must be cut, gathered and carried for miles (Lam. 5:13). They are examples of the many burdens and afflictions the people cry out and plead to God to remember. Remarkably, too, there is that deep commitment and certain hope (Lam. 3:22–26), 'Because of the Lord's great love and compassion we are not consumed, for his compassions never fail. They are new every morning; great is your faithfulness … The Lord is good to those whose hope is in him; it is good to wait quietly for the salvation of the Lord.'

Jerusalem is consumed, the land is consumed, but the Hebrews' faith in God and God's love for his people are not.

Notes

1 **Hareuveni, N** (2006) *Tree and Shrub in Our Biblical Heritage.* Neot Kedumim Ltd. Israel (translation by Helen Frenkley)

2 **Meiggs, R** (1982) *Trees and Timber in the Ancient Mediterranean World.* Clarendon Press, Oxford.

3 **Meiggs** (ibid) cites Herodotus explanation for Sennacherib's army suddenly abandoning the siege of Jerusalem as mice eating the quivers, bows and bow strings, and shield straps. No less a miracle for its timing than the Bible's account.

4 **Evans, J** and **Turnbull, J** (2004) *Plantation Forestry in the Tropics* (3rd edition) Oxford University Press

5 **Zohary, M** (1982) *Plants of the Bible.* Cambridge University Press.

6 **Hepper, N** (1992) *Illustrated Encyclopedia of Bible Plants* Inter Varsity Press, Leicester.

7 We know quite a bit about carving and sculpture of wood, the importance of using a wood which was very stable such as cypress, and that for large statues such as that of Athena (5th C) sheets of gold were detachable. Many contemporary carvings were of ivory overlaid with gold, but wood was the popular choice for small-scale sculptures and Hermes was the most popular 'pocket god' to protect travellers. Even Aesop reflects the prophets' ridicule: 'A man made a Hermes of wood and tried to sell it in the market. No one seemed to want to buy it though he insisted that it would bring blessings and profit to the buyer. Why then, someone asked, did he not keep it himself?'

8 **Thirgood, J V** (1982) *Man and the Mediterranean Forest.* Academic Press, London.

Trees in context and out

Ezekiel was a late contemporary of Jeremiah and delivers his prophecies—and reports a lot of history—in the years immediately preceding and just into the exile. Daniel is written in Babylon during the exile. As for who we rather disparagingly call the 'minor prophets', the timings of their prophecies, when they lived and to whom they were addressing their message, vary. Most were living and writing before the exile except the last three, Haggai, Zechariah and Malachi, who raise issues during or immediately after the return and so were contemporary with or close to the time of Nehemiah. Enough of context, we find in these writings tantalising facts and pictures conveyed through our lens of focussing on trees and forests and their uses—actual and symbolic.

Questionings and riddles

Ezekiel 2, 6, 15–17

Ezekiel's call is nothing if not plain about what he will face. In Chapter 2 verse 6 the pain and poison are palpable, 'And you, son of man, do not be afraid of their words. Do not be afraid, though briers and thorns are all around you and you live among scorpions.' Scratching, tearing, biting and poisoning all speak of difficulties, doubtless as

many and as varied as the plants, shrubs, bushes and trees the ten or so different words in Hebrew describe that our bibles simply have as 'thorns'. Such variety reminds us that Israel is an arid country with a typical flora where many kinds of plants resist browsing with a generous endowment of thorns and prickles or bitter tasting foliage.

The first attacks are not long in coming as Ezekiel starts acting out God's judgments and explains why the people have sinned. His refrain is as Isaiah's and Jeremiah's: 'And they will know that I am the Lord, when their people lie slain among their idols around their altars, on every high hill and on all the mountaintops, under every spreading tree and every leafy oak—places where they offered fragrant incense to all their idols.' (Ezek. 6:13). We may tire of noting this, but the prophets in the Bible are nothing if not consistent.

The first questioning is largely rhetorical in the short Chapter 15. It asks is the wood of a vine better than that of a branch of any forest tree: does it ever have any use? Can it even be used for pegs, small enough items but critically important? Much is symbolic, Israel is frequently likened to a vine, and the reference to a peg harks back to Isaiah 22. But here the vine wood, or more likely the prunings,

FACING PAGE: *Prickly foliage of thorns and spines such as this common lotus jujube a close relative of Christ-thorn*

are burnt and portrayed as the destiny of the people living in Jerusalem. A destiny fulfilled in the sieges of the city in 597 BC when Ezekiel went into exile and then finally in 586 when everything was destroyed and fire was Nebuchadnezzar's main tool.

One wants to pass over the appalling allegory of Chapter 16. The inhabitants of the beautiful country God endowed use the very blessings of fine flour, honey and olive oil (vs13) as offerings to idols and other gods (vs19). They commit lewd acts and prostitution and sacrifice their sons and daughters. But God, in the midst of judgment, still remembers his covenant (vs59) and this sets the scene for a second remarkable allegory in the next Chapter, an allegory of eagles and cedar trees. God sets before the people a parable (Ezek. 17:2).

The riddle is Ezekiel 17:3–4. 'Say to them, "This is what the Sovereign Lord says: a great eagle with powerful wings, long feathers and full plumage of varied colours came to Lebanon. Taking hold of the top of the cedar, he broke off its topmost shoot and carried it away to a land of merchants, where he planted it in a city of traders."' The answer to the riddle is given in verses 12–21. The eagle is Nebuchadnezzar (King of Babylon), he came to Jerusalem (symbolised by Lebanon—because of all the imported cedar?), cedar signifies David's royal lineage and the topmost shoot, King Jehoiakin and his court and ministers, carried into exile (planted) in the city of traders (Babylon). These verses tell us about the first siege of Jerusalem, the second and final one is described in verses 7–10 where the second great eagle is probably the Egyptian pharoah Hophra who came to Jerusalem's rescue in 586 but failed.

Between the two there is another picture where he (the eagle) took seedlings of the land and planted them in fertile soil. They grew like a willow by abundant water, sprouted and became a low spreading vine (Ezek. 17:5–6). The explanation refers to those not exiled at the first siege but left behind and who prospered for a time until their vassal king, Zedekiah, reneged on the treaty with Nebuchadnezzar and sought help from Egypt. This imagery of vigorous willow growth beside a river, of a vine spreading far and wide, bearing much fruit, and sending out its roots, and the scorching

ABOVE: *Euphrates poplar trees*

east wind that came, the well-known desiccating khamsin, (likened to the fury of the final assault of a double-crossed Nebuchadnezzar), encapsulates the symbolism perfectly. Ezekiel's hearers would have immediately understood. So can we when we look again at the translation of willow.

Hareuveni[1] argues that willow refers to the Euphrates poplar. The Hebrew in this verse (*kakh-tzaftzafa*) suggests a tree with characteristics of both willow and poplar. Poplars are members of the willow family (Salicaceae), but importantly occur naturally by the river of their common name, the Euphrates, that flows through Babylon. The foliage of these poplars when young is remarkably willow-like with long slender leaves. Thus he suggests the symbolism that Nebuchadnezzar planted local seed, Zedekiah, in the fertile soil of Judah intending for it to grow into a tree native to Babylon—the 'willow-poplar'. But instead of becoming obedient and submissive, Zedekiah became like a grape-vine (the symbol of Judah) and grew branches and roots in other directions, namely, the alliance with Egypt. All would have been good and peaceful for the remnant as a vassal state of Babylon, but Zedekiah's rebellion unleashed Nebuchadnezzar's wrath. Jerusalem and the temple were liquidated. Zedekiah's fate was awful (2 Kings 25).

Not awful, but awe inspiring, is the nearly identical allegory at the end of the chapter (Ezek. 17:22–24). God takes the initiative. Instead of an eagle God himself takes a shoot from the very top of a cedar, a tender sprig from its topmost shoot, to plant on a high mountain. The familiar symbolism has an unexpected twist: from the house of David (the cedar) a descendant will be made king (planted) in Jerusalem (the high mountain). It is plainly Messianic as it becomes the finest of cedars, it bears fruit and birds of every kind nest and find shelter and shade in its branches. As is recorded in the gospels, e.g. Mark 4:32, Jesus uses similar imagery to describe the kingdom of God. The Messianic promise is seen, too, by all the other trees of the forest acknowledging that the once lowly tree (Israel) God has made grow tall, just as all nations will come to acknowledge Jesus (Phil. 2:10–11).

God does the seemingly impossible. This is underscored by what we know of tree physiology. A shoot taken from the top of a cedar, inserted in soil, cannot be expected to take root and grow. Like most conifers, such easy vegetative propagation simply won't work. It's different for most poplars, willows and, for example, teak in the tropics: take woody shoots of these trees, stick a third or so into the soil and a few weeks later buds will show and a new tree become established. Not so with most kinds of trees and especially not with conifers. Recourse to complex propagation is needed: rooting hormones, sterile growing medium, and weeks of specially controlled temperature, humidity and light levels. Even with all this effort often only a small proportion of cuttings from such trees will root, and cedar of Lebanon is described[2] as 'difficult'. As an aside, success is made even harder by taking shoots from old or mature trees and from their topmost branches. Cuttings from old trees are invariably less successful than from very young ones, as are cuttings taken from high up in the crown compared with low down. Collecting and sowing seeds would have been so much easier, but what God says he will do is the impossible.

Parable of the forest fire
Ezekiel 19, 20 & 24

The rest of Israel does not escape Ezekiel's prophetic warnings, nor do the surrounding nations. The pained contrast of what the Israelites were once like—a wonderfully fruitful vine (Ezek. 19:10–14)—with the vile image worshipping, Sabbath breaking rebels is lamented. Again we read the familiar complaint of a deeply offended God: '... when I brought them into the land I had sworn to give them and they saw any high hill or any leafy tree, they offered their sacrifices, made offerings

ABOVE: *Seedling of cedar of Lebanon: the usual way of propagation and even these need care and protection*

ABOVE: *Foam was laid to slow this forest fire*

that aroused my anger . .' (Ezek. 20:28). It was all because, 'they wanted to be like other peoples of the world, who serve wood and stone.' (Ezek. 20:32). We marvel at such a desire, such a preference and then pause to reflect on some of the life choices we have made.

Ezekiel begins the next parable (Ezek. 20:45–49) by turning his face south to indicate that judgment will come on Judah and Jerusalem too. The invaders, the Babylonians, will come and destroy all before them like a fire destroying a forest, a fire that cannot be quenched. Both 'green' and 'dry' trees will be consumed, i.e. everything, but the emphasis is that the fire will not be extinguished: twice it is repeated, 'it will not be quenched'. This imagery is so appropriate; it is always a struggle to contain forest and bush fires.

Forest fires are hard to cope with: they move rapidly, are frequently life-threatening, and nearly impossible to put out. Water bombing is dramatic but only locally effective, wide fire-breaks are easily breached by sparks blown by winds—fire induced squalls—and even when finally out on the surface, fire can smoulder for weeks in peaty soils only to reignite when the wind gets up.

I once researched forest fire suppression. The two great problems are getting worthwhile amounts of water to the site and then making best use of it. The first is a matter of appropriate transport, the second is how to harness water's cooling effect before it drains off the foliage or soaks into the ground. Three chemical additives can help. One lowers viscosity (which is something washing-up liquid does) and prevents water forming droplets and thus dampens everything on contact very much better. A second does the opposite, it raises viscosity by adding a gel and the water 'sticks' to the foliage and so absorbs more of the fire's heat in evaporating it. The third, a foaming agent, adds bubbles and is another way of helping water to stick and not simply drain away. Quenching forest fires is hard. The Israelites would know this, God knew too and Ezekiel paints a vivid picture of the completeness of their imminent destruction—it could not be stopped.

The remaining chapters of this section contain the most lewd (Ezek. 23) in the Bible. The picture following—of Jerusalem as a cooking pot—recalls a point we made in Chapter 2, that wood is the principal fuel of these times, dung may be second, but there were no fossil fuels of coal, gas or oil. For more heat and long cooking the wood is just piled higher! (Ezek. 24:5, 9 & 10).

Tyre the sea-farers and shipwrights
Ezekiel 26–28

It is easy to forget just how much was traded around the Mediterranean, with shipping the principal means. The prophecies against the port of Tyre, their King, and the lament (Ezek. 26–28) are full of merchants, traded goods, shipwrecks, mariners, oarsmen, sailors and shipwrights, sea powers, coastlands, shores and shorelines. The sea was in their blood, and the traders of Tyre must have had something akin to a Lloyds shipping list to keep tabs on all the places and products: minerals and ores, slaves, horses and mules, ivory and ebony, linen, dyes and precious stones, wheat, honey and olive oil, wine and wool, leather goods, livestock, spices, silver and gold, fabrics, embroidery, garments and carpets (Ezek. 27:12–24). All we would add today are electronic goods, cars and oil tankers! Near the start of this inventory is Tyre itself pictured as a stately ship and the different timbers they employed (Ezek. 27:5–6).

For the shipbuilding some uncertainty of translation, as always, exists. The juniper appears to have come from Mount Hermon (Senir) on modern

ABOVE: *A Phoenician warship, probably from the time of Sennacherib. Note two banks of oars and the prow for ramming* (*British Museum*)

day Israel's northern border, and where this species can still be found. Then follows an interesting reference to a mast of cedar of Lebanon. We know Egypt imported cedars specifically for this purpose and for flagstaffs, and Pliny implies that the tallest cedar ever cut, about 130ft (40 m), was obtained for a mast.[3] The reference to oaks from Bashan for oars is curious. Without doubt Bashan, to the north-east of Galilee, was famed for its oaks but this is an unusual choice of timber for oars where strength must be matched by slender shape, smoothness, and flexibility. Generally young trees would have been used in the round i.e. uncut, a bit like the tapering trunk of a tallish Christmas tree, and fir was the preferred choice either Silver (European) fir (*Abies alba*) in the western Mediterranean or Cilician Fir in Turkey and the Levant. Indeed, Mieggs[4] quotes Theophrastus who describes how oars of fir are fashioned with great care shaving with the annual ring and not cutting into it to maximise strength,

in just the same way that cleft timber split with the grain is stronger, size for size, than sawn timber. No captain, let alone a galley-slave, wanted a trireme's oars to snap as they built speed for ramming: the slave and his oar was the engine. Indeed, so valuable was fir in trireme shipbuilding that an early fourth century BC text bans the Chalcidians (coastal south-east Greece) from exporting the tree except with government permission! Use of oak was confined to the keel because of its toughness when hauling ashore.[5] Of course the ship described by Ezekiel was probably not a man of war which needed to be light, swift and manoeuvrable, but an altogether tougher merchantman for deep sea voyages and long life. As we know from our own naval history, oak is the building timber of choice.

The same verse (Ezek. 27:6) has the only reference in the Old Testament to the island of Cyprus (apart from two in Isaiah) from which Tyre appears to import cypress wood for decking timbers. Again translation is uncertain, as is the spelling of the word in Hebrew: it could be the familiar evergreen cypress or possibly the coastal pine (*Pinus pinea*) which is common in Cyprus. These two verses are not a shipwright's manual, but do offer insight into sea-faring vessels and that skill in caulking was obtained from neighbouring Byblos farther up the coast. In this book's next chapter, Chapter 9, we learn plank by plank and gunwale by gunwale what a first century Galilean fishing boat was made from. It was a discovery almost equalling in significance the Dead Sea Scrolls and certainly that of King Henry VIII's finest battleship, The Mary Rose.

One outcome Ezekiel labours to point out is Israel's eventual freedom from opposition, freedom from 'painful briers and sharp thorns' (Ezek. 28:24), a picture recalling the goads we saw that Ezekiel himself would experience.

Egypt, the felled cedar
Ezekiel 31

Few of our bible's helpful subheadings feature trees! Such subheadings are, of course, not in the original as neither are the subdivision and numbering of chapters and verses, but both help us find our way around. Chapter 31 is all about a great cedar of Lebanon and it is all symbolic. As we have seen many times, the cedar is selected, as Ezekiel does here, because it was the finest and most impressive, the premier of trees. It is centre stage for his fifth oracle about Egypt and it recalls history that once Assyria was like a great well-watered[6] cedar that dominated all: it towered higher, its branches were longer and its spread greater than all others (Ezek. 31:5). It could not be rivalled by other cedars, junipers or plane trees; its beauty was matchless; it was the envy of all the trees (Ezek. 31:8–9). But it fell, it did not last. The verses of prose (Ezek. 31:10–18) describe its downfall. They describe how nations that once felt protected or subjected to the great power, fled. Ezekiel says that just as a new and ruthless power destroyed Assyria so is the destiny of the Pharoah of Egypt: it happened to Assyria, it will happen to you, you will be like a great cedar that falls.

Ezekiel's picture of this great cedar tree resonates with a forester because sometimes in rain forest and

ABOVE: *Oriental plane outside House of the Virgin, Mt Solmissus near Ephesus*

occasionally elsewhere one tree grows high above the canopy of the rest, it is called an 'emergent'. A lone tree towers above all others, it can be seen for miles around, but in great storms it can suffer disproportionately being so exposed. Ezekiel's picture of the great tree's end—branches scattered over the hillside or lying broken in ravines—is just what a site looks like after a clear fell or immediately after a great storm or other catastrophe. If left, wild animals recolonise, birds hop about on the dead hulk (Ezek. 31:13), and beetles burrow in the rotting timber. It reminds me of two visits to Mount St Helens in Oregon (USA), 18 months and 10 years after the volcanic eruption of May 1980. In the first all was as if still freshly destroyed, grey-white ash lying everywhere like snow, trees horizontal from the blast of the pyroclastic flow, and patches of willow-herb the only sign of returning life. After 10 years everything was green, young trees were regenerating, recovery was everywhere and we were told that over 90 per cent of pre-existing wildlife had already recolonised.

The reference to plane trees (Ezek. 31:8) is only the second time in the Old Testament that the species occurs (see Gen. 30:37), and is the Oriental plane. It is probably one of the 'parents' that created the famous hybrid 'London Plane'; the other parent is the American plane (*Platanus occidentalis*). Oriental planes are common in towns and cities of the Mediterranean, grow large and are long-lived, but clearly never the equal of cedar of Lebanon as Ezekiel makes clear!

Restoration and Hope

Ezekiel 34, 36 & 39

The next chapters herald a great change. Gone are the strictures and condemnations. Here we read of hope, of Israel returning, of their re-settling in the promised land. The Lord is Israel's shepherd and one picture of the return to security and safety is likened to ridding the land of wild beasts and being able to sleep unafraid and unmolested in the forests (Ezek. 34:25). Two verses later is the even more familiar and even more welcome news to the exiles that again, 'The trees will yield their fruit and ground will yield its crops' (Ezek. 34:27). The picture of land at peace and settled farming is unmistakeable.

Presenting this scene of quiet rural life and farming, getting on with everyday business, was important. We can forget that a major military tactic throughout the ages is destroying crops, farm implements, and livestock to curtail 'the peasantry' and their supply of resources. Think of Napoleon's or Hitler's armies invading Russia and how this tactic was used to effect, if ultimately causing more harm to invader than the invaded. Farming and war are inextricably linked like the Second World War blockades of convoys to bring Britain to her knees. So Ezekiel's promise and hope of a return is painted in colours and images of an agrarian society.

In Chapter 36 it seems that blessings come to the land itself, the mountains even will be a source of blessing and fruitfulness (Ezek. 36:8). The very places where idolatry was practised— the refrain on every high hill and under every leafy tree—will now be a place of comfort and prosperity. Even more is in store: it seems that fruitfulness of trees and crops cultivated will be increased to the amazement of old antagonists (Ezek. 36:30). What was once laid waste is like a Garden of Eden (Ezek. 36:35).

The great hope of the future culminates in the two factions—Judah and Israel—becoming united once more. Ezekiel writes their names on two sticks and they become joined and appear as one, either miraculously or by the way the prophet holds them. Regardless, the symbolism is clear. And one consequence of all of this, is in a delightful aside. For

BELOW: *Rural life in Israel (recreated Nazareth Village)*

a time at least it'll no longer be necessary to gather firewood, because they will burn their weapons for fuel (Ezek. 39:9–10). Not only swords into ploughshares, but now bows, arrows and javelins, chariots and siege engines turn from warfare to feedstock, from conflict to cooking and keeping warm.

Recalled and foreshadowed—Ezekiel's temple and the tree of life
Ezekiel 40, 41 & 47

In Ezekiel's vision of the re-built temple frequent mention is made throughout Chapters 40 and 41 of the palm tree motif decorating the facing walls of the gateways and carved on the door jambs. It's the same motif as in Solomon's temple (1 Kgs 6:29, 32, 35) and, as noted before, it speaks of beauty and provision, perhaps, too, recalling the Garden of Eden. The inner rooms are panelled with wood (Ezek. 41:16), presumably cedar but we are not told so. Certainly it was imported from Lebanon for the second temple (Ezra 3:7).

The second temple was full of echoes recalling the first, but Ezekiel's remarkable prophecy looks far into the future. It looks to a time when a river will flow from Jerusalem to the Dead Sea. You can visit the place on the Mount of Olives where some believe a rift or chasm will open in the hillside as the water gushes forth (Zech. 14:4 & 8) and then down and down the 25 miles through the Judean desert, just as happens following exceptional rains. The salty sea will turn fresh, the sterile will team with life, and fishing become possible (Ezek. 47:7–12). Where the river flows everything will live, and is symbolised in abundance of trees beside the river (Ezek. 47:7) and in fruit trees which are forever in leaf yielding fruit every month of the year. Their fruit will serve for food, their leaves for healing. It foreshadows, or is repeated in John's depiction of the new heaven and new earth and the city of God in Revelation 22. Ezekiel's river of life flows from the sanctuary, John's from the throne of God and the Lamb (Rev. 22:1). This new depiction of the tree of life is the very last topic in our book.

Nebuchadnezzar's dream of a tree
Daniel 4

Apart from Chapter 1 and the opening verses of Chapter 2, the rest of the first seven chapters of Daniel are in Aramaic in the original. Thus, 'ilan' translated as tree, the tree that is the subject of Chapter 4, is the only place it occurs in the Old Testament. And what a tree is described!

In his dream Nebuchadnezzar saw a tree (Dan. 4:10–15) that stood in the middle of the land, its height was enormous. It grew large and strong, its top reached the sky, it could be seen from the ends of the earth. It was beautiful, fruitful, and provided food for all. Wildlife enjoyed its plenty as well, every creature was fed. And then came its destruction with just the roots and stump left.

Daniel unpacks the symbolism (Dan. 4:20–23) as picturing Nebuchadnezzar himself, what he has achieved and what will happen to him, and how he will eventually be restored (Dan. 4:26). The last part of the chapter describes the dream's fulfilment.

It must have been a particularly terrifying dream, Nebuchadnezzar would be fearful of its meaning because one of his own building inscriptions compares Babylon to a great spreading tree. Its top touching the sky would recall the great temple-towers, the Ziggurats. But the choice of a tree as the image of empire, as of all-providing, is not entirely lost on us.

Ecologically the tree is so four dimensional. The three dimensions of height to tip, lateral spread of branches and depth of roots are plain to apprehend, but the fourth dimension, the dimension of time, is what makes the tree an empire of animals. It is what multiplies the ecological niches to confer on a tree the richness of wildlife so many support. The English oak is celebrated in this regard, a cornucopia of bats, birds and beetles. Through its life and through the years of decay to its eventual demise, different habitats are furnished thus supporting hundreds and hundreds of different organisms.

More thorns and plagues
Hosea and Joel

In Hosea chapter 2 God's judgment of Israel has the

FACING PAGE: *A solitary oak in northern Galilee*

ABOVE: *The 'poor man's figs' on a mature sycomore-fig tree*

familiar picture of ruined vines and fig trees (Hos. 2:12), of thorns and thickets taking over (Hos. 2:6; 9:6 & 10:8) followed by restoration in similarly pastoral imagery (Hos. 2:22–23). The charge about what is wrong is the familiar one: God's people consult wooden idols and 'they sacrifice on the mountaintops and burn offerings on the hills, under oak, poplar and terebinth, where the shade in pleasant.' (Hos. 4:12–13 & 11:2).

The pain of Israel's rejection of God fills many of the pages of Hosea. The call to repentance in the last chapter (Hos. 14) is replete with everything lovely about a restored environment. The similes running through verses 5 to 9 of deep-rooted and fragrant like a cedar of Lebanon, splendour like an olive tree, and flourishing like a juniper—and there are others in these verses— appeal to the hearer to reflect and think. Jewish tradition took these verses as symbolic of greening of the wilderness.[7] Three times Lebanon is mentioned, the land where water was plentiful, and its freshness and vitality longed for in more arid Israel. It was emblematic of Israel's salvation.

Hosea lived in the closing years of the Northern Kingdom, Joel's dates are more uncertain. What is certain though is the appalling impact of locust swarms which occupy the first half of the short prophecy. Whether he was describing an actual plague or using a locust invasion as a clear picture that everyone would understand, the graphic description of devastation is as true today as it was then. Joel 1:12 reads, 'The vine is dried up, and the fig tree is withered; the pomegranate, the palm and the apple (or apricot) tree—all the trees of the field (fruit trees) are dried up. Surely the people's joy is withered away.' It is a picture, says Joel, of 'the day of the Lord'.

But the judgment is temporary. Even trees stripped bare and turned leafless by physical means, as locusts do by devouring the foliage, almost always recover. In some years in Britain newly flushed oaks are stripped from top to bottom by winter moths and oak leaf roller moths; in June the trees are as stark and bare as in winter. By mid-July a second flush of leaves appears and the former appearance only a fading memory. So too in Joel, the subsequent day of the Lord becomes one of immense blessing (Joel 2:28–32), which the Apostle Peter quotes on the day of Pentecost in Acts 2, and the scene is transformed. Indeed, the Lord declares that 'I will repay you for the years the locusts have eaten.' As elsewhere, restoration is portrayed in the return of plentiful harvests and well-watered land even in the desert, 'A fountain will flow out of the Lord's house and will water the valley of acacias.' Acacias, (Heb. *Shittim*), are the desert tree *par excellence*. And *par excellence*, too, is that greatest of invitations Joel, and Peter in his sermon in Acts, both announce, 'Everyone who calls on the name of the Lord, will be saved' (Joel 2:32).

Tending sheep and sycomore-fig trees
Amos

Amos was a true countryman. He tells us he was a shepherd (Amos 1:1) and we learn later on (Amos 7:14) that as well as shepherding he took care of sycomore-fig trees prior to his call to prophesy. We know from 1 Chronicles 27:28 that this was a rural craft where we are told one 'Baal-Hanan, the Gederite, was in charge of the olives and sycomore-fig trees in the western foothills.' What was involved and what, in particular, did Amos do?

The colourful fruits, mainly pale reds and pinks with a hint of translucence, which cling to or sometimes dangle on short stalks or branchlets from the trunk and branches of the sycomore-fig, are edible and were known as the poor man's figs. The main tending work began at the end of summer. With the pasture of the Judean wilderness exhausted, shepherds would take their flocks to the Jordan Plain and Jericho Valley where they would still find green forage. There were also plenty of sycomore-fig trees in the valley, and not only were their leaves good fodder, but the shepherds' arrival coincided with the time of year when the trees would be laden with unripe fruit. To ensure sweetness the embryonic fruit would be pierced and wiped with oil and a juicy fig would ripen over the autumn. It was time-consuming work. But the shepherds could 'moonlight' at it climbing into the branches of the trees while still keeping an eye on their flocks.[8]

In Amos's case, he tells Amaziah (Amos 7:14–15) that this is one of his jobs, a dresser of sycomore-fig trees, he is not 'a professional' earning his living from prophecy. It was God's call on him. It is like Paul's tent-making ministry (Acts 18:3); earning his own keep while exercising the ministry to which he was called.

In Amos we meet again familiar metaphors for apparent stature and strength, cedar and oak, to which the Amorites were likened, but which was no obstacle to God (Amos 2:9). Deadly blight and locusts destroying vines, and fig and olive trees are there, too, as signs of judgment (Amos 4:9). We also meet—and not surprisingly from one who is from the country—with Israel's restoration pictured as planting and provision of abundance of wine and fruit (Amos 9:13–15).

Familiar warnings and great encouragements
Jonah, Micah, Nahum, Habakkuk and Zephaniah

Jonah's leafy plant that shaded him while he waited for Nineveh's downfall and which died, apparently overnight, to his immense annoyance (Jonah 4:6–10), has several possible explanations;[9] but it would not be a tree.

Micah was contemporary with Isaiah and brought to the southern kingdom the same mix of judgment and hope. The land will become wilderness (Mic. 3:12), punishment is pictured in the emptiness of 'planting but not harvesting' (Mic. 6:15) and of lost fruitfulness (Mic. 7:1). Pictured, too, is the pastoral imagery of restoration of again sitting under one's own vine and fig tree (Mic. 4:4) and of a return of good times of old with flocks, forests, and fertile pasture in the well-watered north of the country and the once lush region of Gilead, the plateau to the east of the Jordan (Mic. 7:14).

Micah includes two of the Bible's most famous verses. The first (Mic. 4:3) is pastoral, 'they will beat their swords into ploughshares and their spears into pruning hooks' and immediately precedes the picture of contentment of sitting again under one's own fig tree. The second (Mic. 6:8) has the ingredients of spiritual contentment, 'And what does the Lord require of you? To act justly and to love mercy and to walk humbly with your God.'

In Nahum we are told at the outset that the prophecy concerns the downfall of Nineveh. The great Assyrian city fell in August 612 BC with fire burning parts of Sennacherib's palace as can be seen on the reliefs in the British Museum. This may well be the specific prediction of verses 4–6 and 10 of Nahum chapter 1. In particular in the reference to 'They will be entangled among thorns ... they will be consumed like dry stubble' (Nahum 1:10) is Nahum likening the rapidity and spread of fire to what happens when *seerim* shrubs (*Poterium spinosum*) catch alight?[10] They easily do and in no time everything is destroyed.

Spears of juniper (Nahum 2:3) is a better translation than pine, which would be very sticky with resin and knotty and make an uncomfortable handle, but the verse is obscure and of uncertain translation.

We can't leave Nahum without remarking on Nineveh compared to a fig tree dropping its fruits when shaken (Nahum 3:12). As the NIV footnotes it is a simile for the eagerness with which the victors gather the rich loot of the city. In the end its fall is as easy as gathering ripe figs.

Habakkuk worries at why God seems to ignore the plight of the oppressed and wronged. In particular why he uses the Babylonians of all people to execute judgment. He complains with vehemence, but God's answer is that the Babylonians will themselves be destroyed because of the many appalling evils they have committed two of which are familiar to our theme. They have massively over-exploited, even exhausted the great cedar forests of Lebanon (Hab. 2:17) and they rely on useless idols fashioned out of wood.

Habakkuk is satisfied. His faith is sure and we read at the end of his prophecy (Hab. 3:17) that great affirmation so rich in pastoral terms, 'Though the fig-tree does not bud and there are no grapes on the vines, though the olive crop fails, and the fields produce no food, ... yet I will rejoice in the Lord, I will be joyful in God my Saviour.'

Zephaniah lived just before the time of Jeremiah and prophesies judgment on the whole earth, on Israel and on her neighbours, but concludes with encouragements that will come in the end. Baal worship and child sacrifice to Molek are among the evils judged (Zeph. 1:4–5): they are the last mention of this form of idolatry in the Old Testament though Zechariah does mention idols (Zech. 10:2). And, as if we need reminding, Nineveh's destruction will reveal what they so brazenly exploited (Zeph. 2:14), '... the beams of cedar will be exposed,'

No more spreading trees!
Haggai, Zechariah and Malachi

In these three later prophets after the exile, there is no mention of worshipping under spreading trees in high places. Had the futility, as well as the deep offence to their God, sunk home during the years of exile? However things are far from well. The complaint now is laziness, indifference to God's affairs, half-heartedness. Re-building the temple, paying tithes and complying with the system of sacrifices all take second place to personal interests.

ABOVE: *Most of the prophets included words of encouragement, often with the image of restored rural life and peace. Was this, the picture we used to portray the promised land, perhaps how the Israelites in captivity longingly remembered and talked about their homeland and their hopes for the future as well as thoughts of Jerusalem?*

Though the complaint may differ, the promises are still presented in the familiar terms of prosperous farming and fruitful land which is the envy of the nations (Hag. 2:19; Zech. 8:12; Mal. 3:11).

Haggai voices God's complaint that the returning Israelites have simply got their priorities wrong. They have been building posh houses with fine panelling (Hag. 1:3) while God's house is neglected. Were the leadership setting a bad example by wanting 'to keep up with the Jones's' having seen how luxurious were the cedar-panelled residences in Babylon? Haggai warns them to get their priorities right and instructs them to 'go up to the mountains and bring down timber to build my house' (Hag. 1:8). As we saw in an earlier chapter provisioning

for such an undertaking was no trivial matter. A real change was needed from the top down. The consequence of not doing so, of neglecting God's house, were poor cereal harvests (Hag. 1:5, 10–11) and blighted or hail damaged fruit—grapes, figs, pomegranates and olives (Hag. 2:19). Thus both summer and autumn crops were failing because the people were failing in their priorities.

Zechariah was a visionary in the old sense. Through him God revealed what was going to happen as well as the burden of God's complaint. He was a contemporary of Haggai. He begins by reminding them of the failings of their ancestors (Zech. 1:2–6) and urges them to return to God and he will return to them. Two of his eight visions bear

ABOVE: *The mighty cedar, so much a part of the Old Testament in utility and symbolism*

on our theme, the man on his red horse among the myrtle trees (Zech. 1:8–11) and the gold lampstand flanked by two olive trees. Clearly they are symbolic.

Myrtle never reaches tree size, achieving 2 m at best, but the vision of a ravine is characteristic of where this lovely shrub is found throughout the northern half of Israel. We noted before that it is one of the 'four species' the Israelites were to collect for the first day of Tabernacles. The plant's lovely aroma had many uses and it was so prized that both men and women were named after it.[11] The delicate white myrtle blossom would convey calm and comfort which was the burden of the message

the man brought (Zech. 1:11) and God wanted to convey (Zech. 1:13 & 17).

The pair of olive trees (Zech. 4:3) stand for the priestly and royal offices and symbolise the continuing supply of oil. The branches (Zech. 4:12) probably refer to the individuals then filling the roles, Joshua and Zerubbabel. It is in this vision that God declares, 'Not by might nor by power, but by my Spirit' will God achieve his ends.

After the visions we have the crowning of the high priest, Joshua, with a crown of kingship and who is told by God a message from someone whose name is 'Branch' (Zech. 6:12). This the second mention of the title 'Branch'; earlier we have 'my servant, the Branch' (Zech. 3:8). Both are clearly Messianic references (as indeed is much in Zechariah's prophecy) as we saw in Isaiah (Isa. 4:2).

In Zechariah 10:4 we find two unlikely Messianic images, the 'tent-peg'—see our earlier comments concerning 'peg' (page 92)—and the 'battle-bow'. Both are wooden, both have an explicit purpose, like the 'cornerstone' that introduces this verse, all of which would be well understood by Zechariah's listeners if of less obvious interpretation for us. Tent peg is suggestive of support and the bow, of course, of the warrior; both Messianic qualities.

Immediately following this is a difficult passage (Zech. 11:1). Easy enough to interpret is the picture of forest destruction—all the principal trees of cedar, juniper and oak singled out for ruin and dense forest laid waste, but what it signifies is open to debate. Is it a real destruction in the future or more symbolic of waning of power? We certainly know today that tree cover is sparse and little forest is left in the regions named: Lebanon, Bashan and Jordan.

In the final book of the Old Testament, Malachi invokes the familiar pastoral image of fruitfulness and a delightful land as God's promise (Mal. 3:11–12) if the people will again be faithful, in particular faithful in tithing. It is fitting to conclude the remarks on the Old Testament as Malachi does with the metaphor of judgment of the arrogant and evildoer as 'not a root or a branch will be left to them' (Mal. 4:1). We still speak today of completeness and totality as being 'root and branch'.

Notes

1 **Hareuveni, N** (2006) *Tree and Shrub in Our Biblical Heritage*. Neot Kedumim, Jerusalem. (translated into English by **Helen Frenkley**)

2 **Dirr, M A** and **Heuser, C W** (2006) *The reference manual of woody plant propagation: from seed to tissue culture*. Varsity Press Inc., Cary, N. Carolina, USA. (2nd Edition)

3 **Meiggs, R.** (1982) *Trees and Timber in the Ancient Mediterranean World*. Clarendon Press, Oxford.

4 **Meiggs** (ibid)

5 **Meiggs** (ibid) citing Theophrastus.

6 **Dalley, S** (2013) in her book *'The mystery of the Hanging Garden of Babylon'* (Oxford) suggests that this verse shows that Ezekiel knew all about the famed gardens of Nineveh nourished by remarkably constructed canals, great aquaducts, and re-directed rivers. She argues persuasively that it is Sennacherib's great garden in Nineveh that was the wonder of the world. Only Josephus, writing 700 years later, cites Babylon; no other Classical writer does.

7 **Hareuveni** (ibid)

8 **Hareuveni** (ibid)

9 **Hepper, N** (1992) *The Illustrated Encyclopedia of Bible Plants*, IVP, Leicester.

10 **Hareuveni** (ibid)

11 **Zohary, M** (1982) *Plants of the Bible*. Cambridge University Press, Cambridge.

The natural illustration—trees and wood in Jesus' life and times

The four gospels all have one focus: recording the life and work of the Lord Jesus Christ. In following our theme this chapter covers what is written about his birth and life up to the final week before his crucifixion and the next centres on passion week itself and the resurrection. It continues to impress me that even in such ordinary things as trees and wood and their uses we find encapsulated the elements of the gospel.

The scripture references beneath the subheadings may not always include every relevant reference since many of the incidents occur in several or all the gospels.

Gold, Frankincense and Myrrh
Matthew 2:1–12

Matthew tells the familiar story of the Magi (Matt. 2:1–12) and reports the gifts they bring of which two are tree products. Frankincense achieves the stature of a small tree, but myrrh is, more correctly, a large bush or shrub. Both myrrh and frankincense are exudations, aromatic resins collected by cutting the bark, and both would have come a long way and passed through many hands to be presented to the infant, Jesus. Not only had

the Magi brought them, probably from Babylon, but they would have received them as traded products (think of camel caravans on the famed spice routes of Arabia and the East and Gen. 37:25) from the Arabian Peninsula and the Horn of Africa where these desert plants occur naturally. John in Revelation 18:13 includes both in the cargoes of merchandise traded with Babylon. Certainly neither is found in Israel.

It is surprising to learn that Luke also mentions frankincense, and also in the broad context of the nativity story, because it is the incense burned in the temple as we saw in Exodus. And it was Zechariah, one of the temple priests and shortly to become John the Baptist's elderly father, whose turn it was to burn incense when the angel met him by the altar to announce that his equally elderly wife, Elizabeth, would bear a child (Luke 1:8–10). Incense was and still is widely burned.

Myrrh is the more precious. It is an ingredient of ointments and cosmetics though some suggest it can also be used as an incense. The Egyptians had known it for thousands of years and we meet it again at Christ's death both when mixed with wine as a drink when he was crucified (Mark 15:23) and with

FACING PAGE: *Lone frankincense tree (Oman)* © *M Raffaelli (2004)/Wikimedia Commons*

aloes as part of the ritual for treating or embalming the body of the deceased (John 19:39–40).

Both frankincense and myrrh are obtained in a similar way. The papery bark of the branches or stem is wounded with incisions—oval scars are best for the frankincense tree[1]—to stimulate resin drops (the more opaque the better to produce the 'tears' of frankincense). It's a bit like rubber tapping on a tiny scale. Individual families may be responsible for a number of trees and their management passed down the generations. Over exploitation today of Boswellia trees for frankincense is causing concern and is highlighted in the popular press.[2] Too frequent or too many tapping incisions weaken the tree rendering it more at risk from longhorn beetle attack as well as depressing yields. But it is one of the few products of the desert that earns decent cash.

Much has been made of the symbolism of the three gifts, gold signifying royalty, incense as that which is offered to God by a priest, and myrrh, with its Messianic association (Ps. 45:8), expressing the significance and fact of death. But more important is that the magi came at all. These wise men, not kings, were probably from Babylon and ever since the Israelites were exiled there the Persian intelligentsia would have known about the small Jewish nation's prophecies concerning a Messiah. They knew too the night sky, and when in 7 to 5 BC they observed a succession of astronomical wonders—planetary conjunctions, planetary massings, and finally a comet in the spring of 5 BC—they knew something, or rather someone, very special was about to appear. The astronomy for the star is convincing[3] and we know magi travelled far and wide in the ancient world. How often they travelled with rich gifts fit to present to a king we don't know: for our purpose, is it not fitting that trees and their products were at Jesus' birth, just as they were during his early manhood plying his trade as a carpenter, and in his death, shockingly, as the instrument of execution—trees that as God, he had made and were pleasing to the eye?

The writing tablet Zechariah asked for
Luke 1:63
The ever observant and meticulous Luke includes an interesting detail about the birth of John the

TOP: *Fig. 9.1a Crystals of myrrh resin*
©*G Cornelius (2005)/Wikimedia Commons*

ABOVE: *Stem of frankincense tree showing scarring to stimulate resin release.* © *B Norvell(2008)/Wikimedia Commons*

ABOVE: *Carob tree with its characteristic pods—some straight, some slightly curved and some horn-shaped*

Baptist (Luke 1:63). His father Zechariah, who had been dumb since his encounter with the angel when ministering in the temple, calls for a 'writing tablet'. He surprises the gathered family, apart from his wife, by writing 'John' as the name. The tablet he wrote on was probably a flat piece of wood with a film of wax such as beeswax. Styli have been found for inscribing them.[4] Perhaps it was similar in size to today's tablet computer and sometimes consisted of three of four leaves ('pages'). We see later (page 153) that it was an early pre-cursor to the book form we are familiar with today. Zechariah wrote on a wax film over wood, we write on bonded wood fibres, namely, paper.

John the Baptist in the wilderness
Matthew 3:4, Mark 1:6, Luke 3:7–9
The Judean wilderness ranges from desert to areas of scrub to wadis or narrow valleys, sometimes with rich vegetation like Ein Gedi. At times following very heavy rains high in the hills to the west, torrents flood all the way down to Jericho and the Dead Sea and turn everything green for a few weeks.

There are few plants or shrubs which could provide human food though, as well as honey, some believe the reference to 'locusts' (Matt. 3:4; Mark 1:6) is not the voracious, swarming insect which were once common in Israel, but the locust bean or carob.[5] Although known as 'St John's bread' the carob is a Mediterranean not desert species, growing where there are winter rains, and is common by the coast or in Galilee, so this explanation for 'locust' is unlikely.[6] However, the Hebrew for locust is very similar to that for carob, hence perhaps the confusion, and there is a contemporary story in the Talmud that a Jewish sage, Rabbi Shimeon Bar-Yohai, hid in a Galilean cave with his son to avoid capture by the Romans and was sustained for 12 years on carobs.[7]

We meet the carob again as the food given to swine in the parable of the prodigal son (Luke 15:11–32).

John the Baptist, however he fed himself, did not spare his hearers (Matt. 3:7–10; Luke 3:7–9). His accusation of the Pharisees and Sadducees is stinging, 'You brood of vipers' and what will happen is stark, 'The axe has been laid to the root of the trees, and every tree that does not produce good fruit will be cut down and thrown into the fire.' This contrasts with the remarks about the shoot from the stump of Jesse—the image of a vigorous coppice shoot sprouting from what seems dead and gone— because if you destroy roots even coppicing fails. The sure way to kill a tree is to cut it and extract the root system too. It is a drastic, sometimes necessary way to deal with diseased trees and stumps, such as caused by honey fungus. Subsequently burning everything helps kill the infection and reduce risk of further spread. A picture of complete removal and destruction was indeed painted by John the Baptist.

The Nazarene
Matthew 2:23, John 1:46

Nazareth doesn't get a mention in the Old Testament though it is believed to have existed from Canaanite times. Today it is the largest Arab city within the state of Israel, but its reputation is the place where Joseph and Mary settled on return from Egypt and where Jesus grew up. In those days Nazareth was a small village and somewhat looked down upon, even despised. As John records (John 1:45–46) Nathanael is incredulous when Philip says that Jesus of Nazareth could be the Messiah and exclaims, 'Nazareth, can anything good come from there?' Perhaps the title 'the Nazarene' is to belittle, but perhaps Matthew (Matt. 2:23) had his Jewish readers in mind? They would know that the name Nazareth derives from the Hebrew '*netzer*' meaning twig or branch and so recall Isaiah's Messianic prophecy (Isa. 11:1), 'a shoot will come up from the stump of Jesse, from his roots a Branch (a 'Nazareth') will bear fruit'.

Jesus the carpenter
Matthew 13:55 & Mark 6:3

Although not next in the gospels' ordering of events, in the chronology of Jesus' life he appears to have learned and plied his father's trade before venturing on his public ministry. Indeed, this is clearly suggested by Mark who quotes the derogatory remarks of Jesus' contemporaries in Nazareth (Mark 6:3), 'Isn't this the carpenter?' Matthew's account of the incident has, 'the carpenter's son'

(Matt. 13:55).[8] They were saying, 'Isn't Jesus just an ordinary bloke with brothers and sisters like us?' They had been amazed at his wisdom, but now ridicule his claims, 'Isn't he just a carpenter?' Jesus was surely proficient in carpentry and, in all likelihood, this was his day to day living, though the Greek word also embraces stone mason and smithy, but carpentry is the more common usage. Perhaps local building work was included, but what was it like to be a carpenter in first century Palestine?

Excavations of preserved wood objects, especially from Egypt where decay is prevented by the dry conditions, reveal exquisite craftsmanship and use of the finest timbers, at least for the well-to-do and top officials. As Hepper notes[9] we have no reason to suppose that such standards didn't continue down through the ages, though in Nazareth we are dealing with the everyday. It's no different today from those who can afford solid oak furniture, to oak veneered, to oak looking plastic covered chipboard. In a first century village few could afford anything but the most basic, a stool, a farm implement and it is with these that Jesus worked. It foreshadows him as friend of the man in the street, of you and me— think of his rough and ready disciples. God is not impressed by show or the fine things in life; he looks upon the heart. But back to what being a village carpenter was like.

In the very centre of Nazareth today is an area of virgin farmland which has been found to be an ancient landscape from the early Roman period with three watchtowers, farm terraces, a stone quarry and a wine press. It is now cared for by an American foundation seeking to recreate exactly what conditions would have been like in the first century. The reconstruction has sought to be meticulous, evidence based and archaeologically accurate. Included is a carpenter's workshop.

Amongst several tools on display are first century saws, mallets, an adze, and a rough sawing horse for fashioning all sorts of implements and furniture: yokes, ploughs, winnowing forks, looms, tables, stools, doors and frames etc. Local timbers are used, mostly cypress, but also pine, sycamore-fig, what we call today Christ-thorn wood, and olive for small articles. Palm trunks would be used for roof beams. Jesus would have been familiar with all of

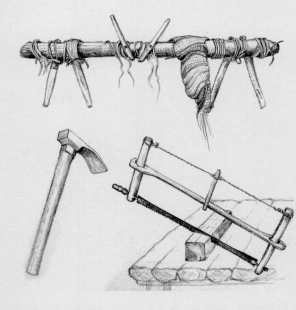

LEFT: *Recreated carpenter's workshop in Nazareth*

RIGHT: *Carpenter's saw and bench, adze, and a donkey's yoke.*

these and, doubtless, the exotic and expensive cedar for special uses, and doubtless too the scratches, blisters and sore thumbs that go with the job! We can surmise this about the timbers from what has been discovered when researching the first century Galilean boat we consider next.

Before doing so, I wonder how Joseph and Jesus obtained the wood they worked with? Did customers bring pieces to be fashioned, was wood re-used such as recovering the sound parts from (say) an old door post, roof beam, or a broken plough to recycle into something smaller? Or did they have access to a few trees, a piece of woodland, or acquire trees when land was cleared? Was tree felling licensed by the Roman occupying authorities? How much was paid for olive prunings to be able to use the branch wood? Did they buy off-cuts from other wood-workers perhaps in the local barracks working on siege engines, spears and the like or from house builders? Perhaps wood was bartered for food.

Also there is one puzzling question. Why didn't Jesus use carpentry examples more often in his many parables? There is the familiar exception in the Sermon on the Mount, and repeated in Luke, warning against hypocrisy in judging others—the speck of sawdust in their eye while ignoring the plank in your own (Matt. 7:1–5; Luke 6:41–42). The likely explanation is that most of his hearers would be more familiar with farming and fishing—crops, livestock, orchards, sowing, ploughing, shepherding, pruning, cleaning nets, setting fish traps—and because Capernaum, where he set up his 'headquarters', had a reputation both for the quality of wheat grown in the locality[10] and its fishing industry. Which leads nicely to the boat.

All about a Galilean boat

Matthew 4:18–22 and many more throughout the gospels

The great African drought of the early 1980s affected Israel too. By 1986 so severe had it become that the Sea of Galilee, the Kinneret in Hebrew, was at an all-time low. The old shoreline was high and dry and much seabed was exposed. Venturing on to it, a military truck got stuck. It took a day to recover, and in the churned up mess two fishermen, brothers from the nearby Kibbutz Ginosar, found Roman coins—they were the widow's mites of Mark 12:41–44. They continued beachcombing and digging in soggy sand: they discovered ancient nails and digging further found a mud encrusted 'strake', a piece of wooden rim. The first archaeologist on site thought it was from a boat that had sunk in the

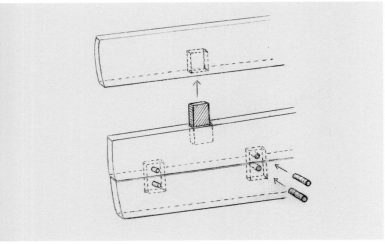

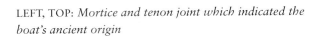

LEFT, TOP: *Mortice and tenon joint which indicated the boat's ancient origin*

LEFT, MIDDLE: *The precious boat cradled on steel supports in the museum*

LEFT, BOTTOM: *A model of what the boat would have been like*

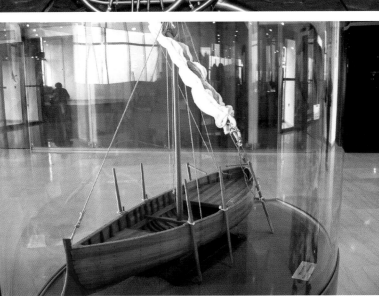

last 200 years, but a week or two later, following a more careful investigation, a marine archaeologist declared it as ancient. This alerted the Department of Antiquities in Jerusalem. In days it was confirmed as likely first century for two reasons: boat builders in those times (a) used mortice and tenon joints and (b) put the outer planking of the hull in place first and then attached the ribs or frame—today we would do it the other way round. The boat in the mud had both these ancient features. Subsequent carbon dating of its timbers showed that the trees from which they had come were felled in the period between 130 BC and AD 90, give or take 100 years for any one sample. Taken together, it confirmed beyond doubt that the boat the fishermen had stumbled upon was first century and contemporary with Christ.

It was an exceptional find. No other boat has been found preserved for 2000 years in the sediments of a fresh water lake.[11] In importance it is at least the equal to the discovery and raising of Britain's Mary Rose, King Henry VIII's great battle ship that sank in the Solent in July 1545.

The wooden boat, 8.2 m long and with a beam of 2.3 m, was salvaged with incredible care, it was so delicate. For eight years it was immersed in preservation fluid to replace the water in the sodden timbers with waxes and other chemicals to add strength and stabilise it when exposed to air. Today it has pride of place in the Yigal Allon Centre on the northern shore of the Sea of Galilee.

As well as how the boat was built, examination of the timber revealed that twelve different tree species had been used. Their identification involved examining wood structure and anatomy and, at the time, experts at the Hebrew University in Jerusalem had just published the authoritative guide.[12] Dr Eller Werker identified the planks as cedar of Lebanon, doubtless chosen because of its ease of working and natural durability, the ribs or frame mainly of Tabor oak, and the keel part carob and part Christ-thorn wood. Other species were only small pieces and probably used when repairs were made. If you visit the museum today, on the left side as you walk to the entrance is a planted row of twelve trees one specimen each of the different timbers found in the boat, though the first, the cedar of Lebanon, was missing when I was there. It's probably never managed to grow: it's far from the cool, high mountains of Lebanon and Syria and woefully ill-suited to the near subtropical climate of the Sea of Galilee. All the other species are native to Israel.

The boat reveals something of Biblical life and times. It is lightly built, the planks of the hull were less than an inch thick, and not like a sturdy sea-going vessel which would have had timbers three times the thickness. It appears to have been constructed in two stages, to a very high standard to start with and then finished off with inferior workmanship revealed by the use of plenty of nails, the builder wanting to make sure it stayed in one piece when afloat! Several of the timbers were secondhand and being re-used, suggesting wood was scarce and costly, that the boat had a long working life, and perhaps that the owner was not wealthy. And if experts can deduce all this (and more) 2000 years on, imagine Jesus, the skilled carpenter, how he would have smiled as he felt a lovely snug-fit mortice and tenon joint or frowned tut tutting over shoddy work made good by extra nails! Of course, he may never have sailed in this particular boat, but how interested he would have been in boat construction, the timbers used, and how well it was finished.

This remarkable boat is unlike relics, with their highly questionable provenances, because here is an artefact dated to the time of Christ and at a place where he ministered. So significant are boats in his story that they are mentioned 50 times in the New Testament:

LIST OF TREES USED IN THE FIRST CENTURY GALILEAN BOAT'S CONSTRUCTION AND REPAIR	
Aleppo pine	one plank of the hull (repair?)
Carob	main keel
Cedar of Lebanon	the most used timber, namely, for almost all the planks of the hull
Christ-thorn	repairs to the keel
Judas tree	small rib and tiny piece of hull plank (repair?)
Laurel	repair of a small rib
Plane	two small repairs
Spiny hawthorn	two ribs of the hull (repair?)
Sycomore-fig	several repairs of hull and ribs
Tabor oak	the boat's frame making the ribs of the hull
Terebinth	two ribs of the hull (repair?)
Willow	a single rib to repair the frame

- from working with boats, Jesus called his first disciples (Matt. 4:18–22)
- from sitting in a boat, Jesus would sometimes teach the crowds (Luke 5:1–3)
- by a boat Jesus crossed the Sea of Galilee to Gadara to heal the demon-possessed man (Mark 5:1–20)
- by a boat Jesus crossed the Sea of Galilee and on a mountainside later in the day he fed the crowd of 5000 who came to hear him (Matt. 14:13; John 6:1)
- it was in a boat that the disciples began to realise Jesus' power and authority (Mark 4:35–41)
- it was in a boat, to which Jesus had walked on the water, that the disciples first worshipped Him as the Son of God (Matt. 14:22–36)
- while fishing in a boat the disciples witnessed a miraculous catch at the start of Jesus' ministry (Luke 5:1–11) and again at the end, after his resurrection, as as sign, a reminder, that it was He as he stood on the shore to summon them and recommission them (John 21:1–14).

All this because of a drought.

Trees and their fruit

Matthew 7:16–20 & Luke 5:43–45

We remarked at the beginning of this book concerning, 'seed bearing plants and trees on the land that bear fruit with seed in it, according to their various kinds.' (Gen. 1:11–12). Jesus takes up this fact to make a point in his great sermons (Matt. 7:16–20; and Luke 5:43–45). You don't pick figs or grapes from thorns or thistles, or obtain good fruit from bad trees, the point being, 'by their fruits you will know them'. Jesus' application was discerning true teaching from the false and to watch out for the false teachers, recognised by their fruit—their lives, behaviour, actions, consistency not matching what they profess. Somewhat tangential to our theme is that it is flowers and fruit, their type and description, that botanists use to classify all plants. They don't use leaves, stems or trunks, or roots, but flowers to classify. It is literally by their fruits you will know them, which is precisely what Jesus says about how to recognise a tree (Matt. 12:33).

A homely example is comparing beech with hornbeam. From a distance the trees look similar and are easily confused. Both have smooth greyish bark, similarly sized oval leaves (though the hornbeam's are slightly serrated), and are often found growing on the same sites in southern England. But their fruits are miles apart: hornbeam with clusters of winged seeds and beech with hard roundish, bristly beechnuts. By their fruits you can be sure.

Parables and pictures with trees

Matthew 13:31–31; Mark 8:22–26; Luke 13:6, 15:16 & 17:6

We've remarked already that Jesus told few parables which he illustrated from wood-working and carpentry, and the same is true about trees more generally. That said, in the gospels there are a few incidents and asides that are close to our theme and we explore each briefly.

The first is the perplexing reference to mustard growing into a tree (Matt. 13:31–32; Mark 4:30–32; Luke 13:18–19). White mustard, the common roadside plant black mustard, and the hoary mustard which colonises waste ground are only ever tall herbs rarely exceeding 1.5 m (5 ft) though some reports suggest black mustard achieving as much

as 10 or even 15 ft.[13] The reference to 'largest of garden plants' in Matthew's account, may suggest Jesus was referring to a local or special cultivar his hearers would have known as it was extensively cultivated in Biblical times for mustard-seed oil and medicament.[14] Zohary[15] comments helpfully, 'since it [black mustard] is conspicuous in the vegetation around the Sea of Galilee and farther north, it suits the context of the parables, as does the small size of its seeds.' Mustards, which are not referred to in the Old Testament, are all in the wall-flower family (*Brassica*) with their cross of four petals in each flower. Seeds are small (1 mm), but not as tiny as many eucalypts for example, and the point Jesus is making is that out of something small and insignificant something great will emerge which,

ABOVE: *Mulberry foliage with its fruits*

He says, is like the kingdom of heaven which His coming inaugurates.

Jesus uses the same analogy of the mustard seed and its potential as a picture of what faith can do. In Matthew (Matt. 17:21) such faith can move a mountain, in Luke's account (Luke 17:6) it is, '... you can say to this mulberry tree, "Be uprooted and planted in the sea." and it will obey you.' This is the only occurrence of a mulberry tree in the Bible[16] apart possibly from the reference to 'wood that will not rot' in Isaiah (40:20). It is not native to Israel and here does not refer to the famous white mulberry used to cultivate silk worms, but the black mulberry (*Morus nigra*) or sycamine tree native to Iran and around the Caspian Sea. They have sweet edible fruit looking like elongated raspberries and were probably introduced to the Levant very early on as were the fig and pomegranate. There is a large mulberry tree, from which my wife and I sampled the fruits, by the entrance to the excavations at Smyrna (modern Izmir) in Turkey. Hepper[17] comments that mulberry is slow-growing, attains great age, and when its gnarled trunk begins to collapse new shoots emerge from the base. It was traditional to pile turves or stones around the base to support the tree and encourage this new growth. It would be extremely difficult to uproot, and hence give point to Jesus' remark.

I think we all smile with sympathy and surely joy at the blind man who Jesus heals at Bethsaida (Mark 8:22–26) and who, as he begins to see, exclaims, 'I see people; they look like trees walking around.' Perhaps in his blindness he had bumped into trees; now he sees what seems to resemble them but moving around. For me this is the kind of detail which no legend would have, it rings authentic and true.

Luke alone tells us the parable of the lone fig tree growing in a vineyard (Luke 13:6). When the owner went to look for fruit it had none so he wanted to cut it down, but the vineyard's manager suggested digging around it, fertilising it and giving it one more year. The meaning probably relates to Israel as the fig tree, or possibly to an individual's guilt. Jesus told it immediately following his remarks about those who had been killed when the tower of Siloam collapsed who were neither more nor less

ABOVE: *Shepherd at the gate of a sheep pen shaded by an Aleppo pine (Nazareth Village)*

guilty of sin than anyone else. All must repent (Luke 13:5). But the parable tells of patience, another year, of care and tending—digging around and fertilising—before judgment. The more interesting of these two improvements is the digging around. While this may refer to weeding or hoeing, deeper digging severs the roots which promotes new root growth and introduces that element of stress which, as we mentioned in the context of beating olive trees (p XXX), can often stimulate flowering. If the fertiliser used was wood ash, perhaps from burning the vine prunings, then this manure, rich in potassium, may also have helped flowering and the next year's crop of figs. Jesus doesn't tell us the end of the story in the parable—whether the digging and fertilising worked—he had made his point about God's patience, love and care.

It is only Luke who tells us the much loved parable of the prodigal or lost son. As we remarked earlier, the pods Jesus was thinking about that the son would have fed to the swine (Luke 15:16)—which the son longed to eat—were probably the protein rich carob. They are still fed today to cattle, pigs and horses, the animals eating the whole pod, husk and all, not just the seeds.

The great 'I ams' of John's gospel

While not wanting to stretch our theme too far, there is something fitting and deeply humbling when, as a scientist, I think about these great sayings of our Lord. The symbolism of each is unrivalled as, of course, is the central point in each case. But what were the actual things to which Jesus compared himself? The list we find in John's gospel is remarkable.

- I am the bread of life (6:36)—the staple food
- I am the light of the world (8:12)—the radiation that underpins the whole universe
- I am the gate (10:7 & 9)—a humble wooden entrance to a sheepfold
- I am the good shepherd (10:11)—a person and an employment of lowly status in Jesus' time
- I am the resurrection and the life (11:25)—an abstract idea about the future of great practical hope for which all long
- I am the way, the truth and life (14:6)—a concept, unique in claim and in import
- I am the true vine (15:1)—a vigorous, productive and fruitful plant

Something wooden is included, perhaps in the

least well-known 'I am'. But what a collection of claims: only God could make them.

Zacchaeus climbs a sycomore-fig

Luke 19:1–10

At breakfast this morning, my wife's daily reading was Luke 19:1–10. She didn't know that I had reached this very passage—I shared the fact with her, and we had to smile! And smile, surely, did Jesus as he saw short Zacchaeus up a tree ahead of him on the road to Jericho. Zacchaeus's intent look of curiosity was soon wiped from his face when Jesus, with the noisy, bustling crowd, stopped right under him. Did a hush descend as Zacchaeus, of all people, was singled out, followed by the wonderful exchange and outcome Luke records? It gave Zacchaeus something to smile about. And I am glad that the incident reminds us that trees are there for climbing, if usually by the younger of us rather than tax collectors and inland revenue staff. Tourists to Jericho are taken to a large, old sycomore-fig which would have been like the one he climbed.

Zacchaeus climbed a tree to see Jesus, and his life was transformed. Our next chapter is about what happened to make this possible.

BELOW: *The large sycomore-fig tree at a road junction in Jericho*

Notes

1 **Hepper, F N** (1992) *Illustrated Encyclopedia of Bible Plants*. Inter Varsity Press, Leicester.

2 **Cumming, Ed** (2012) Gold, myrrh and a tree in danger of extinction. *Daily Telegraph*, 22 Dec 2012.

3 **Humphreys, C J** (1991) The Star of Bethlehem—a comet in 5BC—and the date of the birth of Christ. *Quarterly Journal of the Royal Astronomical Society* **32**, 389–407.

4 **Edwards, B** and **Anderson, C** (2011) *Through the British Museum with the Bible*. DayOne, Leominster

5 Carob in Greek gives us the word 'carat', used for assessing gold and precious stones, because the seeds are unusually uniform in size and consistency and may have been used as a kind of standard or guarantee in gold transactions.

6 **Hepper** (ibid)

7 **Zohary, M** (1982) *Plants of the Bible*. Cambridge University Press, Cambridge.

8 Both are correct of course, but since tradition has it that Mark wrote his gospel from the stories and sermons he heard from Peter, over the years they were together, he is surely right that Jesus too was a carpenter as Peter is probably the best placed person to have known.

9 **Hepper** (ibid)

10 **Lofenfeld, L** and **Frenkel, R** (2007) *The boat and the Sea of Galilee* Gefen Publishing House Ltd. Jerusalem (translation from Hebrew by **Ora Cummings**)

11 (ibid)

12 **Fahn, A, Werker, E** and **Baas, P.** (1986) *Wood Anatomy and Identification of Trees and Shrubs from Israel and Adjacent Regions*. Israel Academy of Sciences and Humanities, Jerusalem.

13 **Darom, D** (undated) *Beautiful Plants of the Bible*, Palphot Ltd, Israel.

14 **Moldenke, H N** and **Moldenke, A L** (1952) *Plants of the Bible*. The Ronald Press Company, New York. [They also note that although black mustard is an annual, in the autumn the stem and branches become stiff and small birds perch on them attracted by the edible seeds.]

15 **Zohary** (ibid)

16 **Musselman, L J** (2012) *A Dictionary of Bible Plants*. Cambridge University Press, New York. [Musselman argues that sycomore-fig is referred to in this verse by Luke, not mulberry.]

17 **Hepper** (ibid)

10

The final journey to a wooden cross

The gospels make clear that Jesus predicted his death on several occasions to warn his disciples what he was going to face. All the gospels have substantially similar accounts of this central and most important of events. While it is in Paul's letters that the full implications of Christ's death and resurrection are spelt out, there is no doubt that the gospels, and Jesus in particular, knew what he was doing and why. All we can do here is to explore some of the details we are given.

The palms of Palm Sunday
Matthew 21:1–11

The narrow road down the west side of the Mount of Olives is steep and winding. To his left Jesus would have seen numerous white tombs, some dating back to King David's time, and ahead of him, on the far hill across the Kidron Valley, the magnificent temple Herod had built. It was centre stage with still bits and pieces of work going on though well over 30 years since Herod the Great had died in 4 BC. Thus the stage is set for that fateful journey on what we call Palm Sunday.

The temple's magnificence contrasts with Jesus riding on a donkey, as the beast hesitantly made its way down the road surrounded by rejoicing crowds laying cloaks and tree branches in honour, in homage fit for a king (Matt. 21:1–11). Palm branches (and perhaps of other trees such as olive as well) were full of symbolism as we have seen in temple motifs, engravings and friezes. Palms were admired for their beauty and graceful appearance as well as valued for the sweet dates, though in the cool climate of Jerusalem the latter develop poorly, and the trees were planted and used for their many other benefits. The crowds, too, would recollect that only two hundred years before the palm was the Maccabees' emblem of victory just as they would sigh that on their Roman coinage the image of a woman seated under a palm signified Judah as an occupied, subject nation. But on this day, as crowds followed Jesus and others pressed on their way to Jerusalem for the passover, they had reason to praise and shout Hosanna, and to cut palm branches: the king was coming.

Two fig tree lessons
Matthew 21 & Mark 11

Much has been made of the fig tree that is cursed by Jesus and withers, to the surprise of the disciples,

FACING PAGE, TOP: *The narrow road descending the Mount of Olives*

FACING PAGE, BOTTOM: *A date palm rich with fruit outside the Dung Gate of Jerusalem*

ABOVE: *Fig tree foliage in southern England—lack of warmth when days are long makes for poor fruiting*

within hours (Matt. 21:18–22; Mark 11:12–14 & 20–22). We find part of the explanation from the lesson Jesus teaches us from the fig and its habit in Matthew 23:32. He tells his disciples about the end times by urging them to be alert to and understand world events, just as they understand that when the twigs of a fig become tender (they fill with sticky, milky latex) and start to flush new leaves, summer is near. The plant, like all plants, is responding physiologically to both increasing warmth, day and night, and to increasing daylength or photoperiod—more hours of light, fewer of dark. These are sensed by plants through a protein called phytochrome which changes its state, particularly as nights get shorter, so they 'know' when to flush and to flower. Jesus' point is that we should be aware of our times, the signs of what is happening, and thus be prepared and not taken by surprise at his return.

This control mechanism of flushing and flowering could be a clue to the cursed fig. Mark

(Mark 11:12–14) tells us that Jesus saw the tree from a distance and it was in full leaf, but had no figs. If these events took place in AD 33, the most likely year,[1] then this fig tree was in leaf in late March (at the beginning of the week leading up to Passover). March is far too early in the year, normal figs flush later than this, so was the tree an unfruitful mutant or sport? Mark's account tellingly adds that, 'it was not the season for figs' i.e. it was too early in the year, yet the tree was already in full leaf. Other explanations are that all Jesus found were the tiny male figs which can overwinter and assumed the trees was infertile or that it was a wild fig or a variety that needed help with pollination, called caprification—see Hepper[2] for details. We may never know for sure, but clearly this fig tree was unusual attracting attention to itself yet offering no good fruit. The theological lesson the incident teaches appears to be twofold. Jesus responds to the disciples' surprise that with faith even greater things will happen, but also it is a picture of the destiny of Jerusalem, apparently flourishing with its new, awe-inspiring temple—its gold gleaming in the noon-day sun—though soon to be utterly destroyed, in AD 70 in fact.

Amusingly, the place where this event occurred has a reputation for unripe figs, Bethphage meaning precisely this, 'the place of unripe figs'.[3]

The olive trees of Gethsemane
All the gospels

There are good grounds for believing that the olive grove in the Garden of Gethsemane, visited by tourists today near the foot of the Mount of Olives, is the site of Jesus' anguished praying just prior to his arrest.[4] The trees are ancient with fat, gnarled 'trunks' testifying to years and years of care and pruning, and they still are so tended. Whether the trees are the actual ones among which Jesus prayed we don't know: they are very old, but as for 2000 years old it is doubtful. Carbon dating suggests the oldest material dates back to about AD 1100, i.e. 900 years old, and this still makes them amongst the oldest olive trees known.[5] The tantalising question is whether, about 900 years ago, some earlier very, very old trees were rejuvenated then (say) by cutting back (coppicing) because they were already considered

LEFT: *Ancient olives in the Garden of Gethsemane*

ABOVE: *A study in olive bark*

very special indeed, to grow into what we see today. It is just possible that today's ancient and evocative olive trees are from the very same stock among which Jesus sweated great drops of blood.

The Garden's location to the east of Jerusalem means that Jesus would surely have seen the arresting party with flaming torches as they made their way in the dark. They would have crossed the Kidron Valley, beneath a star-studded night sky well-lit by a moon two days from full. Jesus could have escaped, hastily retreating through the olive groves up the Mount of Olives, down the far side and into the wilderness of the Judean desert, but he did not. He awaited his assailants: his followers ran away. Graham Usher[6] has it perfectly: comparing the Garden of Gethsemane with Eden, '… we see the main character (Jesus) walking away from his self for the sake of God, whereas Adam walked away from God for the sake of himself.'

What is remarkable, knowing the turbulent history of Jerusalem, is that the site has survived at all. When Jerusalem was sacked by the Romans in AD 70 it is thought that Vespasian had all the olive groves on the east side cut down,[7] which was deeply offensive to the Jews whose laws specifically forbade destroying fruit trees as a military tactic (Deut. 20:19–20). Of course olive will regenerate from a cut stump or fragment of live root still in the ground, thus possibly furnishing the antecedents of the grove we see today. Perhaps equally remarkable, is that the branches and olives produced by today's ancient woody monoliths look as fresh and as healthy as those of any young tree: an olive never dies.

The ancient lineage of the site is reinforced by the name Gethsemane which is Aramaic for olive press. The devotional remarks of that greatest of Victorian preachers, Charles Spurgeon, need no

ABOVE: *Crown of thorns based on Christ-thorn foliage*

elaboration: 'Only the finest olive oil was to be used in the Lord's service. Similarly, the true believer cannot be satisfied with the fake grace of those who say we are naturally good, or the manufactured grace of religious ritual. No, the Christian goes to the olive press of Gethsemane and draws his supply from the One who was crushed there.'

Christ's crown of thorns

Matthew 27:27–31: Mark 15:16–20; John 19:1–5

We do not know for certain from which species of thorny shrub or tree the soldiers hastily tore twigs to fashion a crown, a crown to hurt and to mock the title, 'King of the Jews'. The relics don't help us, they are all of dubious authenticity, including the famous one held in Notre-Dame with a provenance dating back to the early fourth century AD. It is of Palestine buckthorn (*Rhamnus palaestinus*) which has long fearsome thorns and is a common shrub of wilderness. In the Middle Ages a few individual thorns of the Notre-Dame crown were detached and given as the most precious gift a King of France could make. One of these is the Crown of Thorns

Reliquary in the British Museum given as a gift from de Rothschild in 1898. It is set in an exquisite, priceless work of solid gold and jewels that depict the day of judgment.[8] Christ displaying his wounds is at the heart with the long thorn the centrepiece. The problem with this relic and others showing long intact thorns is that plainly this wouldn't be the case as Christ was repeatedly beaten around the head while wearing the crown of thorns (Mark 15:19): the thorns would be broken, snapped and stained.

A more likely candidate for the crown of thorns is another plant in the buckthorn family, the Jerusalem thorn (*Paliurus spina-Christi*) as is suggested by its Latin name. Also known as the European Christ-thorn it still occurs as far south as northern Israel and in New Testament times could well have been found around Jerusalem amongst the scrubby oak of the Judean hills. Other suggestions include boxthorn (*Lycium* spp.), the common thorny burnet[9] (*Sarcopoterium spinosum*) and even the idea that the spines from the base of date palm fronds were used. The latter were readily

ABOVE: *Christ-thorn tree at Korazin. Photo: M. Glass*

available in Jerusalem and could have been woven around a headband, 'to mock Christ's divinity and as well as his Kingship, though it would not have been an instrument of torture in the same way as the other types …'[10]

However, the most plausible candidate remains 'Christ-thorn' itself (*Ziziphus spina-Christi*) and it is what we have illustrated with its mix of upright thorns and recursive, bent-back ones. Specimens of this tree can be found today around Jerusalem as well as very commonly in Galilee. We met the tree in Jotham's parable, the '*atad*' of Judges 9:14–15, and if it is what the soldiers twisted to inflict pain and bleeding, we have a twist indeed. Did the Romans collude with the Jews so that the one earthly crown Jesus wore was the very symbol of bad kingship in Judges and so heap yet one more humiliation and insult on Christ? Jesus the carpenter and country preacher knew the tree well.

The crucifixion
All the gospels

Several times I've been asked, 'What wood was the cross made of?' We don't know for certain though we can make guesses. Crucifixion was the Roman's principal means of execution for all but their own citizens. Ancient literature records countless examples: a hundred years before Jesus was born, almost a thousand Jewish men were crucified on the orders of Janneus;[11] a little later Crassus, in a hideous display of revenge after the Spartacus war, had crucified on the main road north to Rome some six thousand rebels;[12] and when Jesus was a little boy growing up in Nazareth unrest in Jerusalem, Galilee and Perea was viciously quelled by Varus, Governor of Syria,—the ruthless but militarily inept Varus we met before (page 54)— who crucified over two thousands rebels.[13] Despite the frequency and number of crucifixions—and the above are just examples[14]—there is limited archaeological evidence because wood decays. For wooden artefacts to survive either conditions must be exceptionally dry, as for example in the tombs of the Valley of the Kings in the Egyptian desert, or be anaerobic where oxygen is excluded as must have occurred with the miraculously preserved Galilean boat up to its gunwales in silt. Charcoal from wood survives well and of course post holes are common enough, the disturbed soil profile revealing where something wooden had once been.

If archaeological artefacts of crucifixion are limited, that of any human remains was missing altogether until 1968. An accidental discovery of a burial cave at Giv'at ha'Mivtar just north of Jerusalem revealed the remains of a male crucified during the Roman period. This was widely reported including some indication of how crucifixion was carried out in this instance, a nail pinning both ankles together to the cross. A reappraisal of the original research[15] suggested that each ankle was nailed separately, one to each side laterally of the upright, and the arms had been tied. Tiny fragments of wood were found at each end of the ankle nail, the larger of which could be positively identified botanically as olive. Thus the suggestion was made that the upright of the cross was of olive wood, but this too was challenged in the reappraisal given the short stature and great value of olive trees, and because the confirmed fragment of olive came from next to the head of the nail not the pointed end. It appeared to be a plaque or washer to enlarge the nail's head to prevent the victim working the foot loose and, even more cruelly, possibly to staunch the flow of blood. The Romans intended crucifixion to be a slow death: they did not want their victims to die quickly from bleeding. They wanted them to die from excruciatingly painful suffocation, heat stroke or thirst.

This is what has been learned; every detail though may not apply to the cross of Christ. We know Jesus showed his wounds to the disciples, 'look at my hands and my feet' (Luke 24:39) suggesting that all four limbs had been nailed, as well as the spear thrust into his side.

The authors of the reappraisal make a further interesting point:[16] 'Ancient historical sources indicate that the condemned victim never carried the complete cross, as is commonly believed; instead the crossbar was carried, while the upright was set in a permanent place where it was used for subsequent executions. Furthermore, we know from Josephus that during the first century (AD) wood was so scarce in Jerusalem that the Romans were forced to travel ten miles to secure their siege machinery.' The point about the cross-bar (Latin *patibulum*) shows that even this less cumbersome cross-member was too much for the beaten, scourged, and weakened Jesus and Simon of Cyrene was forced to carry it (Matt. 27:32; John 19:17). The point about timber shortage brings us back to the question, of what wood was the cross made? With the number of crucifixions, even assuming continual re-use at least of the uprights,[17] what was the most likely wood available in Jerusalem? The answer is probably cypress though we can't rule out a half dozen other possibilities including cedar and pine. Indeed, was it simply what was most readily to hand?

A case can also be made that the upright was actually a living tree to which the crossbar was affixed, but the tradition of a cross is very strong and it is what the Bible plainly asserts. Perhaps we shouldn't press for other details that are no more than speculation. Wishful thinking and make-believe accumulated in the Dark and Middle Ages

as fast as the relics themselves.[18] In the seventeenth century John Evelyn, in his famous Silva,[19] cites the Venerable Bede that the cross was made of cypress, cedar, pine and box, and Evelyn himself goes on to quote old verse:

'Nailed were his feet to cedar, to palm his hands,
 cypress his body bore, title on olive[20] stands.'

Other tradition holds that wood for the Tree of the Cross came from the Tree of Life[21] which

ABOVE: *Cypress trees behind Domitian's entrance near the large necropolis at Heirapolis in Turkey. Cypresses were widely planted around graveyards and cemeteries. They are common in Israel and is a candidate for the wood from which the cross was made*

ABOVE: *Quiet in the Garden Tomb in Jerusalem. The tree is a terebinth*

is interesting since at least cypress is *Cupressus sempervirens*—the ever-living cypress. Interesting or revealing too is that most supposed 'relics' of the cross turn out to be pine or oak, probably because they're the most widely occurring of trees across Europe. One tradition of possible substance suggests that the wood came from trees on the site now occupied by the fortified eleventh-century (AD) Monastery of the Cross, near today's Israeli Knesset.[22] All in all, cypress is probably the safest guess, but only a guess.

Far more important than the wood is another narrative. We cited it in Chapter 2 and repeat it again because of what John Evelyn means to forestry in Britain and how elegantly he articulated the point. In his famous *Silva* of 1664 he wrote:

> In a word, and to speak a bold and noble truth, trees and woods have twice saved the whole world; first by the ark, then by the cross; making full amends for the evil fruit of the tree in paradise, by that which was born on the tree in Golgotha.

Offered myrrh before and after his death
Matthew 27:34, Mark 15:23, Luke 23:36
The gospels tell us that Jesus cried from the cross 'I thirst' and was offered wine mixed with myrrh (Mark 15:23). Wine was used medicinally as we know from Paul's advice to Timothy about his stomach (1 Tim. 5:23) and from the parable of the good Samaritan. Sometimes it would be flavoured with a resin, such as myrrh, and used as a pain-killer.[23] Others have suggested that myrrh would inflame thirst and inflict more torture.[24] Jesus tasted the drink offered and then refused it.

Joseph of Arimathea and Nicodemus, who took care of Jesus' body, had brought a mixture of spices, myrrh and aloes, for embalming (John 19:39). The quantity was huge, about 35 kg, an amount fit for royalty. Myrrh had been used for this purpose since early Egyptian times. The aloe could be the *Aloe vera* we are familiar with—its oil or juice was extracted from the leaves to perfume the linen used to wrap the body—or it could be the equally precious imported aloeswood (*Aquilaria* spp.) which was known to be used to mask the smell of decay in a tomb.[25]

The garden of resurrection
In Jerusalem the Church of the Holy Sepulchre shelters the probable site of the tomb where the body of Jesus was laid, but the Garden Tomb can also make a plausible claim from its location outside the city wall, its proximity to a 'Golgotha'—a small hill looking like a human skull, and that it was a 'garden' in the first century with a tomb cut into the rock. The church is devoid of trees of course, though full of much human elaboration, the garden with its many trees and shrubs is a haven of tranquillity and peace from the bustle of the street outside.

Whichever is the place where Jesus rose on that first Easter Sunday, there are several details in the accounts which are plainly those of eyewitnesses. One is in Luke and John who both refer to the grave clothes, strips of linen, still being inside the tomb. John's account adds a further detail that the cloth, '... that had been wrapped around Jesus' head. The cloth was lying in its place, separate from the linen.' (John 20:6–7).

This remark has led to much speculation, one of which is that it symbolised that Jesus' work was well and truly finished. It has been suggested that in the first century when a carpenter had finished his work, for example on a stool, a table, or an implement, he signified that it was ready for inspection, that all 'was done and dusted', by placing his turban on the article. Was this what the separate head cloth implied? It is nothing but speculation. What it, and the other linen clothes, definitely do imply is resurrection. If the body had been stolen there would be no grave clothes, if Jesus had somehow managed to recover, the linen would have been unwrapped, like Lazarus (John 11:44), and the head cloth would certainly not be 'lying in its place'.

Commissioned fisherman
John 21
Much of what took place at the start of the gospels is where much of what we learn about the risen Lord finishes, on the shore of the Sea of Galilee. The risen Jesus would meet his disciples there (Matt. 28:10) and John tells how it happened (John 21). For me it nicely brings together three of the main points we have been following. Jesus was cooking a meal (John 21:9) and I wonder if he lit the fire with

Christ-thorn twigs which make excellent kindling, readily catching fire and generating much heat with little smoke.[26] There would have been many such trees about, and a proper use for them rather than a crown of thorns. The disciples were back in their fishing boats, but their future lay as fishers of men, though how grateful we are that one of the boats of their time survived to tell its story. And Peter's death, predicted by Jesus (John 21:18–19) to be on another cross of wood, would remind him and us all of the supreme sacrifice of all.

ABOVE: *The shrub-lined shore of the Sea of Galilee beneath the Mount of Beatitudes. A little farther west (out of the picture to the left) is where tradition says that Peter was re-instated and where Jesus cooked breakfast for his disciples*

Notes

1 **Humphreys, C J** (2011) *The Mystery of the Last Supper—reconstructing the final days of Jesus*. Cambridge University Press, Cambridge.

2 **Hepper, F N** (1992) *Illustrated Encyclopedia of Bible Plants*. Inter Varsity Press, Leicester.

3 (ibid)

4 **Montefiore, S S** (2011) *Jerusalem, the biography* Phoenix, Orion Books Ltd, London

5 **Anon** (2012) Jerusalem Olive Trees amongst oldest in the World. *Reuters*, Saturday 20 October 2012

6 **Usher, G B** (2012) *Places of Enchantment—meeting God in landscapes*. SPCK, London.

7 **Hepper, F N** (ibid)

8 **MacGregor, N** (2010) *A history of the World in 100 objects*. The British Museum, BBC Radio 4, Penguin Books

9 **Musselman, L J** (2012) *A Dictionary of Bible Plants*. Cambridge University Press, New York. [Mussleman argues the case for thorny burnet as a very common, low-growing spiny shrub in Jerusalem with wiry, flexible twigs; it was both easily available and easily fashioned into a 'crown of thorns'.]

10 **Hepper** (ibid)

11 **Devine, A-J** (1998) Visions of Kingdoms—from Pompey to the First Jewish Revolt. In M D Coogan (ed) *The Oxford history of the Biblical World*. Oxford University Press, Oxford. 352–387.

12 **Marr, A** (2012) *A History of the World*, BBC/Macmillan, London

13 **Devine, A-J** (ibid)

14 **Evans, C A** and **Wright, T** (2008) *Jesus, the final days*. The Society for Promoting Christian Knowledge (SPCK), London. (An excellent account of the historical data concerning Jesus' crucifixion, death, burial and resurrection)

15 **Zias, J** and **Sekeles, E** (1985) The Crucified Man from Giv'at ha-Mitvar: A reappraisal. *Israel Exploration Journal* 35(1) 22–27.

16 (ibid)

17 Re-use of the means of execution is common. In Britain gibbets were continually re-used and stood as a warning.

18 **Montefiore** (ibid) (p177) summarises the reports of how in the fourth century the pious Empress Helena scoured Jerusalem for Christian memorabilia: 'She discovered three wooden crosses, a wooden plaque that read 'Jesus of Nazareth, King of the Jews, and the actual nails ... From now on all Christendom craved holy relics ... No archaeologist has ever approached her success.' There is no record of how these crosses, including the one claimed to be the one true cross, were successfully preserved, stored, or hidden away for 300 years before their 'discovery'.

19 **Evelyn, J** (1664) *Silva or Discourse of Forest Trees* The Royal Society, London.

20 Mention of olive is interesting as the *Titulus crucis* relic is of olive wood, but carbon 14 tests date it only to early medieval (Bella, F and Azz. C (2002) ^{14}C of the *Titulus Crucis*. *Radiocarbon* **44**(3): 685–689)

21 **Usher** (ibid)

22 **Montefiore, S S** (ibid)

23 **Hepper** (ibid)

24 **Musselman** (ibid)

25 **Musselman** (ibid) [Aloeswood could also be what is translated 'aloes' in Num. 24:6; Ps. 45:8 and Prov. 7:17]

26 **Hareuveni, N** (2006) *Tree and Shrub in Our Biblical Heritage* Neot Kedumim, Jerusalem (transl. **Helen Frenkley**)

11

Faith, flotsam and a future in the tree of life

Notes from the early Church

Acts 1–12

The need to replace Judas after his betrayal is reported by Luke at the beginning of Acts where comment is added in parentheses about how Judas met his death. The only other account of what happened is given by Matthew (Matt. 27:1–10). Both describe the purchase of a field with the blood money, the thirty pieces of silver, but they differ a little as to how Judas died—by hanging himself or, in graphic and gruesome detail, '… falling headlong, his body burst open and spilled the intestines.' (Acts 1:18–19). They are not irreconcilable: perhaps the tree or branch on which Judas hanged himself broke, the fall might have been from some height e.g. hanging over a ledge, and the ground rocky with the gory result. From this incident grew the story of the Judas tree (*Cercis siliquastrum*), but it is never named in the Bible.

The tree just makes 20 ft so might have been big enough, and long tradition does have it that it was what Judas used. Perhaps the deep pink flowers led to the name. They often grow directly on the trunk, the phenomenon of cauliflory just like the figs of sycamore-fig, and are pea-like with a slight resemblance to drops of blood. It is native to Judea, and sometimes called 'Judea Tree'. The name 'Judas tree' is mistaken according to Hareuveni,[1] who labels it Mediterranean Redbud, while Nature in Israel's delightful leaflet '*Trees and Shrubs in Israel*' calls it Juda's Tree.[2]

'Hanging on a tree' made a deep impression on Jesus' followers as they surely reflected on all that the crucifixion meant. Luke quotes Peter twice using this expression (Acts 5:10 & 10:39), Peter uses it himself in his first letter (1 Pet. 2:24) as does Paul when writing to the Galatians (Gal. 3:13). This translation of 'hanging on a tree' is the familiar one from the Authorised, Revised Standard and older New International versions. Many modern translations, including the 2011 NIV, give 'hanging on a cross' except in the case of Galatians where Paul is quoting from the curse in Deuteronomy (Deut. 21:22–23) which the new NIV now translates as 'hanging on a pole'. These are refinements recognising that in the Greek the normal word for tree '*dendron*' was not used but '*xulon*', which has the broader meaning of wood or timber, as well as tree: it is what is translated 'wood' in 1 Cor. 3:12 but still 'tree' in 'tree of life' in Revelation 22. The

FACING PAGE: *The ruddy pink flowers and flower buds of the Judas tree*

ABOVE: *Oak woods in Devon once coppiced for their bark for tanning*

main point though is clear. Jesus' crucifixion was an appalling execution Peter witnessed (Acts 10:39), as he did the resurrection. As he appeals to his hearers he goes on to tell them what it meant (Acts 10:43): '... everyone who believes in him receives forgiveness of sins through his name.'

Peter's audience were Cornelius' household in Caesarea Maritima (Acts 10:23–48). He had been summoned there while staying farther down the coast in Joppa at the house of Simon the tanner (Acts 9:43; 10:6 & 32). While Peter must have felt at home since the house was beside the sea, he may have been uncomfortable if bold knowing his host dealt with the skins of dead animals and so was 'unclean' in Jewish eyes. And Peter would have been

reminded of this every hour of every day by the smell that must have been on Simon's working clothes as well as from the tannery.

Tanning leather is a messy business, and the key chemical a polyphenol, tannin, is usually extracted from tree bark. Most green plants have tannins—just think of drinking tea—but the concentration varies. One of the best sources of tannin comes from oak bark and in New Testament times with three native oaks in Israel, Tabor oak was probably the most important,[3] and supply would have been plentiful except in desert regions where Acacia bark and pods would be good alternatives. (I wonder if Joseph and Jesus ever sold bark for tanning from the logs and branches they used, or just kept it for kindling or added it to all the sawdust and shavings for bedding for livestock?) The process of tanning then differs only in detail from that practised right up to the 20th Century when synthetic chromate based 'tannins' took over. Indeed, it was this switch one hundred years ago that led to the decline in coppicing of many of Britain's western oakwoods still extant around Dartmoor and Exmoor and the coastal or upland oak woods of Wales and the Lake District.

Oak trees are felled when the sap has risen and the bark is easy to peel. Bark from trunks and branches, along with any acorn cups lying around (another good source of tannins), is then boiled to produce a brown tannin rich liquid. Animal hides, which have been scraped and had fatty tissues, fur and hair removed by soaking for days in lime or even livestock urine, are then immersed in the tannin rich soup. The tannin stabilises the collagen proteins in the skin turning it to leather that will not readily decay. Tanned hides are removed, stretched out and dried to produce leather. I expect Peter got to know the process well. An appropriate introduction, if ever there was one, to his vision when praying on the roof of Simon's house of the clean and unclean animals which was so central to the advance of the gospel beyond the Jews to the gentiles.

The seafarers

Acts 13–28

The second half of the books of Acts is awash with 'ships' and 'sailing' with twenty-one and twenty-eight mentions respectively. They tell, of course, of Paul's journeys around the Mediterranean, much of it with his companion, the ever alert and careful recorder, Luke. We learn about wooden ships, first century trade and commerce, how voyages were undertaken and what could go wrong.

The impression of much shipping activity, both naval and merchant, comes across: Paul only has to turn up at a port and there is a ship ready to board. This is only possible if piracy is under control and it was a crime the Romans neglected for too long. Indeed, in 67 BC pirates were so bold that they defeated a Roman fleet in the mouth of the Tiber River—only miles from the city of Rome itself. This

appears to have been too much and not long after, fleets were stationed permanently and strategically at Ravenna, where there was also much useful pine forest for shipbuilding in the vicinity, and at Misenum to patrol the sea lanes.[4] This relative security of passage lasted half a millennium, right up to the 5th Century AD. So Paul travelled in some safety, though he was buffeted enough in other ways including three shipwrecks (2 Cor. 11:23–29).

We read in classical literature of many naval engagements around the time of Christ and of new fleets being built, which straightaway begs the question about sourcing timber. Had they changed from the time of Jonah and his voyage 500 years before, or when Solomon was rafting logs down the coast another 500 years before that? We have a few clues.

We know that in 313 BC Theophrastus was concerned about depletion of accessible stocks of ship timber so it is surprising that one hundred years later the Romans burnt enemy fleets rather than keeping them as prizes, suggesting no real timber shortage.[5] At the time of Paul's journeys Pliny (AD 23–79) reviewed timber resources in the Mediterranean basin revealing a westward shift to the forests and wooded slopes of Corsica, the Pyrenees and elsewhere for shipbuilding. Crete and Lebanon still provided some supplies but the Atlas Mountains in North Africa were described as exhausted. But always accessibility was key and coastal forest resources were exploited first. By the first century there was generally less forest cover and less immediately accessible forest.

Choice of trees for shipbuilding was thus determined by a mix of utility and availability. Off north-west Sicily two third century BC Roman ships have been uncovered and found to contain a wide variety of timbers—pine for planking, tenons and dowels of oak, and both oak and maple for the ribs.[6] Plant material in the hold to stop the ballast of rocks rolling about included myrtle, phillyrea and bracken. The crew and soldiers manning the ships appeared to have enjoyed olives, pistachio and hazel nuts! As Hepper points out[7] by New Testament times wooden sea-going merchant vessels were sizeable craft able to carry a cargo of wheat and around 300 people (Acts 27:37). No wonder James

ABOVE: *The utilitarian date palm. As well as its sweet dates, almost every part of the tree was useful*

marvelled how a small rudder could steer so great a ship (Jas. 3:4).

Luke gives some more facts about boat construction in his account of the storm and shipwreck in Acts 27. After hoisting in the lifeboat, 'they passed ropes under the ship to hold it together'. Also ropes would have been used for the sea anchor, for taking soundings, holding the rudder, hoisting the sails and other rigging which are all mentioned. We know from Egyptian tombs that much rope was made from papyrus rind, and it was tough when one thinks of what the Egyptians built(!), but it is equally as likely that the ropes of Paul and Luke's ship were made of date palm fibre which was widely used in ancient Mesopotamia, Egypt and even today. (Samson's famous escape from being tied up with ropes is another story.[8,9]) The story of the shipwreck ends with the stern breaking up and everyone on board getting to shore in Malta; those who couldn't swim make it by clutching at flotsam, planks, and parts of the ship thanks to their being wooden.

Paul's letters

Paul did not come from country stock. As he says he was a pharisee and a son of a pharisee (Acts 23:6), an academic through and through and arguably the finest brain of his day who gave up all and faced trials of all kinds for the sake of his Lord. He weaves few agricultural metaphors and allegories into his letters and I wonder whether Jesus' own humble occupation was initially a challenge (did he muse, like Nathanael, 'Nazareth, can anything good really come from there?'), making his subsequent commitment to and zeal for Him the more remarkable. We have already mentioned how Paul draws out the parallel of hanging on a cross with the curse in Deuteronomy (Deut. 21:23) and what it means (Gal. 3:13). In full it is : 'Christ redeemed us from the curse of the law by becoming a curse for us, for it is written: "Cursed is everyone who is hung on a pole."' This is Paul's priority not trees, forests, timber and their uses, but in two places even these, humble as they are, are part of the story because they help illustrate a subject close to Paul's heart: the ultimate salvation of his own people, the Jews (Romans 11).

ABOVE: *A study in watercolour of Mediterranean landscape*

Olive branches and grafting

Romans 11

Grafting has a long history. For millennia it has been a commonplace horticultural practice to attach fruitful or productive material, the scion, to a rootstock that itself may not yield much but may be more hardy, or well established or useful in other ways. Grafting is how the attachment is done and, whatever method, all aim to bind the tissue of the scion to that of the rootstock to create a union that flourishes. Technically what happens is that new cambial cells develop from the wound parenchyma cells at the point of grafting to produce new conductive tissue, that is new xylem and phloem cells. The plant can then continue to function so

that water, nutrients, and the products of the leaves' photosynthesis pass unhindered. The bond remains for rest of the olive tree's long life.

For grafting olives in biblical times rootstock branches were cut off, small incisions made, and the scion of the desired type, inserted and bound or sealed in place. The key was to ensure that rootstock bark and scion bark were held in contact and prevented from drying out while the 'wound' calloused over and a bond formed.[10] It's a bit like human organ transplants, without the complications, and as successful when done properly. Paul's Roman readers would know well the essentials of grafting: their attention, though,

would be arrested when he turns the process on its head, as he acknowledges (Rom. 11:24).

What Paul does is to compare Gentiles (non-Jews) to wild olive branches, the scions, that are grafted into a fertile and fruitful olive rootstock—the Jews and their status as God's chosen people. It works well, wild olive branches could be grafted this way. Even though his readers would think it the wrong way round, normally fruitful strains of olive are grafted onto wild olive rootstock, they would get the point: they are grafted in and become part of God's chosen people. And Paul goes on, if branches of wild olive can be so grafted, how much easier is it for the cultivated or good

ABOVE: *Delicious olives ripe for picking*

FACING PAGE: *Early writing tablet in book form on slivers of wood (British Museum)*

olive's own branches to be re-united by grafting: Israel, the Jews, will one day be restored.

This contrast is all the more exquisite as metaphor for knowing that wild olive (*Olea europaea* var. *sylvestris*), which occurs throughout the Mediterranean, has small fruits with large seeds, and little edible flesh which can be bitter. It grows in rocky places amongst the scrub vegetation known as maquis. Despite this unpromising situation scions from wild olive can be grafted on to cultivated ones, though there is no horticultural reason for doing so, only the spiritual one Paul makes.

Wood, hay and straw

It is interesting that Paul includes wood with hay and straw in the symbolically weak and largely worthless for laying a foundation because they are combustible unlike gold, silver and precious stones that are not (1 Cor. 3:12). The analogy drawn is that of the Day of Judgment and the value or otherwise of a Christian's discipleship and service.

Writing materials

2 Timothy 4

In the British Museum is a small item which should have been included in MacGregor's *A History of the world in 100 objects*.[11] It points to the beginning of books, and the early church may have been pivotal in this development and their demand for a codex.[12] A codex is a way of housing or assembling manuscripts in book form rather than as a scroll to be unrolled—as Jesus had to when he read from Isaiah in his local synagogue (Luke 4:17). Scrolls

were not easy to transport and it appears that the early church wanted to bind together their sacred books, particularly the four gospels, in this way for ease of use and carriage. This 'demand' led to the codex superseding scrolls and may have been the way Paul's parchments (Latin *membranae*) were bound together and which he was so anxious for Timothy to bring to him (2 Tim. 4:13).

In the British Museum is a wooden writing tablet with four leaves or 'membranae'—an early notebook.[13] Was this a forerunner of the book-like codex and would they have been bound between wooden boards to protect the fragile papyri and parchments they held? Or were even very thin slivers of wood used like the horde discovered so well preserved at Vindolanda, the Roman fort close to Hadrian's Wall?

Paul wrote to Timothy in the early 60s of the first century. Within 100 years codices, the book format that we would recognise, had become the norm. As well as its probable wood covers, it touches on our theme because the book of today, both cover and pages, are wholly tree products. Paper and cardboard are made from wood fibres. In biblical times paper as we know it was not known to the Greeks and Romans, but its precursor, papyrus, from the which paper gets its name, had been for thousands of years. Papyrus 'paper' is more like matting than a true paper in which plant fibres are separated, mechanically or chemically, and then reconstituted or settled out to bond together in a flat sheet. The invention of paper itself dates back to about 100 BC in China where the plant fibres used came from hemp. Paper making technology was brought to the west through Islam around the 9th or 10th Century.

Wooden rudders and forest fires

James 3

James uses three striking metaphors to describe what boasts we can make and what havoc we can wreak by what we say: the bit and bridle that directs a horse, the tiny rudder that turns a ship, and the smallest of sparks that ignites a forest (Jas. 3:5). James's point about the tiny rudder is probably something we've all wondered about, if only from watching the film, 'Titanic'. A naval architect will

ABOVE: *A tiny rudder can be see at bottom left of this marble relief of a 2nd Century AD in-shore trading boat —seemingly small in proportion, but powerful in effect (British Museum)*

typically design a rudder with an area of just two per cent of the product of the ship's length times draught. Much bigger than this and it causes drag. So a ship of the size Paul and Luke might have boarded, say 20 m long with 3 m draught, would need a rudder of 20 x 3 x .02 = 1.2 m². With a rudder's height usually a little less than twice its length, our ship would be well steered by one of just 1.4 x 0.8 m or no more than 5 x 3 ft. (Of course its actual rudder would have probably been a pair of long 'oars' lashed to the stern, hence Luke's reference to, 'the ropes that held the rudders' (Acts 27:40).) I recall from my rowing days, as bow or three in the school's first eight, what a tiny rudder the cox had to steer the boat, and yet recall too the immediate check when he put it hard over.

James's remark about sparks is equally apposite. We've mentioned forest fires before, but the point is how something so tiny sets a great forest, even a whole countryside, ablaze. One strike of lightening is enough, a match will do, and even a single spark from a steam engine. Countless Westerns have included American steam engines with their angular urn shaped funnels so designed as a spark arrester. In my first job in the South Wales valleys, it was still well remembered that up to the 1960s a forest worker on a bike would follow every train up the Afan Valley branch line just to dowse any fires the engine would cause. Sadly the vast majority of forest fires were and are from arson.

James, who may have been Jesus' brother, concludes his ire about taming the tongue with two analogies he may well have heard his brother articulate some 30 years before (Jas. 3:9–12). 'Out of the same mouth come praise and cursing, My brothers this should not be … . My brothers, can a fig-tree bear olives, or a grapevine bear figs?' The point is self-evident: with fruit trees it can't happen, so why does it with us?

Fruit trees without fruit
Jude
Jude, who also may have been one of Jesus' brothers, presents a picture of those who corrupt others by their example and teaching. In verses 12 and 13 five comparisons are drawn of what they are like of which 'autumn trees, without fruit and uprooted—twice dead' is particularly graphic. That which appears wholesome and promising, in the end is worthless. Just like an apple or pear orchard when poor pollination in spring or a late frost catches the blossom, the trees continue to grow and occupy valuable space, but yield little harvest. Last year in Britain, 2012, was such an example: much top fruit was disappointing because of cold, wet weather in April and May. Jude implies worse to come when the failed crop is followed by autumnal gales destroying the trees—worse than useless or 'twice dead'. A deadly picture of false teaching leading many astray, like John Bunyan's 'bypath meadow' in *Pilgrim's Progress*, seductive but destructive.

Revelation, recapitulation and resolution
Revelation 2, 5–7, 9, 11 & 18
The alliterative heading sums up for our theme the last book of the Bible. We meet a new tree species, we revisit symbolism and imagery, and in the final chapter we reach the climax—the perennially fruitful tree of life the leaves of which are for the healing of nations.

In one of the letters to the seven churches, the letter to the church in Ephesus, a right to eat from the tree of life is the promise made (Rev. 2:7). The tree

is located in the paradise of God, and what is now promised is the very thing which Adam and Eve were denied. As we've remarked before the word paradise derives from the Persian word for pleasure garden, a place of peace and bliss, and the whole scene is of restored fellowship between God and man.

Next, in Revelation chapter 5, where there is much about scrolls, we meet 'the Lion of the tribe of Judah, the Root of David, who has triumphed.' (Rev. 5:5) The following verse referring to the Lamb that was slain, namely Christ, makes clear that 'The Root of David' (or Jesse, David's father, as Paul quotes it in Romans 15:12) refers to Christ's lineage, his family tree—as we use the same metaphor! Reminiscent of Palm Sunday, is the great multitude standing before the Lamb who are holding palm branches (Rev. 7:9) with all the symbolism of victory and joy they represent.

The book of Revelation is a vision full of imagery and symbolism which is not always readily understood, certainly not by this writer. One is a picture of the end of the world (Rev. 6:20), 'and the stars in the sky fell to earth, as figs drop from a fig-tree when shaken by a strong wind.' John was probably thinking of what happens to the small winter figs when the tree is shaken violently. The awe of the celestial picture is captured perfectly by C S Lewis in his children's story, *The Last Battle*,[14] as night falls on Narnia,—like figs plummeting earthwards. We find, too, as punishments and doom are unleashed on the earth, that trees are singled out. They do not escape (Rev. 8:7) but are also symbolically protected (Rev. 7:1 & 3, 9:4). Does this suggest special significance? Probably no more than that trees are part and parcel of the biblical narrative from beginning to end, so perhaps it is not so surprising after all.

Perhaps inevitably man-made idols, including of wood (Rev. 9:20), again intrude about which the prophets despaired as we saw earlier in this book in Chapters 7 and 8 (pages 97–99).

The two olive trees (Rev. 11:4) are quoted from Zechariah's prophecy (Zech. 4) and stand for priestly and royal offices representing the necessary continuous flow of oil (page 120).

Thyine wood, scented wood, perfumed wood and citron wood are some of the translations we find for a kind of wood included in the list in Rev. 18:12 which is mentioned nowhere else in the Bible. It is from a tree species we've not met before. Several much prized tree products are listed in this waybill of trade and commerce—costly wooden articles, myrrh, frankincense, olive oil—and 'citron wood' is rightly included. It is a valuable furniture wood, dark, dense, durable, and aromatic. It was used for inlay work often with ebony. And it was the cabinet wood of choice of the super-rich.

Confusingly known as '*citrus*' wood by the Romans, '*thyon*' by the Greeks, citron wood comes from a conifer native to North Africa, *Tetraclinis articulata*. It is mentioned by Homer, but Pliny is surprised that Theophrastus doesn't, 'because citrus tables had been the talk of the town since the days of Cicero'.[15] Its great value led to overexploitation by the Romans, especially once Julius Caesar featured it extravagantly in his triumphal processions after conquering Gaul, even though the tree didn't occur in Gaul! Its use became high fashion with two kinds in particular being sought: pieces with wavy-grain called 'tiger wood' and that with little spirals called 'panther wood'. Citron wood was said to be worth its weight in gold.[16] It shows what valuable commodities, what luxuries were traded two thousand years ago, and why John lists it as symbolising the god of extravagance-fuelled commerce, identified as Babylon in Revelation 18. The tree today is protected in Algeria and Morocco, and there are tiny enclaves in Malta and Spain, but the great forests have long gone.

The real tree of life
Revelation 22

We began with the tree of life and now end with the tree of life (Rev. 22:2–3). Its description is remarkable, exulting in munificence, twelve crops of fruit and yielding its fruit every month. The term 'tree of life' is collective,[17] as in the account in Ezekiel 47:12, and indicates many trees, an avenue, or parkland, even a heavenly 'Capability Brown' landscape. And then we have added a great claim, 'And the leaves of the tree are for the healing of the nations.' Is this more than symbolic, more than hyperbole of the glory of Eden restored, of heaven itself? Yes, all these symbols apply, in principle, to this present age.[18] It is a question worth asking because the leaves of the tree are singled out and singled out for healing (as they were too in Ezekiel). So how might this be?

Concluding this book with this question introduces my own life-long research interest. It is the question, is it sustainable to grow (and harvest) successive crops of trees on the same site again and again? The question has taken me around the world and taken me to Swaziland in southern Africa more times than I can recall. In Swaziland, very fast growing sub-tropical pine plantations have been assessed for more than 45 years through four successive crops, or rotations as foresters call them, raised on the same site. The conclusion is clear: each crop of pine trees has grown as well or better than its predecessor, with a few minor exceptions, without the need for fertilisers or other treatment, just sensible management.[19] This good result is true across the world, again with just one or two exceptions. It shouldn't be a surprise. Farmers harvest the nutrient rich parts of their crops (seeds, tubers, fruits) for us to eat and be nourished: foresters harvest the nutrient poor parts (the trunk) and leave behind on site the nutrient rich bits—leaves, twigs, nuts and cones. The Victorians knew that trees were soil improvers, we had forgotten.

Trees improve soil largely through their leaves. As leaves, twigs and needles drop they return nutrients to the soil and help build up organic matter. Physically they protect the soil from water erosion and encourage infiltration, a benefit augmented by tree roots and the presence of undergrowth and understorey shrubs. It is why forest clearance (deforestation) is so destructive. But leaves do far more:

- leaves, through their numerous, pin-prick size holes on the surface called stomata, absorb carbon dioxide and by photosynthesis store the carbon as wood, and so help slow climate change;
- leaves, through the same stomata, emit oxygen into the atmosphere;
- from leaves water is lost through the same stomata—as we all know when we put flowers in a vase and forget to replenish the water or our Christmas tree dries out and sheds its needles. The process is called transpiration and thanks to the physics of evaporation cooling takes place;

BELOW: *A little bit of paradise; cool among the laurels and Syrian ash around the pools of Tel Dan.*

ABOVE, LEFT: *Left intact, the great natural forests of the world bless the environment largely thanks to the leaves of the trees. Rainforest in Papua New Guinea*

ABOVE, RIGHT: *An old picture of Banias Falls in late winter fed from the melting snows of Mt Hermon. It is one of the River Jordan's three tributaries and a river of life providing Israel with fresh water and the dry countryside moisture to be green. An oriental plane tree stands on the tiny island between the gushing torrents Photo: W. Stewart*

- all the leaves together that make up the crown of a tree and the canopy of a whole forest help scrub particulates and other pollutants from the atmosphere: they clean the air.

We can say even more. Trees and forests with their canopy of leaves help the cycling and re-cycling of moisture, they can mitigate downstream flooding, they help reduce wind speed, they provide shelter and shade in the heat of the day. They are a home for wildlife: leaf-eaters (both insect or animal herbivores) provide food for higher up the food chain. By planting trees these benefits can be harnessed to help initiate the process of recovery of eroded land and denuded landscape. We could go on for we are describing what are today called 'ecosystem services', an enormous benefit trees and forests provide that are at last being properly recognised.

Leaves do all these things. They reverse many of the negative effects of what we do to the environment; a healing of harms.

These things are temporal. The great spiritual reversal, the Bible's great story, is how harm was undone by the One who hung upon a tree. It gives the believer the right to the tree of life and a share in it (Rev. 22:14 & 19). And the One who extends this invitation, 'I Jesus', describes himself (Rev. 22:16) with a final metaphor on our theme, 'the Root and Offspring of David'.

Notes

1 **Hareuveni, N** (2006) *Tree and Shrub in Our Biblical Heritage.* Neot Kedumim, Jerusalem. Transl. Helen Frenkley.

2 **Kishenbaum, N** (2007) *Trees & Shrubs in Israel.* Nature in Israel, Jerusalem

3 **Hepper F N** (1992) *Illustrated Encyclopedia of Bible Plants,* Inter Varsity Press, Leicester.

4 **Meiggs, R** (1982) *Trees and Timber in the Ancient Mediterranean World.* Clarendon Press, Oxford.

5 **Thirgood, J V** (1981) *Man and the Mediterranean Forest—a history of resource depletion.* Academic Press, London

6 **Hepper** (ibid)

7 **Hepper** (ibid)

8 It is believed that the 7 ropes to tie down Samson (Judg. 16:4–9), which he said must be green and freshly cut, came from the shrub yitran (*Thymlea hirsuta*). Samson knew this would create problems because the Philistines couldn't just go to the market and buy dried ones. They would have to cut and fashion enough rope all in a day and so occupy many people and attract great interest. Samson was good at PR as well as strong!

9 **Hareuveni** (ibid)

10 For a time, grafts are weak, liable to break and must not be unwound or left unsupported too soon. Last year we bought a variegated Salix graft, but it shrivelled as wind stressed the bond and the leaves couldn't get enough sap.

11 **MacGregor** (2010) *A History of the World in 100 Objects.* The British Museum/BBC Radio 4/Penguin Books.

12 **Hill, C E** (2010) *Who Chose the Gospels?* Oxford University Press, New York

13 **Edwards, B** and **Anderson, C** (2011) *Through the British Museum with the Bible.* DayOne, Leominster.

14 **Lewis, C S** (1956) *The Last Battle* Bodley Head/Penguin, Middlesex

15 **Meiggs** (ibid)

16 **Thirgood** (ibid)

17 **Hendriksen, W** (1940) *More than Conquerors—an interpretation of the Book of Revelation.* The Tyndale Press, London (1962).

18 **Hendriksen** (ibid)

19 **Evans, J** (2009) Sustainable silviculture and management. In **Julian Evans,** (ed.) *Planted Forests: Uses, Impacts & Sustainability.* CAB International, Wallingford, and United Nations Food and Agriculture Organisation, Rome. Chapter 8 summarises the issues including my most recent account of the Swaziland sustainability research.

A personal afterword

In coming to the end of our theme of trees, forests and wood in the Bible, I am reminded of C S Lewis's famous remark. He said of his faith, 'I believe in Christianity as I believe that the sun has risen, not only because I see it but because by it I see everything else.' As a forest scientist, appreciating better the trees we find in the Bible's narrative has helped me appreciate better its far greater story.

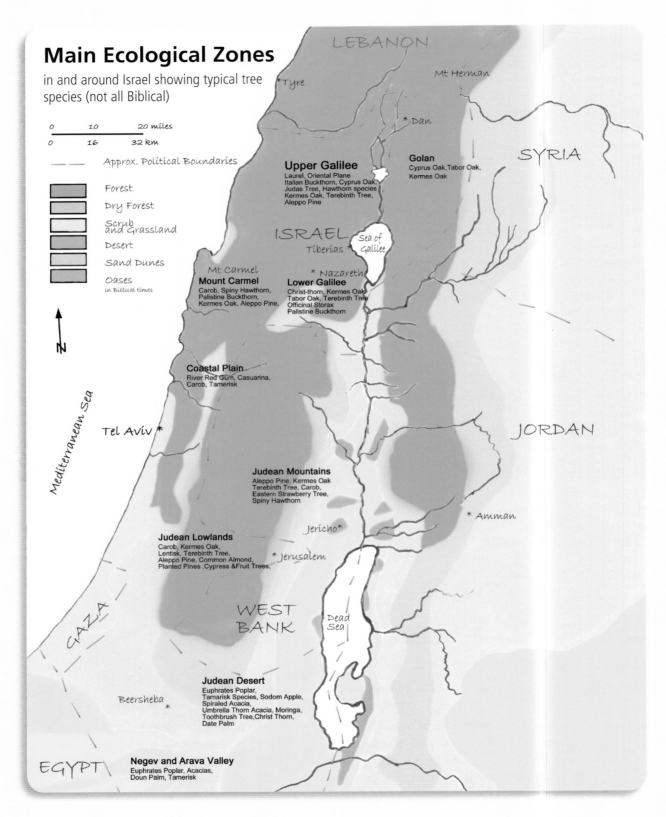

Main Ecological Zones

in and around Israel showing typical tree species (not all Biblical)

0	10	20 miles	
0	16	32 km	

— — — — Approx. Political Boundaries

Forest
Dry Forest
Scrub and Grassland
Desert
Sand Dunes
Oases
in Biblical times

N

LEBANON

Tyre

Mt Herman

Dan

SYRIA

Upper Galilee
Laurel, Oriental Plane
Italian Buckthorn, Cyprus Oak,
Judas Tree, Hawthorn species
Kermes Oak, Terebinth Tree,
Aleppo Pine

Golan
Cyprus Oak, Tabor Oak,
Kermes Oak

ISRAEL

Tiberias

Sea of Galilee

Mt Carmel

Nazareth

Mount Carmel
Carob, Spiny Hawthorn,
Palistine Buckthorn,
Kermes Oak, Aleppo Pine,

Lower Galilee
Christ-thorn, Kermes Oak
Tabor Oak, Terebinth Tree
Official Storax
Palistine Buckthorn

Coastal Plain
River Red Gum, Casuarina,
Carob, Tamerisk

Mediterranean Sea

Tel Aviv

JORDAN

Judean Mountains
Aleppo Pine, Kermes Oak
Terebinth Tree, Carob,
Eastern Strawberry Tree,
Spiny Hawthorn

Amman

Jericho

Judean Lowlands
Carob, Kermes Oak,
Lentisk, Terebinth Tree,
Aleppo Pine, Common Almond,
Planted Pines ,Cypress &Fruit Trees,

Jerusalem

GAZA

WEST BANK

Dead Sea

Judean Desert
Euphrates Poplar,
Tamarisk Species, Sodom Apple,
Spiraled Acacia,
Umbrella Thorn Acacia, Moringa,
Toothbrush Tree,Christ Thorn,
Date Palm

Beersheba

EGYPT

Negev and Arava Valley
Euphrates Poplar, Acacias,
Doun Palm, Tamerisk

Above: A hand-drawn map of the approximate ecological zones of Israel and adjacent regions showing where the main kinds of trees and larger shrubs occur. All boundaries, ecological and political, are indicative only. (Note that in desert regions some species only grow next to water by rivers and at oases e.g. Euphrates poplars and palms).

Compendium

Trees and shrubs are listed in alphabetical order of their common name in English. They are grouped into three:

- Those in the Bible that are named or may be implied.
- Some other native species of the eastern Mediterranean.
- Some other trees and shrubs that visitors to the eastern Mediterranean may come across.

The latter two are not exhaustive.

For each entry we try to provide some helpful notes without being a definitive field guide. The notes are based on personal observations, those of others and several excellent guides and books which are listed at the end. Some of the entries are illustrated, some are not but were earlier in the book and some, notably the few at the end about some other trees and shrubs visitors might come across, are not. Comment is made about occurence in UK. All may be found in large countries e.g. USA wherever climate is suitable.

Many of the illustrations in the first section concerning biblical trees and shrubs were photographed in the Jerusalem Botanic Garden.

It bears repeating that certain identification of biblical species is not always possible.

Trees and larger shrubs in the Bible—named and may be implied

ACACIA

NEGEV ACACIA
Acacia gerardii

COMMON ACACIA
Acacia raddiana

UMBRELLA THORN
Acacia tortilis

A huge genus of trees across the world, but species of the Eastern Mediterranean are mostly confined

Top: Negev Acacia (*Acacia gerardii*) Photo: F. Leung

Middle: Common acacia (*Acacia raddiana*) Photo: F. Leung

Above: Umbrella thorn (*Acacia tortilis*)

to desert and semi-desert environments. Desert acacias are hardy, and very long lived and are found in and around wadis and oases. The '*shittim*' in

Hebrew. Three species are common in Israel, and the Bible doesn't distinguish between them.

All acacias have pinnate leaves (like walnut or ash though much finer) with each leaf itself made up of rows of tiny leaflets. The foliage is thorny to resist browsing, but is very palatable to livestock being rich in nitrogen. Flowers are usually white or creamy and produce the familiar pods characteristic of the pea (legume) family. Negev acacia pods are long and banana shaped, those of common acacia and umbrella thorn are curled. The Negev acacia looks rather disordered in growth habit compared with the more familiar 'mushroom' shapes of the other acacias.

Wood of desert acacias is durable, stable and can be used for furniture.

Bible: many references in Old Testament. e.g. Exod. 26:15.

UK: No desert acacias hardy enough, but an Australian acacia, mimosa (*A. decurrens*), succeeds in the milder south and west.

ALGUM AND ALMUG

A tree(s) only named in connection with Solomon's timber imports in connection with the temple. The 2011 NIV considers the names as variants of each other. Others make a good case for two species: algum as possibly either Grecian juniper (*Juniperus excelsa*) or boxwood (*Buxus sempervirens*) imported through King Hiram for making the steps and stairs in the temple, and almug as the Indian red sandalwood (*Pterocarpus santalinus*) imported from Ophir (India?) for its fragrant, scented wood with exceptional working qualities fit for musical instruments.

Bible: 1 Kings. 10:11–12; 2 Chron. 2:8 & 9:10–11.

UK: Box is native, Grecian juniper can be found in a few arboreta. Sandalwood is not hardy.

ALMOND

Prunus dulcis (syn. *Amygdalus communis, Prunus amygdalus, P. communis*)

Wild almond found scattered throughout Israel. It is the widely cultivated variety (usually labelled *P. dulcis*) that is famous for its nuts and also its profuse white blossom in late winter, a herald of spring. Indeed it flowers close to Israel's national tree day (Tu Bishvat), which in 2013 fell on 26 January, and goes on flowering for up to a month. Flowering almonds do not occur in the Sinai (though they do grow on the hills of the Negev), but they may once have because 'almond-shaped' was a key decoration of the candelabrum for the Tabernacle fashioned when the children of Israel were wandering in the desert.

Both the Hebrew '*shaked*' and '*luz*' are safely identified as almond, the words derive from different roots in semitic languages.

Bible: Num. 17:8; Eccles. 12:5

UK: Almond is quite common, especially in southern England where it flowers in early March well before the leaves flush. Has very dark almost black bark. Tree is short-lived.

ATLANTIC PISTACHIO—SEE TEREBINTH

APPLE

Malus domestica

Probably introduced into Israel from Turkey or Iran in late Neolithic times. Many guides to biblical species refer to *Malus sylvestris* (crab apple), but its distribution is no further south than northern Turkey and the Caucasus. For example charred fruits of the sweet 'domestic apple' have been found near Kadesh Barnea (southern Israel) dating to the 10th Century BC. There are numerous varieties and cultivars producing the fruit we love, but it seems that selection and domestication of the apple was much later than figs and olives.

Eve didn't take an apple; we don't know what forbidden fruit tempted her.

Bible: Song 2:5; Joel 1:12

UK: Both apple orchards and our native crab apple are common.

BALSAM (BALM OF GILEAD)

Commiphora gileadensis

A tropical tree that was once widely cultivated around Jericho and the Jordan Valley for its precious healing resin. Many classical writers refer to the balm groves. Legend accords the Queen of Sheba as introducing the tree when she visited Solomon and it is likely that Queen Hatshepsut introduced it to Egypt from Punt (probably Eritrea or Somalia) around 1465 BC.

Bible: several references e.g. Gen. 37:25. Some translations wrongly cite Balsam as the trees to guide David when attacking the Philistines (2 Sam. 5:23–24). They were Euphrates poplars.

UK: not hardy.

FALSE BALSAM
Balanites aegyptica
Musselman (2012) in his *Dictionary of Bible Plants* (CUP) suggests that the Balm of Gilead referred to by Jeremiah (Jer. 8:2 & 46:11) is the resin of terebinth trees. This is probably the large woody shrub *Pistacia lentiscus* found in oak-terebinth woodland in Gilead (the mountains to the east of the River Jordan and now in Jordan).

BEAN TREE (ALSO BEN OIL TREE, HORSE RADISH TREE OR, SIMPLY, MORINGA)
Moringa peregrina
A dozen or so Moringa species occur in the Horn of Africa, India and SW Asia. Several are valued in the drier tropics and sub-tropics in agro-forestry e.g. *Moringa oleifera*, for rapid growth, enrichment of soil by nitrogen, livestock feed, fuelwood etc. Some species have seeds which cause flocculation of sediment and impurities in water. In Ancient Egypt ben oil was used in cooking and cosmetics. Bean tree in Israel occurs in desert wadis, e.g. Ein Gedi, and has very long pods up to 30 cm.

Bible: may have been the 'tree' or 'piece of wood' Moses used to turn sweet the bitter waters of Marah (Ex. 15:25)

UK: not hardy. Not to be confused with the Indian Bean tree from America (*Catalpa bignonioides*)

BRIERS—SEE THORNS

BROOM (WHITE)
Retama raetam
Fairly tall desert and wilderness shrub in Israel, Arabia and, indeed, around the Sahara. Often in dry river beds, rocky areas and sandy soils. Can be small tree in favourable conditions. Fragrant white flowers. Famed for its thick long roots which help stabilise sand dunes and make excellent firewood

with embers retaining heat for an unusually long time.

Bible: 1 Kg. 19:4; Job 30:3–4. May have been the bush under which Hagar laid Ishmael when they were dying of thirst (Gen. 21:14–15)

UK: not hardy.

CAROB (ALSO CALLED 'ST JOHN'S BREAD, AND ALGARROBA BEAN)
Ceratonia siliqua
Open woodland species with edible fruit in long straight or curly pods. Often planted. Uniform seeds once used as measuring weights.

May have been the food John the Baptist ate in the wilderness and the pods Jesus refers to in the parable of the prodigal son.

Bible: Matt. 3:4; Luke 15:16. Surprisingly not mentioned in the Old Testament.

UK: not hardy.

CEDAR
Atlas cedar (*Cedrus atlantica*)
Cedar of Lebanon (*Cedrus libani*)
Two true cedars of the Mediterranean which intergrade in characteristics of foliage and cone

Above: Atlas cedar (*Cedrus atlantica*)

Top: Cedar of Lebanon *(Cedrus libani)* Young cedars in Jerusalem Botanic Garden

Above: Male flowers and cones on foliage

shape and size. Male flowers emit clouds of yellow pollen. Cones born on top of branch, like the firs, and breakdown *in situ* so are rarely found fallen on the ground. Famed throughout Classical times as the most prized of timbers, especially cedar of Lebanon which only occurs naturally in the mountains of Lebanon, Syria, southern Turkey and possibly Cyprus. Atlas cedar is the cedar of Morocco and North Africa, but the species do intergrade. The similar deodar cedar occurs in the western Himalayas.

Many other conifers have cedar in their name e.g. western red cedar (*Thuya plicata*) and pencil cedar (*Juniperus virginiana*), as do several tropical timbers called 'cedar': none has any botanical relation with the true cedars, the name is used or copied to indicate quality!

Bible: Many references to cedar of Lebanon in Kings and Chronicles for building Solomon's temple, palaces, and the second temple. Many symbolic references, as the finest of trees, in the prophets. Cedar of Lebanon would be the largest and most impressive tree known to people living in the Levant.

UK: Both cedars, and intermediate forms, widely planted and very popular in 18th and 19th Century as ornamental in gardens and estates of great houses and stately homes. An original introduction of cedar of Lebanon from 1638 is still growing vigorously in the grounds of Old Childrey Rectory, near Wantage.

CHRIST-THORN (CHRIST'S THORN JUJUBE, SIDDER)

Ziziphus spina-Christi

Many *Ziziphus* or jujube species occur in the drier more semi-arid parts of the Eastern Mediterranean and elsewhere. All are thorny shrubs or small trees of the wilderness and desert. Christ-thorn achieves tree stature and like so many plants with spiny or thorny foliage to resist browsing it is most prickly near ground level. High up in the crown thorns and spines are few: the same is true of holly in Britain. Christ-thorn bears edible fruits, but the tree has the undesirable characteristic of preventing other plants growing in the vicinity. It is the first to be cleared from land that is needed for farming.

Top and above: Christ-thorn (Christ's Thorn jujube, Sidder) *Ziziphus spina-Christi*   **Right:** Cypress foliage (Evergreen or Italian cypress)

Bible: probably the '*atad*' in the Hebrew and the tree of Jotham's fable (Judg. 9:7–15). Candidate for Christ's crown of thorns (John 19:2).

UK: not hardy.

CITRON
Tetraclinis articulata
A small, rare conifer confined to north Africa with tiny populations also in south-east Spain and in Malta where it is the national tree. Much sought-after for cabinet wood in Classical times; so valuable as to be worth its weight in gold. Sometimes called thuya wood or thyine wood. In Roman times unsustainable quantities were shipped to Greece and Italy from north Africa.

Bible: Rev. 18:12
UK: rare

Not to be confused with same English name, citron, of fruit of *Citrus medica*.

CYPRESS (EVERGREEN OR ITALIAN CYPRESS)
Cupressus sempervirens
Striking tree throughout the Mediterranean, particularly the columnar form with its dark, cigar-shaped appearance. Once native to Israel and one of the conifers probably included in the Hebrew term '*berosh*'. Paul, the other apostles and disciples would have often seen it on their travels. Both the wood of Noah's Ark and that of the cross may have been cypress.

Bible: Probably *not* imported for building the temple, when Solomon ordered cedar, juniper and fir, because local sources were likely to be available in Israel as the tree was common at the time.

Top: Sycomore-fig *(Ficus sycomorus)*

UK: although thought to have been introduced about 1500 it is uncommon and only occasionally seen in parks and gardens of stately homes. It can grow to 20m. Recommended for topiary work by RHS. Ornamental narrow forms used in landscaping.

DATE PALM (SEE PALM)

EBONY
Diospyros ebenum or possibly *Dalbergia melanoxylon*
Not the tropical ebony, but a single mention in the Bible as an important traded timber (Ezek. 27:15). Uncertain species identification. Clearly the wood was strikingly black and much valued.

FIG
COMMON FIG
Ficus carica
SYCOMORE FIG
Ficus sycomorus
The fig genus (*Ficus*) is large, about 750 species, and very largely tropical where many species grow by clambering up and entwining other trees for support and then taking them over. The world's oldest planted tree of which we have reasonably sure records is the Bodhi tree in Sri Lanka (*Ficus religiosa*). In the Bible we meet two figs, the common fruiting fig and the sycomore-fig.

The common fig has been cultivated for its sweet fruit, which can be eaten freshly picked and when dried, from the very earliest of times. Pollination and reproduction is complex and involved. It will go on fruiting for about 50 years before showing signs of decline. The Sycomore-fig also produces edible fruit, achieves substantial tree size and furnishes an everyday timber which was used for coffin boards in ancient Egypt and for general purpose use across the eastern Mediterranean. Very widely distributed.

Both figs have large leaves, the sycomore-fig's can be over a foot across, larger than an A4 sheet.

Bible: The common fig is the first identifiable tree (Gen. 3:7) and numerous later mentions. One of the 'seven species' of the promised land (Deut. 8:8). Feature in several incidents in the New Testament, while the sycomore-fig is famous as the tree Zacchaeus climbed in order to see Jesus (Luke 19:4).

UK: Sycomore-fig is not hardy, but common figs grow well on sunny south facing walls and will even achieve large size, up to 20 ft, and can produce edible fruit in a warm summer.

FIR, CILICIAN
Abies cilicica
One of the conifers probably included in the

Above: Fir, Cilician *(Abies cilicica)*

Above: Fir, Cilician *(Abies cilicica)*

Top and above: Judas Tree *(Cercis siliquastrum)*

Hebrew term '*berosh*'. Occurs in the same stands in the mountains of Syria, Lebanon, and possibly Turkey, as cedar of Lebanon and juniper and probably exploited with these other species. This is a true fir of the *Abies* genus, but many conifers are loosely and lazily called 'fir trees' which really are pines, cypress, juniper or spruce for example.

Bible: certain identity not sure, but may have been used in building the temple (1 Kgs & 1 Chron.)

UK: rare, confined to tree collections, but will make an elegant tree capable of exceeding 100 ft.

FRANKINCENSE
Boswellia sacra
Incense was a traded commodity and came mainly

from the frankincense tree. Not native to Israel or Egypt, where it was much used, but to the Horn of Africa and Arabian peninsula.

A small tree of the semi-desert and today much over-exploited and endangered.

Bible: Many references to burning incense in Old Testament e.g. Exod. 30:34 and as one of the gifts presented to the infant Jesus (Matt. 2:11).

UK: not hardy

JUDAS TREE
Cercis siliquastrum
A small tree displaying lovely pink pea-shaped flowers, slightly resembling drops of blood, which grow directly on the trunk or branch. The dark crimson flower buds may persist unopened for

Top: Grecian juniper *(Juniperus excelsa)*

Above: Phoenician juniper *(Juniperus phoenicia)*

JUNIPER
GRECIAN JUNIPER
Juniperus excelsa
PHOENICIAN JUNIPER
Juniperus phoenicia

Two juniper species may feature in the Bible but neither is explicit though the 2011 NIV does translate '*berosh*' as juniper in connection with the timber imported for the temple.

The Grecian juniper is a tall tree and occurs quite widely in the mountains from the Balkans to Asia Minor and may grow in mixture with cedar of Lebanon and Cilician fir. Has an aromatic wood of high quality. Was imported by Solomon for the temple and his palace, but was probably also present in the forests on Mt Hermon.

The Phoenician juniper is a woody shrub of the desert margins occurring throughout the Eastern Mediterranean and North Africa. It is common in northern Sinai, and may be the 'cedar' in Leviticus, used as part of the ritual for cleansing mildew from houses because of strongly aromatic foliage possessing some anti-fungal properties when used as a fumigant, and in the water of cleansing in Numbers.

Bible: Phoenician juniper: possibly Lev. 14:51 and Num. 19:6. Grecian juniper: 1 Kgs. 5:8 and 2 Chron. 2:8.

UK: Both very rare and only in collections. Our native juniper, *Juniperus communis*, is very widely distributed and can even be found in Asia Minor (Turkey) but is not a biblical species.

MORINGA (SEE BEAN TREE)

MULBERRY
Two species have long been cultivated in Israel, but neither is native.

BLACK MULBERRY OR SYCAMINE
Morus nigra
WHITE MULBERRY
Morus alba
White Mulberry is the tree cultivated for silk industry.

Only the black mulberry is mentioned in the

weeks, so prolonging the 'looking like drops of blood' phase. Has typical pods (10 cm) of the pea (legume) family and paired heart-shaped leaves but without a tip. Only achieves about 6 m (20 ft) in Israel. Association with Judas Iscariot is questionable.

Bible: not named

UK: Introduced before 1600 (by the crusaders?) and frequent in parks and gardens of the south. Flowers in May. Some specimens achieve 10 m (30 ft).

Bible. It is quite a common tree producing edible fruits rather like elongated raspberries. When ripe they are darkish red. The tree is difficult to uproot.

Sycamine (black mulberry) is no relation of sycomore-fig, or sycamore (of the maple family), but similarity of names is source of confusion.

Bible: Luke 17:6?, possibly the durable wood referred to in Isaiah 40:20.

UK: Black mulberry is quite common in parks and gardens in the south and can grow up to 12 m (40 ft)

MUSTARD

Not a tree or really a shrub, see text page 130.

MYRRH

Commiphora myrrha

Several species of myrrh, but the incense, cosmetics and ointments come from myrrh occurring in Somalia, Oman and Yemen as a large woody shrub of the semi-desert. Exudations of myrrh are stimulated by cutting the bark and the reddish aromatic resin that oozes out is collected in baskets.

One of the three gifts presented to the infant Jesus; myrrh is more precious than frankincense. Solomon greatly appreciated it using it several times as a metaphor for the preciousness of his lover in the Song of Solomon. The Egyptians had known it for thousands of years and it was used at Christ's death both when mixed with wine as a drink when he was crucified and with aloes as part of the ritual for treating or embalming the body of the deceased.

Bible: Several Old Testament e.g. Gen. 37:25, Ps. 45:8 and Song. 1:13. New Testament Matt. 2:11, Mark 15:23 and John 19:39–40. Also. Rev. 18:13

UK: Not hardy.

MYRTLE

Member of the *Myrtaceae* family to which myrtle gives its name. The family includes the huge genus, *Eucalyptus*.

COMMON MYRTLE

Myrtus communis

A delightful evergreen shrub or small tree of drier parts. Foliage is scented owing to numerous tiny

Above: Kermes oak *(Quercus calliprinos)*

glands in the leaves. Has delicate creamy-white flowers with a prominent spread of stamens.

Bible: Isaiah 41:19 & 55:13 where it is prophesied as replacing scrub and thorny plants; and it is one of the species used in the Feast of Tabernacles (Neh. 8:15).

UK: Uncommon, but available from larger garden centres. This lovely shrub will need protecting from frost, and especially cold persistent winds.

OAK

A huge genus of many hundreds of species of which three oaks are native to Israel, and are also widespread in eastern Mediterranean countries. Probably only two mentioned in the Bible.

CYPRUS OAK

Quercus boissieri syn. Q. infectoria subsp. veneris—may not be mentioned in Bible. Also known as Aleppo oak.

KERMES OAK

Quercus calliprinos syn. *Q. coccifera* subsp. *calliprinos* evergreen. Also known as Palestine oak.

TABOR OAK

(*Quercus ithaburensis* syn. *Q. aegilops*. Also known as Vallonea oak.

Cyprus oak is confined to northern Israel, both the Kermes or evergreen oak and Tabor oak are widespread in the Judean hills, Upper Galilee and towards the sea. In drier parts Kermes oak is often no larger than a prickly shrub with leaves resembling holly, but in favourable conditions it achieves large size e.g. on lower slopes of Mt Hermon. Tabor oak generally achieves greater stature and is often seen as a fine individual, just like a hedgerow oak in England, as well as in open woodland. Both oaks have the familiar acorns (the Tabor oak's are large) and the familiar fissured bark.

Several other species of oak are found around the Mediterranean and North Africa. In Classical times oaks were often accorded sacred status thus wreaths were often of oak leaves, sometimes fashioned in gold, and the oak leaf motif decorated many a Greek and Roman temple. The wreaths referred to in Acts 14:13, which the priest of the temple of Zeus tried to present to Paul and Barnabas, thinking they were the gods Hermes and Zeus, were probably of oak leaves and possibly of gold.

Bible: Oak trees feature often as places of commemoration and as where the wayward Israelites offered sacrifices to and worshipped other gods. Sometimes terebinth trees are called 'oak' in the bible, but they are not true oaks; they just look a bit like them both in general appearance and in their bark.

UK: Kermes and Tabor oak are rare, occurring in some gardens and arboreta. Present in the national oak collection in the Hillier Gardens, Hampshire.

OLIVE
Olea europaea
The oldest tree in cultivation? Hard olive stones found in many archaeological excavations of very early civilizations. The olive family, *Oleaceae*, is large and almost all the genera have species with opposite leaves and include familiar trees and shrubs such as common ash, lilac, privet and forsythia.

Widely cultivated in orchards and groves. Can achieve very great age (>1000 years) and can cope with very varied moisture conditions. Trees have remarkable abilities of recovery and rejuvenation through coppice shoots and root suckers, but many orchard trees are managed as a form of pollard with shoots cut back at about 2–2.5 m above ground—so that new growth sprouts out of reach of goats! Traditionally olive trees are never cut down or uprooted. One tree yields about 10–20 kg of olives from which 1–2 kg of oil can be pressed. Good harvest years alternate with poorer ones. Olives have numerous uses: the oil from pressed olives is used in cooking, cosmetics, and illumination; the wood is excellent for carving and handicrafts.

Bible: Numerous references. One of the 'seven species' of the promised land—a land of olives (Deut. 6:11 & 8:8). Olive branches symbolise peace and hope. Mount of Olives to the east of Jerusalem and Gethsemane (the olive press).

UK: Not common, but several varieties hardy enough. Seen in parks and gardens.

PALM
Well-known and easily recognised trees which fall into two main groups, those with leaves (branches) like the date and coconut palms and those where the leaves form a fan like the doum palm.

DATE PALM
Phoenix dactylifera

DOUM PALM
Hyphaene thebaica
Only the date palm is referred to in the Bible, though the Israelites would have been familiar with the doum palm from all their years in Egypt where it was and still is very common on the banks of the River Nile. As well as fans of leaves, the doum palm usually has a widely forked trunk. Date palm is one of the 'seven species' of promise (Deut. 8:8)—'honey' refers to a sugary liquid made from dates, not to honey from bees as widespread as that would have been.

Date palms are the quintessential tree of desert oases and wadis throughout northern Africa and the Middle East. Long cultivated for its sweet dates, while its trunk and branches are put to many uses—rough building, matting, ropes, roofing materials etc..

Bible: Many references, notably Jericho the 'city of palms' (Deut. 34:3) and Palm Sunday (John 12:13).

UK: Not hardy

Top left and right: Aleppo or Jerusalem pine
(Pinus halepensis)—native to Israel

Left and above: Stone or Umbrella pine *(Pinus pinea)*

PINE

A large conifer genus and amongst the most important for commercial timbers worldwide. Several Mediterranean pine species, only one is native to Israel, but others may be mentioned or implied in the Bible.

ALEPPO OR JERUSALEM PINE
Pinus halepensis—native to Israel

CANARY ISLAND PINE
Pinus canariensis

CYPRUS PINE
Pinus brutia.
Also called Turkish or Calabrian pine.

STONE OR UMBRELLA PINE
Pinus pinea

All four pines are commonly seen in Israel and throughout the Mediterranean. Aleppo pine has been much used in afforestation and looks a little like Britain's native Scots pine (*Pinus sylvestris*) with orange bark and similar sized needles. Stone pine is readily identified from its umbrella shaped crown in older trees—anyone holidaying in the Mediterranean will have seen it, notably by the coast. The seeds inside the large cones of stone pine are edible and are often on sale. Cyprus pine is similar and closely related to Aleppo pine and has also been used in afforestation. Canary Island pine used in recent plantings in Upper Galilee.

Bible: The tree name *'tirzah'* in Hebrew appears only in Isaiah 44:14 and may be stone pine. 2011 NIV has it just as pine but there is uncertainty. Aleppo pine may be the correct translation for the five mentions of *'etz shemen'* in the Old Testament, rather than 'wild olive' (Neh. 8:15) or 'olive wood' in 1 Kgs. 6:23 & 31, according to Zohary (1982). In the latter case Aleppo pine would certainly be suitable for fashioning the cherubim and the doors of Solomon's temple. Aleppo pine was much commoner in Israel in biblical times than it is today.

UK: All four pines can be seen in arboreta and botanic gardens.

PISTACHIO (SEE TEREBINTH)

PLANE (ORIENTAL PLANE)
Platanus orientalis
In the natural environment, a handsome long-lived tree of river banks often seen with white poplar and willows. Has been widely planted as specimen or individual trees in parks and towns throughout the Mediterranean. Has typically large, indented, hand-shaped (palmate) leaves like those of London Plane (of which it is probably one of the parents of this famous hybrid). Its fruits are balls, almost golf ball size, hanging on a long stalk like a Christmas tree bauble. Israel's tallest native tree is an oriental plane.

Bible: Jacob included peeled plane tree branches in breeding sheep (Gen. 30:33). One of the trees that could not rival the cedars in the garden of God (Ezek. 31:8).

UK: Seen from time to time in parks and gardens of the south. Better known as one of the parents of London plane.

POMEGRANATE
Punica granatum
Long cultivated for its fruit. On most soils it yields two harvests each year and with its bright scarlet flowers seems always to be in production. Pomegranate orchards are very colourful.

Bible: Pomegranate motifs were woven into and hung from the hem of the priest's robe (Exod. 28:33–34). One of the seven species of promise (Deut. 8:8) and included in the fruits the spies brought back (Num. 13:23). A metaphor of beauty and desire in the Song of Solomon (Song. 4:3). Many references along with other fruit trees.

UK: Not hardy, but some do survive in London suburbs.

POPLAR
A large genus of mostly fast growing trees usually associated with streams and riversides. Two species native to Israel and present throughout Middle East.

WHITE POPLAR
Populus alba

EUPHRATES POPLAR
Populus euphratica

Above: Pomegranate (*Punica granatum*)

Top and above: Leafless Tamarisk *(Tamarix aphylla)*

to be at garden boundaries and in parks. Has many varieties.

SYCAMINE (SEE MULBERRY)

SYCOMORE (SEE FIG, SYCOMORE)

TAMARISK

LEAFLESS TAMARISK
Tamarix aphylla

JORDAN TAMARISK
(Tamarix jordanis) (not mentioned in the Bible)

Known as leafless tamarisk because it is the twigs that are green and photosynthesise. A tree of the desert and wadis. Tolerant of saline (salty) soil conditions i.e. a halophyte. It excretes salt through glands in its 'leaves' which, as the moisture evaporates, cools the air making it a lovely shade tree in the hot desert. Small white flowers bloom in the autumn.

Top and above: Atlantic terebinth or Atlantic pistachio *(Pistacia atlantica)* (see page 174)

Both poplars can make striking specimens. Impressive white poplars trace out the course of the Dan river in northern Israel. When young, Euphrates poplar is willow-like with long sinuous leaves. Can be seen beside the River Jordan especially the more southerly stretches towards the Dead Sea as the tree has some tolerance of salty water.

Bible: Jacob included peeled white poplar branches in breeding sheep (Gen. 30:33). Euphrates poplar was the tree on which the harps were hung in exile in Babylon (Ps. 137:1–3) and where David was instructed to muster his army when fighting the Philistines (2 Sam. 5:23–24). Possibly the willow of the 'four species' of the feast of Tabernacles.

UK: White poplar was an early introduction and is quite common, but being a large tree tends

Jordan tamarisk is a common small tree or shrub occurring on many stream sides and riverbanks in the Jordan, Hula Valley and Golan regions.

Bible: Leafless tamarisk is the tree Abraham planted in Beersheba (Gen. 21:33) to mark the treaty.

UK: Not hardy. Other tamarix shrubs can grow in UK.

TEREBINTH

ATLANTIC TEREBINTH OR ATLANTIC PISTACHIO
(Pistacia atlantica)

PALESTINE TEREBINTH
(Pistacia palaestina)

LENTISK BUSH
(Pistacia lentiscus)—a possible balm of Gilead source.

The Atlantic terebinth is the 'terebinth' of the Bible, but often 'oak' in older translations. Terebinth in this book refers to this species. The confusion arises from the Hebrew '*elah*' and '*alah*', which should be rendered terebinth, being similar to '*elon*' and '*allon*' which are the true oak. Further confusion occurs because from a distance the tree looks like an oak and it has oak-like bark – see page 173!

A large spreading tree with pinnate leaves. Some species achieve great age with gnarled and knobbly trunks.

Bible: Many references. It was under terebinths

Above: Walnut, common (*Juglans regia*)

that foreign gods were buried (Gen. 35:4), much idolatry occurred, and also convenants renewed (Josh. 24:26). Absalom caught his hair in the branches of a terebinth as he rode away from battle (2 Sam. 18:9).

UK: Not hardy.

THORNS

Many species of the Middle East bear spines, thorns or prickles to resist browsing by goats sheep and camels. Trees and shrubs include acacias, spiny broom, Palestine buckthorn, prickly burnet, spiny hawthorn (*Crataegus*), Christ-thorn and lotus jujubes (*Ziziphus* spp.), and the prickly foliage of some oaks.

Bible: Many references to wilderness, thorns and briers in inhospitable or uncultivated land.

WALNUT, COMMON
Juglans regia

Widely cultivated nut species throughout Mediterranean. It is native from eastern Turkey to central Asia and probably introduced into the Levant in Bronze Age times. In Israel mostly seen as single trees, though Josephus, writing in the 1st Century AD, mentions groves of walnuts cultivated in the valley of Genesaret. It was a greatly prized food throughout the Roman Empire. Leaves are strongly pinnate. The familiar globular nuts are inside a woody shell, itself enclosed by a green-yellow husk that stains the hands when peeled.

Bible: One probable reference in Song of Solomon 6:11.

UK: Fairly common in sunnier and warmer south. Introduced by Romans. Yields some fruit but most valued for its prized timber. The last tree species to flush in spring, usually in late May or early June. Frost tender in UK. Selected good fruiting forms were often cultivated at monasteries.

WILLOW

A huge genus of 300 species across north temperate to Mediterranean regions.

COMMON WILLOW
Salix acmophylla (probably the willow of the Bible).

Above: *Salix acmophylla* (probably the willow of the Bible)

WHITE WILLOW
Salix alba

Both species are common trees of riverbanks, wetlands and around oases; often seen beside the River Jordan in the upper parts in the vicinity of the Sea of Galilee. Willow branches are one of the four species of the Feast of Tabernacles.

Bible: Five mentions with willow the translation of the Hebrew '*aravah*' e.g. Lev. 23:40 and Is. 44:3–4. The question of correct translation of Ps. 137:2 was noted earlier (page 173).

UK: *Salix alba* is native to UK as well as much of Europe and Middle East. Weeping willow is a variety of it as is 'cricket bat' willow. The so-called weeping willow, *Salix babylonica*, is a Chinese tree that grows poorly in UK and has nothing to do with Babylon (Euphrates poplar was the tree on which harps were hung during the exile), but is a cultivated tree in Israel.

Above: Sweet chestnut (*Castanea sativa*)

ASH
Fraxinus angustifolia subsp. *syriaca*
Occurs in Israel in the moister north e.g. Dan Reserve. Not as large as English ash but has similar characteristic 'keys', the bundles of winged seeds.

LAUREL OR BAY
Laurus nobilis
Occurs in moister parts e.g. Upper Galilee. Tough fragrant dark green leaves. Leaves were woven for victors' wreaths. Paul writing of the 'victor's crown' in 2 Tim. 2:5 and possibly Peter referring to the 'crown of glory' (1 Pet. 5:4) may have had such wreaths of laurel leaves in mind.

My mother would add a couple of laurel leaves to the water in which potatoes were boiled to add flavour: we had a laurel bush in our back garden in south-east London.

MAPLE, CRETAN
Acer sempervirens
Common tree of south-east Europe and west Asia as far south as southern Turkey. Very drought and heat tolerant for a maple. Has typical maple leaves palmate in shape, very similar to but much smaller than those of common sycamore.

OLEANDER
Nerium oleander
A shrub of stream sides and semi-desert shrub with lovely pink flowers. Occurs around Petra (Jordan), as constituent of riverine vegetation in Upper Galilee and in seasonal watercourses in vicinity of Mt Carmel. Mentioned in the Apocrypha. A poisonous plant especially its sap.

PHILLYREA
Phillyrea latifolia
Small tree with tiny hard dark-green leaves. The leaves are a little prickly and not unlike those of Kermes oak except that they are in opposite pairs

STRAWBERRY TREE

Above: Yew (*Taxus baccata*)

Arbutus andrachne
Has sweet edible fruits. Quite common in the vicinity of Mt Carmel and Upper Galilee. The strawberry tree of Ireland (*Arbutus unedo*) is the only species native to that country which isn't native to the UK.

SWEET CHESTNUT
Castanea sativa
Cultivated for its nutritious nuts. Introduced to UK by the Romans. A species demanding acid soils for good growth. Widely managed or regenerated by coppicing. Has a very durable timber looking much like oak, and substituted for it in many instances.

TOOTHBRUSH TREE
Salvadora persica
Very common large bush of semi-desert. Branch tips once used as tooth brushes. Recognised from a distance as a bush 'plonked' in the desert like the top of a mop.

YEW
Taxus baccata
The common English yew occurs throughout Europe and around the Mediterranean to North Africa and east to Iran.

A few other common trees visitors may see

APRICOT
Armeniaca vulgaris syn. *Prunus armeniaca*
Included here because apricot orchards are a fairly common sight, but the tree itself was probably not introduced into the Mediterranean basin until 3rd Century BC. Some have held that the Hebrew '*tappuah*' refers to apricot (Prov. 25:11—'apples of gold'— and several references in Song of Solomon) but unless special stands are implied, this fruit tree from China and east Asia wasn't available in Old Testament times.

CASUARINA

Casuarina equisetifolia
Casuarina cunninghamiana
Casuarina glauca

Australasian trees, the she-oak of Australia, widely used for stabilising sand dunes and planting on poor sites. Has dense wood which makes a good fuel. Enriches soil through fixing nitrogen. Leaves are like long fine needles, fruits not dissimilar to cypress cones but Casuarina is not a conifer. *C. equisetifolia* is a coastal shore-line species in eastern Mediterranean, other species planted more inland.

GUM TREES

RED RIVER GUM
Eucalyptus camaldulensis

BLUE GUM
Eucalyptus globulus

Australian gum trees (eucalypts) have been successfully planted throughout the world wherever winters are not severe. There are over 500 species but Red river gum for drier parts and blue gum for cooler locations are common throughout the Mediterranean. Blue gum so-called because young juvenile foliage is bluish and leaves much broader than the dark green, leathery and long, sinuous adult leaves. Blue gums are one of the few trees that goats will not browse.

JACARANDA

Jacaranda mimosifolia

The decorative town tree *par excellence* with stunning bluish-lilac flowers bedecking trees before the leaves emerge. Very popular throughout the Mediterranean and the towns and cities of the tropics and sub-tropics.

PEPPER TREE

Schinus molle

An excellent street and roadside tree seen throughout the tropics and sub-tropics as well as the Mediterranean. Leaves are very starkly pinnate.

Some guide books and information sources to trees and shrubs of the Bible

Seeing and growing biblical trees and shrubs

Alon, Azaria (2008) *Israel—National Parks & Nature Reserves*. A Carta Guide, Jerusalem. [A comprehensive guide to parks and reserves with a section headed 'Vegetation' in every entry. Less helpful for tree and plant identification, but good on what to expect to see.]

Darom, D. (undated) *Beautiful Plants of the Bible, from Hyssop to Mighty Cedar Trees*. Palphot Ltd. Herzlia, Israel. [Attractive well-illustrated booklet]

Hepper, F. Nigel (1992) *Illustrated encyclopedia of Bible Plants*. Inter-Varsity Press, Leicester. [The finest reference work on biblical trees and plants, their ecology and their uses.]

Hareuveni. Nogah (2006) *Tree and Shrub in Our Biblical Heritage*. Neot Kedumim, Lod, Israel. English translation by Helen Frenkley. [The book to have to go deep into Old Testament thinking and understanding about trees and shrubs, their significance and uses. Numerous citations of traditions of rabbis, sages and reference to other literature such as Midrash and Rabbinical writings.]

Kirshenbaum, N. (2007) *Trees and Shrubs of Israel—a Pocket Guide to Common Species*. Nature in Israel. [An excellent, inexpensive fold-out pocket guide to common trees and shrubs. A 'must' for first-time visitors.]

Musselman, L.J. (2012) *A Dictionary of Bible Plants*. Cambridge University Press, New York. [An up-to-date but *very* expensive book, both much shorter and adding little to Hepper (ibid). It has a helpful history of biblical plant literature.]

Zohary, Michael (1982) *Plants of the Bible*. Cambridge University Press. [A useful complement to Hepper (ibid) with emphasis on Hebrew etymology in identifying biblical species correctly.]

Outside of the Mediterranean basin only a few regions have a comparable climate—warm, wet winters and hot, dry summers—where biblical species will grow well. These include parts of California, the Cape region of South Africa, south-west Australia, and central Chile.

However, many of the species in this book have a wide natural distribution e.g. sycomore-fig across much of Africa, or are resilient and tolerant of many kinds of sites such as olive and cedar trees. Cedar is especially interesting as the cedar of Lebanon has only a small natural range, but is hugely adaptable and can be found widely planted, being such a beautiful tree, in European countries and the United States for example.

Almost all countries have national or regional collections of native and introduced plant species. They are known as botanic gardens or, if confined mainly to trees, as arboreta. Examples include The Royal Botanical Gardens, Kew, the Jerusalem Botanic Garden, and the Arnold Arboretum in USA. Such plant or tree collections have a scientific purpose and will often display their collections by regions. Biblical species will be found in the 'Mediterranean collections' and also where special greenhouses provide, say, a desert environment.

Owing to the supreme place of the Bible in our life and society, many have created biblical plant collections such as Neot Kedumim near Tel Aviv, the Bible Path in the Jerusalem Botanic Garden, and at St George's Cathedral, Jerusalem, all in Israel itself. Outside Israel such collections are often established in the grounds of cathedrals, abbeys, churches and monasteries. They will be only as complete as the climate permits. It is worth remembering that Israel is a very varied country from cool, moist hills and mountains to harsh, hot desert. In the UK we are able to grow quite easily

FACING PAGE: *The Garden Tomb, Jerusalem, where many biblical trees and shrubs grow*

about one-third of the species in this book such as cedar, fig, plane and walnut.

To find collections of biblical plants near you, use an internet search engine and enter: botanic garden, arboretum, bible plant collections.

Creating a biblical arboretum

Readers are referred to Nigel Hepper's *Planting a Bible Garden* Candle Books (2000) for a general bible garden, but if you are wanting to concentrate on a collection of trees and larger woody shrubs, to create your own biblical arboretum, the following are worth trying in a temperate climate. One or two are questionable concerning their biblical credentials.

Likely to succeed: almond, apple, black mulberry, box, cedar, fig, Judas tree, laurel, oriental plane, walnut, white poplar

Definitely worth a try: Aleppo pine, Italian cypress, olive, stone pine, Tabor oak,

Might succeed with care and protection: kermes oak, myrtle, pomegranate

In general for more tender species, choose south-facing, sheltered locations which are not frost pockets. Avoid windy conditions or places where winds funnel. Any reasonably well-drained soil should be suitable, but avoid very calcareous (chalky/limestone) ones.

Index

Index of Scriptural References

Genesis

1	4, 21
1:11–12	4, 130
1:11–13	4
1:12	8, 37
1:30	5
2, 3	7
2:8–25	7
2:9	8
2:9a	7
2:9b	8
3:6	3, 8
3:7	11, 166
3:17–18	11, 12
3:22	80
4	12
4:17	15
4:21	15
5–50	15
6	15
6:7,18	16
6:14	15
6:15–16	15
8:11	16
10–12	18
12:6	18, 46
13:18	20
14:7	45
14:13	20
14, 21, 23	19
18	20
18:4	20
18:8	20
21:14–15	163
21:15	19
21:33	19, 174
22:7	32
22:13	32
23:17	20
23:17–20	20
28:19	45
30 & 31	21
30:33	172, 173
30:37	113
30:37–43	21
31:12	21
35:4	18, 58, 174
37:25	123, 163, 169
43:11	35
46:29–30	21
49:29–32	21

Exodus

	15
2:2–3	15
3:1–3	22
3 & 15	22
9:24	79
15:22–25	23
15:25	163
16:27	24
20: 4–6	38
25:5; 35:4; 36:3	25
25:9; 27:8	25
25–27, 35–39	24
25, 30, 31, 37	26
25: 31–36; 37: 17–22	26
25–38	15
25–40	24
26:15	162
26:15–16	24
28:31–34; 39:22–25	26
28:33–34	172
30: 22–38; 37: 25–29	26
30:34	167
35:34	25
35–39	25
36:1–2	25
36:2	25

Leviticus

1–6	29
1:7 & 17; 3:5; 4:12	29
6:12–13	29

14	32
14:38	33
14:51	168
19:23; 23:40; 26:20; 27:30	33
19:23–25	33
19, 23, 26, 27	33
23:40	34, 74, 175
26:4, 20	34
27:30	34

Numbers

13	36, 44
13:23	172
13:27	37
14:7	37
15:32	29
17:8	162
17 & 20	35
19:6	33, 168
20:9–11	36
24:6	145
33:49	45

Deuteronomy

2:36	45
6:11; 8:8	37, 170
8:6–9	44
8:8	37, 166, 170, 172
13	38
13, 16	37
16:21	38, 46
19:5	38
19:20	41
19, 20, 22	38
20:19	38, 104
20:19–20	66, 137
20:20	39
21:22–23	39, 147
21:23	150
22:6–7	38
28:20–24	34
34:3	41, 45, 170

Joshua

1–24	41
2:1	24, 45
6:24	41
9:21, 23	59
13–19	41
13–21	44
13:26	45

15:33; 17:8	45
17:15, 18	44, 59
17:18; 18:1	7
18:1–10	44
19:7	45
19:33	45
21:45; 23:14	44
22:12	41
24:15	45
24:26	18, 45, 174
14–19	45
16:2	45
19:15, 21:35	45
24	45

Judges

1–10	45
3:13	41
4:5	45
6	46
6:11	45
6:26	46
6:31	46
7:22	45
9	47
9:6	18, 45
9:7–15	165
9:8	47
9:14–15	139
9:15	48
9:37	46
9:46–49	48
9:49	67
14	41
16	48
16:3	48
16:4–9	159
19	46

Ruth

1–4	48
1:6	48
2:7	49
2:23	51
3:7	51

1 Samuel

10	53
14:2	54
14:2; 22:6	46
14, 22, 31	54

14:24–45	55
17:2	45
22:5	45
22:6	55
31:13	55

2 Samuel

5	53
5:11	55
5:23–24	53, 163, 173
5:24	54
17–18	56
17:29	56
18	56, 57
18:6	45
18:9	56, 174

1 Kings

4	167
4: 29–34	57
5	57
5:6	59
5–7	60
5–8	55
5:8	58
5:9	60, 168
6	60, 62
6:7	62
6:15	58
6:18	62
6:19–22	62
6:23, 31	63
6:29, 32, 35	172
6:34	115
7:2–5	63
10	85
10:11–12	64
18:22	64, 162
18, 24	64
19:4	64
	163

2 Kings

2:19–22	23
2:21	23
3:4	48
6:5	39
12:2 & 22:6	64
12, 16–18, & 22	64
16:4; 17:10	64
17:16–17	64

18:13	65
24:10	65
25	109
25:21	67

1 Chronicles

	167
14:1	55
14:8–17	53
16:8–36	64
17:1	55
22:4	60, 63
22, 28	58
27:28	117
28	55

2 Chronicles

1, 2, 9	64
1:15; 9:27	64
2	59
2–3	55
2–7	58
2:8	59, 168
2:8; 9:10–11	64, 162
2:8–11	67, 85
3–4	62
3:5	79
3:16	62
7:14	58
9:23	79
28:5–8	88

Ezra

	69
1–10	69
3:7	62, 69, 115
5:8	69
6:3	69

Nehemiah

	69
2	70
2:8	70, 84
8:15	74, 169, 172
8:15–16	74
10:34	70
13:31	70

Esther

	69

1–9	69
2:12	83

Job

14:7–9	74, 88
14:8–9	74
14, 19, 40	74
19:10	75
19:25–26	75
30:3–4	163
40:15	75
40: 21–22	75

Psalms

1	99
1:3	76
1, 37, 52, 74, 83 & 92	76
29, 50, 96, 104, 105, 148	79
37	77
45:8	83, 124, 145, 169
50:10	79
52:8	77
74	78
74:5–6	78
83:14	78
92:12	78
92:12–14	97
92:13–14	67
96:12	79
104:16	79
104:17	79
104:20	79
105:32–33	79
105:33	79
137:1–3	173
137:2	175
148:9	80

Proverbs

3, 11, 13 & 14	80
3:18; 11:30; 13:12; 15:4	80
7:17	145
25:11	177

Ecclesiastes

2, 3, 11 & 12	80
2:4	73
2: 4–7	84
2:4–7	80
2:5	70

3:2	80
10:9	16
10:10	60
11:3	82
12:5	83, 162
12:7	83

Song of Solomon

1–3, & 5	83
1:13	169
1:13–14	83
1:17	83
2:3	83
2:4	85
2:5	162
2:11	84
3:9	84
4:3	172
4:6	84
4:13	70
4:13–14	84
5:4	84
5:5	84
5:10–16	84
6:11	84, 174

Isaiah

1, 2	87
1:29	79, 87
1:30	87
2:11	88
2:13	87
2:17	88
4:2	100, 121
6–11	88
6:13	88
6:29	74
7	88
7:13	88
7:17	88
7:23	88
9	88
9:6	92
9:10	88
9:18–19	88
10:15	88
10:18–19	89
10:33–34	89
11:1	51, 88, 89, 126
11:1, 10	75
13–24	89

13–35	89	1–10	97
14:8	89, 93	1:11	97
14, 17, 22, 29, 32, 35	89	2:20	97
15:7	93	2:27	97
17:6	90	3:6, 9	97
22	89, 91, 107	4:3	97
22:8	83, 91	4:29	98
22:22	92	5:6	98
22:23, 25	91	5:17	98
22:25	92	6:6	98
24:13	90	7:18	98
29:17	90	7:20	98
32:15	91	7:30–33	98
35:1–2	91	8:2; 46:11	163
36:16	93	10: 2–5	99
36, 37	93	10:3	60
36–39	93	11, 12, 15, 17	99
37:24	90, 93	11:16	99
37:36	98	11:18–23	99
40:19–20	93	12:2	99
40:20	131, 169	12:8	99
40, 41, 44, 53, 55	93	12.13	99
40–55	93	12:15	99
41:19	93, 96	15:1	99
41:19; 55:13	169	17:1–2	99
41:20	93	17:7–8	76
44:3–4	91, 175	17:7, 8	99
44:4	93	21:14	99
44:12–20	93	21, 22	99
44:14	172	22:7, 14, 15	100
44:19	94	22:16	100
44:23	94	22:23	100
45:20	94	23	100
53	94	23:5	100
53:2	89, 94	24	101
53:12	92, 94	26:8	102
55	94	29:11–14	103
55:1	94	31:5	103
55:12	94	31:15	103
55:12–13	94	31:31–34	103
55:13	94, 95	32	103
56:8	95	33:15	103
57:5	95	39:8	103
57, 60, 61, 65	95	46:22–23	103
60:13	96	49:19	103
61:3	96	50	103
65:17–25	97	50:44	103
65:22	97	50, 52	103
		51:37	103
Jeremiah		51:58	104
		51:64	104
1–5, 7, 10	97	52:16	104

Lamentations

	103
3, 5	105
3:22–26	105
5:1	105
5:6	105

Ezekiel

2:6	107
2, 6, 15–17	107
6:13	107
15	107
16	108
16:13	108
16:19	108
16–23	64
16:59	108
17:2	108
17:3–4	108
17:5–6	108
17:7–10	108
17:12–21	108
17:22–24	108
19:10–14	109
19, 20, 24	109
20:28	109
20:32	110
20:45–49	110
20:47	110
23	45
24:5, 9, 10	110
26–28	110
27:5–6	110
27:6	110
27:12–24	111
27:15	110
28:24	166
31	112
31:5	112
31:8	112
31:8–9	113, 172
31:10–18	112
31:13	112
34:25	112
34:27	113
34, 36, 39	113
36	113
36:8	113
36:30	113
36:35	113
39:9–10	113
	115

40, 41, 47	115
41:16	115
47:7	115
47:7–12	115
47:12	156

Daniel

4	4, 115
4:10–15	115
4:20–23	115
4:26	115

Hosea

	115
2	115
2:6; 9:6; 10:8	116
2:12	116
2:22–23	116
4:12–13; 11:2	116
10:12	97
14	116
14:5–8	79
14:5–9	117

Joel

	115
1:12	117, 162
2:28–32	91, 117
2:32	117

Amos

	117
1:1	117
2:9	117
4:9	117
7:14	117
7:14–15	117
9:13–15	117

Jonah

	118
4:6–10	118

Micah

	118
3:12	102, 118
4:3	118
4:4	118
6:8	118

6:15	118
7:1	118
7:14	118

Nahum

1:4–6, 10	118
1:10	118
2:3	118
2:15	118
3:12	66
	118

Habakkuk

2:17	118
3:17	118
	118

Zephaniah

1:4–5	118
2:14	118
	118

Haggai

1:4	118
1:5, 10–11	100
1:3	119
2:19	119
	119

Zechariah

1:2–6	118
1:8–11	119
1:11	120
1:13 & 17	120
3:8	120
4	121
4:3	156
4:12	120
6:12	120
8:12	120
10:2	119
10:4	118
11:1	121
14:4 & 8	121
	115

Malachi

3:11	118
	119

3:11–12	121
4:1	121

Matthew

2:1–12	123
2:11	167, 169
2:23	126
3:4	125, 163
3:7–10	125
4:18–22	127, 129
7:1–5	127
7:16–20	130
11:5	96
12:33	130
13:1–23	97
13:31–31	130
13:31–32	130
13:55	126
14:13	129
14:22–36	129
17:21	131
21	135
21:1	45
21:1–11	135
21:18–22	136
23:32	136
24:37–39	17
26:61	58
27:1–10	147
27:27–31	138
27:32	140
27:34	143
28:10	143

Mark

1:6	125
4:30–32	130
4:32	109
4:35–41	129
5:1–20	129
6:3	126
8:22–26	130, 131
11	135
11.1	45
11:12–14	136
11:12–14; 20–22	136
12:41–44	127
14:32–42	45
15:16–20	138
15:19	138
15:23	123, 143

15.23	169

Luke

1:8–10	123
1:63	124, 125
2:1–3	54
3:7–9	125
4:17	153
5:1–3	129
5:1–11	129
5: 43–45	130
6:41–42	127
7:22	96
13:5	132
13:6	131
13:6, 15:16; 17:6	130
13:18–19	130
15:11–32	125
15:16	132, 163
17:6	131, 169
17:26–27	17
19:1–10	133
19:4	11, 166
21:37 & 22:39	45
23:36	143
23:43	70
24:39	140

John

1:45–46	126
1:46	126
6:1	129
6:36	132
8:12	132
10:7, 9	132
10:11	132
11:25	132
11:44	143
12:13	170
14:6	132
14:26	25
15:1	132
19:1–5	138
19:2	165
19:17	140
19:39	143
19:39–40	124, 169
19:41	7
20:6–7	143
21143	
21:1–14	129

21:9	143
21:18–19	144

Acts

1–12	147
1:18–19	147
2	91
5:10 & 10:39	147
5:30	13
9:43; 10:6, 32	148
10:23–48	148
10:39	148
10:43	148
13–28	149
14:13	85, 170
18:3	117
23:6	150
27	150
27:37	149
27:40	154

Romans

8:21–22	79
11	150, 151
11:24	152
15:12	155

1 Corinthians

1:27	89
3:12	147, 153

2 Corinthians

11:23–29	149

Galatians

3:13	13, 147, 150

Philippians

2:10–11	109

1 Timothy

5:23	143

2 Timothy

2:5	176
4	153
4:3	102
4:13	153

Hebrews

10:10	32

James

2:10	70
3	153
3:4	150
3:5	153
3:12	4
3:9–12	154

1 Peter

2:24	3, 13, 92, 147
5:4	176

Jude

	154
12, 13	154

Revelation

2, 5–7, 9, 11, 18	154
2:7	154
5	155
5:5	89, 155
6:20	156
7:1 & 3, 9:4	156
7:9	156
8:7	156
9:20	156
11:4	156
18.12	165
18:13	123, 169
22	115, 147, 156
22:1	115
22:2	80
22:2–3	156
22:3	9
22:14, 19	158
22:16	51, 158

Index of tree species and some woody shrubs

A

Abies alba	111
Abies cilicica	96, 166
Acacia	21, 25, 77, 93, 117, 148, 161, 174
Acacia gerardii	161.
See Acacia	
Acacia raddiana	24, 161.
See Acacia	
Acacia tortilis	161.
See Acacia	
Acasia decurrens	162
Acer sempervirens	80, 176
Alder	74
Aleppo oak	51, 169
Aleppo or Jerusalem pine	171
Aleppo pine	74, 129, 132, 171
Algarroba bean	163
Algum	64, 162
Almond	21, 27, 33, 35, 83, 162
Almug	64, 162
Aloeswood	143
American plane	113
Amygdalus communis	162
Apple	81, 162
Apricot	177
Aquilaria spp.	143
Araucaria angustifolia	64
Arbutus unedo	177
Armeniaca vulgaris	177
Ash	3, 74, 170, 176
Atlantic pistachio	162, 174.
See Terebinth	
Atlantic terebinth	174
Atlas cedar	163
Australian acacia	162
Australian gum tree	95, 178
Azalea	77

B

Balanites aegyptica	163.
See False balsam	
Balm of Gilead	162.
See Balsam	
Balsam	162, 163
Baobab	8
Bay / laurel	176
Bean tree	163
Beech	44, 74

Ben oil tree. See moringa	
Birch	103
Blackberry	23
Black mulberry	131, 168, 169
Black mustard	130
Blackthorn	27
Blue gum	95, 178
Bodhi tree	166
Boswellia	124
Boswellia sacra	26, 167
Box	80, 141, 162
Boxthorn	138
Boxwood	162
Bracken	149
Brassica	130
Briers	163
Bristlecone pine	80
Broom (white)	163
Buxus sempervirens	80, 162

C

Canary Island pine	171
Carob	125, 129, 132, 163
Castanea sativa	176, 177
Casuarina	178
Casuarina cunninghamiana	178
Casuarina equisetifolia	178
Casuarina glauca	178
Catalpa bignonioides. See Indian Bean tree	
Cedar	58, 63, 79, 83, 87, 93, 100, 112, 117, 141, 163
Cedar of Lebanon	3, 22, 33, 48, 52, 57, 60, 63, 69, 78, 79, 87, 109, 113, 129, 163, 164
Cedar wood	33
Cedrus atlantica	163
Cedrus libani	3, 163, 164
Cercis siliquastrum	147, 167
Cherry	75, 81
Christ-thorn	47, 48, 107, 129, 138, 139, 144, 164, 174
Cider gum	95
Cilician fir	96, 111, 168
Citron	34, 156, 165
Citrus	34, 81
Coastal pine	112
Coast redwood	80
Commiphora	27
Commiphora gileadensis. See Balsam	
Commiphora myrrha	26, 83, 169
Common acacia	161.
See Acacia	
Common thorny burnet	138
Crab apple	162
Crataegus	174
Crataegus sinaica	22

Cretan maple   80, 81
Ctrus medica   34, 165
Cupressus sempervirens   15, 80, 143, 165
Cypress   3, 15, 22, 73, 93, 95, 96, 141, 143, 165
Cyprus oak   169
Cyprus pine   171, 172

D

Dalbergia melanoxylon   166
Date palm   33, 41, 79, 135, 138, 150, 166, 170
Desert acacia   24, 76
Dictamnus albus   22
Diospyros ebenum   166
Douglas fir   59
Doum palm   170

E

Ebony   166
English oak   20, 58
Eucalyptus   4, 77, 95, 130, 169
Eucalyptus camaldulensis   95, 178
Eucalyptus gunnii   95
Eucalyptus nitens   74
Euphrates poplar   160, 172, 173, 175
European Christ-thorn   138
Evergreen cypress   80, 165

F

False balsam   163
Ficus carica   11, 166
Ficus religiosa   38, 166
Ficus sycomorus   11, 166
FIg   11, 33, 36, 38, 44, 101, 124, 131, 136, 156, 166,
     173
Fir   58, 83, 93, 96
Fir, Cilician   166
Forsythia   170
Frankincense   26, 123, 124, 156, 167
Fraxinus angustifolia   176
Fraxinus excelsior   74

G

Gas-plant   22
Gopher wood   15
Grapes   36
Grape-vine   11, 109
Grecian juniper   64, 162, 168
Gum trees   178

H

Hawthorn   103

Hazel   74, 149
Henna   83
Hoary mustard   130
Hornbeam   130
Horse radish tree   163
Hyssop   33
Hyssopus officianalis   33

I

Indian Bean tree   163
Italian cypress   165, 180

J

Jacaranda   178
Jacaranda mimosifolia   178
Jerusalem thorn   138
Jordan tamarisk   173, 174
Judas tree   129, 147, 167
Juglans regia   84, 174
juniper   22, 33, 58, 63, 90, 93, 94, 96, 112, 168
Juniperus communis   33, 168
Juniperus excelsa   22, 64, 162, 168
Juniperus phoenicea   33, 168
Juniperus virginiana   164

K

Kermes oak   51, 58, 94, 169, 170
Knightwood oak   19

L

Larch   63
Laurel   129, 157, 176
Laurus nobilis   176
Lawsonia inermis   83
Leafless tamarisk   173, 174
Lentisk bush   174
Leucaena   9
Lilac   170
Locust bean   125
London plane   172
Loranthus acacia   22
Lotus jujube   107, 174
Lycium spp.   138

M

Malus domestica   162
Malus sylvestris   162.
     See Crab apple
Maple   169
Maple, Cretan   176
Mediterranean Redbud   147

Mimosa   162
Mistletoe   22
Moringa   24, 163, 168
Moringa oleifeira   24
Moringa oleifera   163
Moringa peregrina   24, 163
Morus alba   168
Morus nigra   131, 168
Mulberry   131, 168, 173
Mustard   169
Myrrh   26, 83, 84, 123, 124, 143, 156, 169
Myrtaceae   95, 169
Myrtle   34, 74, 93, 95, 120, 149, 169
Myrtus communis   169

N

Negev acacia   161, 162.
   See Acacia; See Acacia
Nerium oleander   176
Norway spruce   80

O

Oak   3, 17, 45, 49, 56, 64, 73, 74, 80, 87, 92, 93, 95,
   96, 103, 117, 143, 148, 149, 169
Oak-terebinth   163
Olea europaea   8, 63, 153, 170
Oleander   176
Olive   8, 11, 12, 14, 16, 26, 33, 36,
   37, 39, 44, 45, 47, 48, 59, 63, 67, 74, 77, 80, 90, 93,
   98, 99, 104, 108, 110, 117, 118, 120, 126, 127, 132,
   135, 136, 137, 138, 140, 145, 149, 151, 152, 153,
   156, 170, 172, 179, 180
Oriental plane   172
Origanum syriaca   33

P

Palestine buckthorn   138, 174
Palestine oak   169
Palestine terebinth   174
Paliurus spina-Christi   138
Palm   4, 34, 74, 78, 166, 170
Parana pine   64
Peach   81
Pencil cedar   164
Pepper tree   178
Phillyrea   149, 176
Phillyrea latifolia   176
Phoenician juniper   168
Phoenix dactylifera   41, 170
Picea abies   80
Pine   3, 4, 63, 73, 79, 95, 141, 143, 149, 171
Pinus aristata   80

Pinus brutia   171
Pinus canariensis   171
Pinus halepensis   171
Pinus pinea   112, 171
Pinus sylvestris   171
Pistachio   149, 172
Pistacia atlantica   3, 58, 174
Pistacia lentiscus   163, 174.
   See False balsam
Pistacia palaestina   174
Pistacia terebinthus   15
Plane   21, 46, 112, 129, 172
Platanus occidentalis   113
Platanus orientalis   21, 172
Pomegranate   26, 27, 36, 44, 54, 84, 131, 172
Poplar   3, 4, 21, 54, 73, 74, 108, 109, 172
Populus alba   172
Populus euphratica   21, 172
Poterium spinosum   118
Prickly burnet   174
Privet   170
Prunus amygdalus   162
Prunus armeniaca   177
Prunus communis   162
Prunus dulcis   21, 162
Pterocarpus santalinus   64, 162
Punica granatum   26, 172

Q

Quercus aegilops   58, 169
Quercus boissieri   51, 58, 169
Quercus calliprinos   58, 169
Quercus coccifera   58, 169
Quercus infectoria   51, 58, 169
Quercus ithaburensis   58, 169
Quercus macrolepis   58
Quercus petraea   58
Quercus robur   20, 58
Quercus spp.   80

R

Red river gum   95, 178
Red sandalwood   64, 67, 162
Redwood   80
Retama raetam   19, 163
Rhamnus palaestinus   138
Rhododendron   77
Rubus sanctus   23

S

Salicaceae   108
Salix acmophylla   174

Salix alba 175
Salix babylonica 175
Sallow 103
Salvadora persica 177
Sarcopoterium spinosum 138
Schinus molle 178
Scots pine 77, 171
Seerim shrub 118
Sequoiadendron giganteum 80
Sequoia sempervirens 80
Sessile oak 58
She-oak of Australia 178
Shining gum 74
Sidder 164
Silver (European) fir 111
Sinai hawthorn 22
Sitka spruce 77
Spiny broom 174
Spiny hawthorn 129, 174
Spruce 63
St John's bread 125, 163
Stone or umbrella pine 171
Strawberry tree 176, 177
Sweet chestnut 74, 176, 177
Sycamine 168, 169, 173
Sycomore 173
Sycomore fig11, 21, 38, 64, 73, 79, 101, 103, 116, 117, 126, 129, 133, 147, 166, 169, 179
Syrian ash 157

T

Tabor oak 50, 51, 53, 58, 87, 88, 101, 129, 148, 169, 170
Tamarisk 19, 21, 55, 173
Tamarix aphylla 19, 173
Tamarix jordanis 173
Taxus baccata 80, 177
Teak 109
Terebinth 3, 18, 45, 56, 58, 64, 73, 95, 129, 142, 162, 172, 174
Tetraclinis articulata 156, 165
thicket 102, 107, 116
Thorns 163, 174
Thorny burnet 145
Thuya plicata 164
Thymlea hirsuta 159
Toothbrush tree 177
Tree of knowledge of good and evil 8, 11
Tree of lifevii, 8, 9, 14, 38, 80, 115, 141, 147, 154, 156, 158
Turkish of Calabrian pine 171
Turpentine tree 15

U

Umbrella thorn 161.
  See Acacia

V

Vallonea oak 169

W

Walnut, common 84, 90, 162, 174
Western red cedar 164
White broom 19
White mulberry 168
White mustard 130
White poplar 172
White Willow 175
Willow 16, 34, 74, 108, 109, 129, 174
Willow-poplar 108

Y

Yew 80, 177
Yitran 159

Z

Ziziphus spina-Christi 47, 139, 164

General Index

A

Aaron's staff 21
Abimelek 18, 67
Abraham 3, 18, 19, 20, 21, 174
Absalom 54, 56, 174
Adam and Eve 8, 11, 155
Aesthetic values 8
Afforestation 20
Africa 71
Agriculture 12, 34, 72, 80
Akkad 55
Alexander the Great 71
Algeria 156
Amanus (Syria) 55, 58, 84
America (USA) 59, 154
Annon River 48
Annual rings 30, 72, 111
Apollonia 6
Arabia 163
Arabian Peninsula 123
Aristotle 57
Ark of the covenant 15, 21, 24, 58
Armenia 17
Artaxerxes, King 70
Asaph 70, 71, 72, 73
Asherah poles 38, 46, 99
Ashurbanipal 71
Ashurnasirpal 9
Ashurst 44
Asia Minor 168
Assyria 55, 70, 79, 88, 89, 90, 93, 112
Atacama desert 77
Atlas Mountains 149
Attenborough, David 103
Australia 5, 74, 95
Axe 16, 38, 39, 48, 58, 60, 78, 88, 89, 90, 103, 126

B

Baal 38, 46, 64, 118
Babylon 27, 62, 67, 71, 85, 90, 103, 107, 108, 109, 115, 119, 121, 123, 124, 156, 173, 175
Balawat 48, 70
Balkans 168
Banias 54, 75, 93
Banias Falls 158
Bark 124, 130, 148
Bar-Yohai, Rabbi Shimeon 125
Bashan 88, 111
Bazaioi 71

Bedgebury National Pinetum, Kent 33
Beersheba 19
Bethlehem 48, 49, 53, 103, 133
Beth Shan 55
Bitter water 21, 22, 23, 163
Boundaries 20, 45, 173
Branch(es) 56, 74, 90, 92, 100, 112, 120, 151
Brazil 64
Britain 63, 64, 74
British Museum x, 9, 22, 48, 49, 51, 62, 66, 67, 70, 71, 85, 111, 118, 133, 138, 145, 152, 153, 154
Broadleaves (angiosperms) 4, 9, 74, 78
Brocklesby Park 80
Brown, Capability 156
Buerk, Michael 5
Bunyan, John 154
Burning bush 21, 22, 23
Byblos 112

C

Caesarea Maritima 148
Caesarea Philippi 88
Caesar, Julius 156
Cajander, A J 37
California 4
Canaan 18, 36, 37
Carbon dating 17, 128, 136, 145
Carpentry 16, 126, 127, 129, 130, 143
Caspian Sea 131
Caucasus 162
Charcoal 30, 31, 140
Childrey Rectory, Wantage (UK) 100
Chile 4, 57, 77
China 177
Christian Aid 31
Church of the Holy Sepulchre 143
Cilicia 55, 69
Coffin (Egyptian) 21, 22, 38, 166
Conifers (gymnosperms) 4, 15, 22, 55, 64, 78, 96, 109, 164, 165, 166, 167
Coppice 30, 74, 83, 89, 94, 126, 136, 148, 149, 170, 177
Corsica 149
Crassus 140
Crete 149
Cross of Christ 9, 39, 69, 92, 140, 141, 143
Crown of thorns 138, 144, 165
Crucifixion 69, 140, 147, 148
Cyprus 55, 58, 111, 112

D

Damascus 90

Dan River   4
Darius, King   69
Dartmoor (UK)   149
Date honey   41, 170
David   51, 53, 54, 55, 56, 57, 58, 163, 173
Dead Sea   48, 56, 83, 115, 125, 173
Deforestation   6, 13, 44, 89, 156, 157
Desert   22, 24, 29, 31, 36, 44, 48, 74, 77, 91,
    93, 98, 115, 117, 124, 125, 137, 140, 148, 160, 161,
    162, 163, 164, 167, 168, 169, 170, 173, 177, 179
Domestication (trees)   11, 12, 27, 162
Domitian   141

E

Ecological zones   160
Ecosystem services   158
Eden   4, 7, 11, 27, 63, 113, 115, 137, 156
Egypt   ix, 17, 21, 22, 23, 24, 26, 27, 33, 35, 36, 38,
    55, 60, 62, 79, 80, 96, 101, 103, 108, 109, 111, 112,
    126, 150, 163, 166, 167, 170
Ein Gedi   125, 163
Elim   24
En Gedi   83
England   45, 49, 62
Ephesus   6, 155
Eritrea   163
Etham   85
Ethiopia   5, 13, 29, 31
Euphrates   16, 108
Evelyn, John   16, 141, 143
Exile, The   62, 67, 69, 103, 105, 107
Exmoor (UK)   149

F

Felling trees   16, 38, 58, 59, 60, 63, 72, 78, 112, 127
Fertile Crescent   12
Finland   37
Firewood 5, 9, 20, 29, 30, 31, 32, 64, 66, 72, 95, 105,
    115, 163
Flood   15
Forest fires   78, 88, 99, 109, 110, 153, 154
Forest law   71, 72
Forest management   71, 72
Forest of Ephraim   56
Forest of Hereth   55
Forest products   5
Forest resources   149
Forests and history   54
France   59
Fruit trees 33, 37, 39, 41, 48, 54, 80, 83, 84, 104, 115,
    117, 118, 130, 137, 154, 172
Fumigation   33, 168

G

Galilean fishing boat112, 127, 128, 129, 140, 144, 150
Galilee   47, 115, 125, 139, 140
Garden of Eden   4, 7, 11, 27, 63, 113, 115
Garden of Gethsemane   136, 137
Garden of resurrection   143
Garden Tomb   142, 143, 179
Gaul   156
Geldof, Bob   5
Gethsemane   7, 74, 137
Gibeah   53
Gideon   45, 46
Gilgal   53
Gilgamesh, Epic of   15
Giv'at ha'Mivtar   140
Golan   174
Gospel Oak (UK)   45
Grafting   151, 152, 159
Greece   33

H

Hadrian   72
Hadrian's Wall   17, 153
Hail damage   79, 80, 119
Hammurabi   71
Hampshire (UK)   44, 53, 60
Hardwood   4
Hareuveni   108, 147
Harrison   80
Hatshepsut, Queen   26, 162
Heirapolis   141
Helena, Empress   145
Hepper, Nigel   26, 64, 96, 126, 131, 136, 149
High Place of Dan   96
Hillier Gardens, Hampshire   81, 170
Hinnom Valley   95
Hiram, King of Tyre   55, 58
Hitler, Adolf   113
Home gardens   34
Homer   39, 156
Honey (bees)   55
Horn of Africa   26, 123, 163
Horticulture   80
Hula Valley   174
Hussain, Saddam   6

I

Idolatry   3, 37, 38, 64, 93, 95, 97, 98, 113, 116, 118,
    174
Impalement   69, 70
Incense   26, 27, 83, 84, 123, 124, 167

India   32, 163
India (Ophir)   64
Iran   56, 131, 177
Iraq   49, 56
Israel   24, 42, 44, 163
Izmir   131

J

Jacob   18, 21, 35, 172, 173
Janneus   140
Jehoiakin   108
Jericho   41, 48, 125, 133
Jericho Valley   117
Jerusalem   48, 53, 55, 63, 64, 69, 95, 102, 103, 115,
    128, 137, 140, 179
Jerusalem Botanic Garden   67, 79, 161, 164, 179
Jesus Christ   3, 11, 17, 25, 27, 31, 32, 35, 51, 85, 89,
    123, 129, 132, 135, 143, 158
Johanan, Rabbi   79
John the Baptist   96, 123, 124, 125, 126, 163
Joppa   69
Jordan (country)   24, 44, 163, 176
Jordan Plain   117
Jordan Valley   162, 174
Joseph   21, 35
Joseph of Arimathea   143
Josephus   6, 17, 85, 121, 140, 174
Jotham   45, 47, 48, 139, 165

K

Kadesh Barnea   162
Karnak (Egypt)   60
Kennedy, President John F   59
Kenya   46
Kibbutz Ginosar   127
Kidron Valley   96, 135, 137
Knesset   143
Korazin   92, 139
Korem (Ethiopia)   5

L

Lachish   39, 64, 65, 66, 67, 98
Lake District   149
Leaves   157
Lebanon 55, 58, 60, 62, 69, 79, 84, 96, 115, 129, 149,
    167
Lesseps, Ferdinand Marie, de   59
Levant (Israel, Lebanon and Syria) 12, 55, 58, 111, 131,
    164, 174
Lewis, C S   9, 156, 159
Linnaeus, Carolus   58
Logging   60, 62

Log rafts   62
Log trade   55, 69
London   103
Lotubai   46
Lyndhurst   44

M

Magi   27, 83, 123, 124
Mali   31
Malta   150, 156
Mamre   20
Marah   21, 23, 24, 163
Mecca   32
Medicinal trees   32, 33, 80, 143
Mediterranean   3, 4, 5, 6, 11, 20, 33, 57, 80, 82, 83,
    90, 95, 110, 111, 113, 125, 149, 153, 161, 163, 164,
    165, 166, 168, 169, 170
Meiggs, Russell   6, 57, 111
Melchizedek   20
Memphis   38
Mesopotamia   7, 150
Messianic images   94, 100, 109, 120
Middle East   12, 20
Midian   22
Miletus   6
Mina   32
Moab   48
Moccas   71
Monastery of the Cross   143
Moreh   18, 46
Morocco   156
Moses7, 15, 21, 22, 23, 24, 25, 27, 35, 36, 41, 44, 46,
    163
Mount Ararat   17, 18
Mount Carmel   64, 73, 176, 177
Mount Gerizim   47
Mount Hermon   4, 58, 84, 158, 170
Mount Hermon (Senir)   110
Mount of Beatitudes   144
Mount of Olives   45, 115, 135, 136, 137, 170
Mount Sinai   24, 39
Mount St Helens (USA)   112
Mount Tabor   53
Mount Zalmon   48

N

Napoleon   55, 113
Navarra, Fernand   17
Nazareth   50, 51, 113, 126, 127, 132, 140
Nebuchadnezzar   108, 115
Negev   30, 31
Nelson, Horatio, Lord   59

New England (USA) 83
New Forest (UK) 19, 72
Nicodemus 143
Nineveh 62, 66, 89, 93, 118
Noah 14, 16, 18, 58
Noah's Ark 15–16, 24, 38, 165
Nogah Hareuveni 88
North Africa 5, 80, 168, 170
North America 38, 77, 80

O

Oakhanger (UK) 45
Oars 111, 154
Odysseus 39
Old Childrey Rectory, near Wantage (UK) 164
Olive oil 26, 37, 59, 90, 110, 120, 138, 156, 170
Olive wood 63, 170, 172
Olympic National Park, Washington, USA 82
Oman 24
Orchards 84, 98, 170, 177
Oregon (USA) 112

P

Packard, Vance 99
Palace of the Forest 83, 85, 91, 99
Palestine 62
Palm Sunday 135, 155, 170
Panama 59
Paper making 153
Papua New Guinea 20, 34, 158
Paradise 4, 70, 155, 157
Paul, Apostle 5, 39, 102, 117, 135, 143, 147, 149, 150, 152, 153, 154, 155, 165, 170, 176
Persia 69
Peter, Apostle 39, 91, 117, 144, 147, 148, 149, 176
Petra 176
Petrie, Flinders 31
Petts Wood 103
Place names 44
Planting (trees) 20, 26, 31, 34, 59, 95, 97, 108, 109
Pliny 111, 149, 156
Pliny the Elder 57
Pollarding 30, 49
Prodigal son 125, 132, 163
Promised Land 18, 27, 34, 36, 37, 41, 44, 45, 64, 113, 166, 170
Propagation 9, 11, 109
Publius Quintilius Varus 54
Punt 26, 163
Pyramids 3, 17
Pyrenees 149

Q

Queen of Sheba 64
Quintus Curtius 71
Quirinius 54

R

Ravenna 149
Red Sea 36
Regeneration 7, 30, 59, 72, 74, 82, 88, 103, 112, 137, 177
Richmond (UK) 71
River Jordan 4, 41, 48, 75, 158, 163, 173
River Nile 62, 170
River Tigris 62
Rooting 11, 77, 109, 131
Root of David 89, 126, 155, 158
Rope 41, 150
Rothschild, Ferdinand James Anselm Freiherr, de 138
Royal Botanical Gardens, Kew 179
Rudder 153, 154
Russia 17
Rwanda 34

S

Sacred trees 9, 45, 46
Sahara 163
Sahel 20, 32
Samson 48
Sargon 55, 71
Saudi Arabia 24
Scotland 44
Sea of Galilee 75, 127, 128, 129, 130, 143, 144, 175
Seedlings 83, 108
Seeds 97, 109, 130, 157
Senegal 32
Sennacherib 39, 62, 65, 66, 71, 79, 89, 90, 93, 98, 100, 118, 121
Seti 60
Shade 20, 45, 49, 54, 74
Shechem 18, 45, 67
Shipbuilding 110, 149, 153
Shredding 49, 50
Sicily 149
Siege 38, 39, 48, 65, 66, 98, 100, 104, 108
Sinai Peninsula 24, 31
Sinkiang 32
Smyrna 131
Softwood 4
Soil erosion 5, 12, 34
Soil survey 44
Solomon 53, 57–58, 79–80, 164

Somalia 163
South Africa 77
South Africa's Western Cape Province 4
South Pacific 20
Spain 156
Sparrow Wood 103
Spartacus 140
Spices 83, 123, 143
Spurgeon, Charles Haddon 79, 137
Star of Bethlehem 124
Staverton 71
Stewardship 5, 39
Stumping back 89
Sudan 20
Suez 59
Sustainability 156, 159
Swaziland 80, 156
Sweden 80
Symbolism 35
Syria 24, 54, 55, 58, 60, 129, 167

T

Tabernacle 24, 25, 162
Tanning 148
Taurus Mountains (Turkey) 58
Taxonomy 57
Taylor, John 90
Tearfund 5, 31
Tel Arsuf 6
Tel Aviv 6, 95
Tel Dan 157
Tel Dan Nature Reserve 4, 18, 65
Temple 53, 58, 62, 69, 115, 118, 164
Temple Mount 58
Teutoberger Forest (Germany) 54
Theophrastus 57, 111, 149, 156
Thirgood, J V 6
Tiber River 149
Tigris 16
Timber extraction 60, 119
Timber imports 21, 55, 58, 69, 96, 100, 111
Tolkein, JRR 56
Tree age 80, 97, 170
Tree form 52
Tree growth 30, 37, 72
Tresco Gardens, Isles of Scilly 70
Tropical rain forest 4, 11, 37, 82, 112
Turkey ix, 1, 6, 17, 33, 52, 55, 58, 67, 69, 79, 90, 111, 131, 141, 162, 164, 167, 168, 174, 176
Tuscany (Italy) 3
Tyre 110, 111

U

Upper Galilee 58, 170, 172, 176, 177
Ur 18
Usher, Graham 137

V

Valley of Rephaim 53
Valley of the Kings 26, 140
Varian disaster 54
Varus, Governor of Syria 140
Venerable Bede 141
Vespasian 137
Vindolanda (UK) 153

W

Wadi Felik 6
Wadi Nash 31
Wales 149
Werker, Dr Eller 129
West Africa 20
Wilberforce Oak 19
Wilberforce, William 19
Wilderness 29, 76, 94, 107, 117, 125, 164
Wildlife 5, 12, 98, 112, 115, 158
William the Conqueror 72
Windthrow 75
Wood carving 38, 63, 105, 170
Wooden peg 92, 107, 121
Wood properties 16, 22, 24, 38, 63, 79, 111, 126, 149, 162
Woodworking tools 126
Wreaths of leaves 85, 170, 176
Writing tablet 124, 152, 153

Z

Zacchaeus 11, 133
Zedekiah 108
Zohary, M 74, 83, 130